New Language Learning and Teaching Environments

Series Editor
Hayo Reinders
Department of Education
Department of Languages
Anaheim University
King Mongkut's University of Technology Thonburi
Anaheim
Bangkok, USA

New Language Learning and Teaching Environments is an exciting new book series edited by Hayo Reinders, dedicated to recent developments in learner-centred approaches and the impact of technology on learning and teaching inside and outside the language classroom. The series aims to:

- Publish cutting-edge research into current developments and innovation in language learning and teaching practice.
- Publish applied accounts of the ways in which these developments impact on current and future language education.
- Encourage dissemination and cross-fertilisation of policies and practice relating to learner-centred pedagogies for language learning and teaching in new learning environments.
- Disseminate research and best practice in out-of-class and informal language learning.

The series is a multidisciplinary forum for the very latest developments in language education, taking a pedagogic approach with a clear focus on the learner, and with clear implications for both researchers and language practitioners. It is the first such series to provide an outlet for researchers to publish their work, and the first stop for teachers interested in this area.

Linh Phung • Hayo Reinders
Vu Phi Ho Pham
Editors

Innovation in Language Learning and Teaching

The Case of Vietnam and Cambodia

Editors
Linh Phung
Eduling International
Pittsburgh, PA, USA

Vu Phi Ho Pham
Faculty of Foreign Languages
Van Lang University
Ho Chi Minh City, Vietnam

Hayo Reinders
Faculty of Liberal Arts
King Mongkut's University of
Technology Thonburi
Bangkok, Thailand

ISSN 2946-2932 ISSN 2946-2940 (electronic)
New Language Learning and Teaching Environments
ISBN 978-3-031-46079-1 ISBN 978-3-031-46080-7 (eBook)
https://doi.org/10.1007/978-3-031-46080-7

© The Editor(s) (if applicable) and The Author(s), under exclusive licence to Springer Nature Switzerland AG 2024
This work is subject to copyright. All rights are solely and exclusively licensed by the Publisher, whether the whole or part of the material is concerned, specifically the rights of translation, reprinting, reuse of illustrations, recitation, broadcasting, reproduction on microfilms or in any other physical way, and transmission or information storage and retrieval, electronic adaptation, computer software, or by similar or dissimilar methodology now known or hereafter developed.
The use of general descriptive names, registered names, trademarks, service marks, etc. in this publication does not imply, even in the absence of a specific statement, that such names are exempt from the relevant protective laws and regulations and therefore free for general use.
The publisher, the authors and the editors are safe to assume that the advice and information in this book are believed to be true and accurate at the date of publication. Neither the publisher nor the authors or the editors give a warranty, expressed or implied, with respect to the material contained herein or for any errors or omissions that may have been made. The publisher remains neutral with regard to jurisdictional claims in published maps and institutional affiliations.

Cover image (c): Getty Images / VU PHAM VAN

This Palgrave Macmillan imprint is published by the registered company Springer Nature Switzerland AG.
The registered company address is: Gewerbestrasse 11, 6330 Cham, Switzerland

Paper in this product is recyclable.

CONTENTS

1 An Overview of the Innovation in Language Teaching and Learning in Vietnam and Cambodia   1
Vu Phi Ho Pham, Hayo Reinders, and Linh Phung

Part I Program and Curriculum Developoment   13

2 Using Environment and Needs Analyses to Innovate an Intensive English Course in Transnational Bachelor's Programs   15
Tuan Nhat Nguyen and Huong Thi Bao Dinh

3 Out of the Ordinary: Implementation of a New Japanese Language Program in Higher Education in Vietnam   33
Eriko Yamato

4 A Trilingual K-12 Program in Siem Reap: Reflecting on Successes and Failures   51
Stephen Louw, Raksmey Rath, and Wenwen Tian

5 Harnessing Partnerships and Technology to Establish a New Language Program in Cambodia   73
Joseph Ng and Patrick Mannion

v

vi CONTENTS

Part II   Materials Development and Teaching Methodology   91

6   A Culturally and Linguistically Responsive Approach to
Materials Development: Teaching Vietnamese as a Second
Language to Ethnic Minority Primary School Students   93
Thao Phuong Do, Hoa Do, and Linh Phung

7   Pronunciation Teaching Innovation in the English as a
Foreign Language Classroom   115
Loc Tan Nguyen

8   Using a Mock Conference as an Innovative Internship
Activity for Translation Education   135
Nguyen Thi Nhu Ngoc

Part III   Technology Integration   155

9   Enhancing Student Participation in Online Collaborative
Learning Groups, Using a Design Framework and
Accessible Technologies   157
Vu Thi Thanh Nha

10   Revitalizing Language Education: An Exploratory Study
on the Innovative Use of Mobile Applications in English
Language Teaching at a State University in Vietnam   183
Nghi Tin Tran, Phuc Huu Tran, and Vu Phi Ho Pham

11   Factors Affecting EFL Lecturers' Implementation of
Blended Learning in Vietnamese Universities   209
Thi Nguyet Le

12   Innovation in Language Teaching in Vietnam and
Cambodia: Key Themes   235
Linh Phung, Hayo Reinders, and Vu Phi Ho Pham

Index   243

Notes on Contributors

Huong Thi Bao Dinh Dean of the Postgraduate Studies Department of Hanoi University, Hanoi, Vietnam, obtained her PhD in Education from RMIT University, Australia, in 2015. She has been teaching a range of courses for both undergraduate and postgraduate students, and supervising MA and PhD students in English Studies. Her main areas of interest are ICT in English teaching and TESOL Methodology. She can be contacted at huongdtb@hanu.edu.vn

Hoa Do has been working as an English language teacher for 15 years, helping students of different age groups and levels in Vietnam and Australia to improve their general and academic language skills. She gained her Master's degree in Applied Linguistics in 2013 from Victoria University of Wellington, New Zealand, and is currently a PhD student at Department of Languages and Cultures, La Trobe University, Australia. Her main research interests include instructed second language acquisition, teacher training, heritage language maintenance, language-in-education policy and family language policy among transnational migrant communities.

Thao Phuong Do is a lecturer at Faculty of Vietnamese Studies, Hanoi National University of Education. She completed a Master in Linguistics degree and a Bachelor in Philology from Faculty of Philology, Hanoi National University of Education. She earned a Doctorate in Education with a focus on the theory and teaching methods of literature and Vietnamese at Hanoi National University of Education. Her dissertation is titled "Develop Vietnamese lexical competence for Korean students from the perspective of Cognitive Linguistics." She has researched and taught Vietnamese language for foreigners since 2009. She has over ten articles and three co-authored books. Her research focuses on Linguistics, Vietnamese language, and teaching Vietnamese as a first and a second language. She can be reached via email at thaodp@hnue.edu.vn

Thi Nguyet Le has been working as a senior lecturer of English language at People's Security University, Vietnam, for over 20 years. She achieved a doctoral degree at School of Education, Edith Cowan University, Western Australia. She has also been in charge of teaching and supervision for postgraduate candidates at other Vietnamese universities. Her research interests focus on blended learning, TESOL methodology, ESP and EMI.

Stephen Louw is a lecturer and researcher at King Mongkut's University of Technology Thonburi, Bangkok. He has taught English as a foreign language since 1992 in countries across Africa and Asia. His area of expertise is teacher education, particularly intensive pre-service teacher training of EFL teachers. His current interest is teacher development in Cambodia.

Patrick Mannion has been an EFL instructor for over 20 years and language educator for about 3 years. His research interests include language teacher education, multimodality, and genre approaches to literacy. He taught language teacher education courses in Cambodia as a fellow in the US State Department's English Language Programs.

Joseph Ng has been teaching and heading up the English Department at Life University, Sihanoukville, Cambodia, from 2017. Certified as an OCELT instructor and a PTCT and TESL trainer with TESL Ontario, he has taught settlement English, prepared internationally trained professionals for the Canadian workplace, and developed online curricula of late.

Nguyen Thi Nhu Ngoc is currently vice-dean cum chair of the Department of Translation and Interpreting at the Faculty of English Linguistics and Literature, University of Social Sciences & Humanities, Vietnam National University Ho Chi Minh City. She has taught the English language and worked as a translation teacher and part-time translator since 1997. She was also a co-author of some ESP textbooks published by VNUHCM Publisher and used at her university. Her main research interests are Translation Studies, Comparative Linguistics, and Intercultural Communication. Email: nhungoc@hcmussh.edu.vn.

Tuan Nhat Nguyen is the director of the International Education Center, home to transnational programs at Hanoi University. Nhat Tuan holds a PhD in Translation Studies, granted by Dublin City University (Ireland). His areas of expertise include translation studies, curriculum and syllabus development, TESOL, and EMI. He can be contacted at tuannn@hanu.edu.vn

Loc Tan Nguyen is a senior lecturer at the School of Foreign Languages, UEH University, Vietnam. Dr. Loc Tan Nguyen obtained his PhD in Applied Linguistics from Victoria University of Wellington, New Zealand, in 2019. He has been teaching a range of English courses (both undergraduate and graduate levels), including phonetics and phonology, pronunciation, academic writing, and curriculum design. Loc's research focuses on pronunciation teaching and learning, academic writing, teacher cognition, second language teacher education, corrective feedback, and professional learning for language teachers. He can be contacted at loc.nguyen@ueh.edu.vn

Vu Thi Thanh Nha obtained a PhD in Education at the University of New South Wales, Australia, in 2014. She is also the dean of the Faculty of English, VNU University of Languages and International Studies, VNU-HN. Her research interests include educational change, classroom-based research, technology-based teaching, English as a medium of instruction, and professional development at the tertiary level.

Vu Phi Ho Pham vice dean of the Faculty of Foreign Languages, associate professor, Van Lang University, Vietnam, vice president of AsiaCALL International Conference. He has also served as the vice president of Ba Ria—Vung Tau University and the vice president at Van Hien University, Vietnam. Pham has published 64 research articles in both local and international journals (ISI/Scopus-indexed), and nine books and course books, three course books were used for both the undergraduate and graduate levels at Van Lang University, HCMC Open University, Vietnam, and Lourdes College, Higher Education Department, Cagayan de Oro City, Philippines. He has international experience in teaching English at Suranaree University of Technology, Thailand, and Gyeongju University, South Korea. He is the vice president for Administrative Affairs of AsiaCALL and the managing editor of its online journal. He is now the editor-in-chief of the international journal of TESOL & Education. He is a peer reviewer for some international journals indexed in ISI/Scopus such as Computer Assisted Language Learning, Open Sage. His main interests include academic writing, peer responses, translation, teaching methodologies, and technology-enhanced learning. His CV may be found at https://www.phamho.com/c-v; his Orcid ID; Scopus ID; Google Scholar profile

Linh Phung is founder of Eduling, an organization offering English language instruction, services, and technologies to language teachers and learners from all over the world and assistant professor of TESOL at Anaheim University. She also has experience in directing the English Language Program at Chatham University for 12 years and currently serves as an English Language Specialist with the U.S. Department of State. Her research interests include learner engagement in second language learning and teaching, task-based language teaching, educational technology, and international education. She has published research in high-impact journals, language learning and children's books, and a task-based app called Eduling Speak with over 1000+ tasks for language development and research. She can be reached at ltp252@gmail.com or www.eduling.org/drlinhphung.

Raksmey Rath is school director of the Westgate International Schools in Siem Reap, Cambodia. He has been involved in school management for over 20 years, and has developed and opened 12 languages and K12 schools in Cambodia and Vietnam.

Hayo Reinders (www.innovationinteaching.org) is TESOL professor and director of Research at Anaheim University, USA, and professor of Applied Linguistics at KMUTT in Thailand. He is founder of the Global Institute for Teacher Leadership and editor of *Innovation in Language Learning & Teaching*. He has published 31 books and over 200 articles in the areas of out-of-class learning, technology, and language teacher leadership.

Wenwen Tian holds her MA and PhD in Applied Linguistics as well as certificates in CELTA and TEFL. She is currently an associate professor in the School of Foreign Studies, Northwestern Polytechnical University, China. Over the last 20 years, she has worked as an English lecturer and coordinator for international affairs in China, Saudi Arabia, and Thailand. Her research interests include discourse analysis, academic supervision, intercultural communication, and teacher development.

Nghi Tin Tran Dean of the Faculty of Foreign Languages, Ho Chi Minh City University of Industry and Trade. Dr. Nghi Tin Tran is an experienced educator and researcher interested in second language acquisition and pedagogy. His work focuses on developing and implementing effective teaching methodologies, using corpus-based techniques in language teaching, AI in education, and the role of literacy in second language learning. He has a strong record of scholarly publications in prestigious Scopus-indexed journals. His commitment to ongoing professional development is evident through his active involvement in leading organizations like VietTESOL, STESOL, and VietCALL. Dr. Nghi Tin Tran can be contacted at nghitt@huit.edu.vn. (Orcid), (Scopus), (Google Scholar)

Phuc Huu Tran is currently the Rector of University of Foreign Language Studies—the University of Da Nang. He is also the chairman of the CTESOL, a part of the Association of Vietnam Universities and Colleges. He holds a PhD in Applied Linguistics, granted by University of the West of England, Bristol, UK, in 2013. His research interests are teaching English as a foreign language, corpus linguistics, and cognitive linguistics. He can be contacted at thphuc@ufl.udn.vn (Scopus), (Google Scholar)

Eriko Yamato is a senior lecturer at RMIT University Vietnam, specializing in digitally enhanced Japanese language learning. Her research interests include cultural studies, critical pedagogy, and innovative approaches to cultural and language exchange.

LIST OF FIGURES

Fig. 4.1	Summary of the trilingual transitional immersion curriculum	57
Fig. 9.1	A typical lesson structure for a Zoom session	168
Fig. 9.2	Reported benefits of group work	171
Fig. 11.1	A conceptual framework for the Vietnamese university lecturers to manage their implementation of blended learning in EFL education	227

LIST OF TABLES

Table 2.1	Checklist for situation (environment) analysis	21
Table 2.2	Examples of learning outcomes	27
Table 6.1	Example practice activity	104
Table 6.2	Percentage of teachers rating the materials as meeting criteria	106
Table 6.3	The necessity of the materials	106
Table 6.4	Feasibility of materials use	107
Table 7.1	Celce-Murcia et al.'s (2010, p. 45) CPT framework	120
Table 7.2	The teachers' proportion of lesson planning	121
Table 9.1	Descriptions of communication tools for online group work	163
Table 9.2	Examples of group setup by theme	167
Table 9.3	Assessment criteria for group assignment	167
Table 9.4	A summary of students' responses to the evaluation questionnaire	170
Table 9.5	Favorite aspects of group work	172
Table 9.6	Unfavorable aspects of group work	173
Table 10.1	Demographic characteristics of participants	188
Table 10.2	Frequency of mobile app usage	189
Table 10.3	Most useful mobile apps for language learning	190
Table 10.4	Frequency and duration of mobile app usage in language learning	190
Table 10.5	Perceived improvement of language learning outcomes through mobile app usage	191
Table 10.6	Advantages and disadvantages of mobile app usage	192
Table 11.1	Underlying factors negatively affecting the EFL lecturers' implementation of BL	223

xv

CHAPTER 1

An Overview of the Innovation in Language Teaching and Learning in Vietnam and Cambodia

Vu Phi Ho Pham, Hayo Reinders, and Linh Phung

RATIONALES FOR INNOVATION IN LANGUAGE TEACHING

Innovation in language teaching refers to the planned adoption and integration of effective pedagogical strategies, technological advancements, and methodology to improve the learning process. It entails the inventive adaptation of instructional approaches, the use of innovative instruments, and the acceptance of developing trends in language education. Innovation in language teaching often seeks to promote engagement, competency, and cultural awareness in addition to addressing the learners' changing

V. P. H Pham (✉)
Faculty of Foreign Languages, Van Lang University, Ho Chi Minh City, Vietnam

H. Reinders
Faculty of Liberal Arts, King Mongkut's University of Technology Thonburi, Bangkok, Thailand

L. Phung
Eduling International, Pittsburgh, PA, USA

© The Author(s), under exclusive license to Springer Nature Switzerland AG 2024
L. Phung et al. (eds.), *Innovation in Language Learning and Teaching*, New Language Learning and Teaching Environments, https://doi.org/10.1007/978-3-031-46080-7_1

needs. According to Thornbury (2006), innovation in language teaching extends beyond conventional approaches, inspiring teachers to consider creative means of presenting material, encouraging interactive learning, and making the most of digital resources. Language teachers contribute to a dynamic and adaptable learning environment by regularly re-evaluating and improving their teaching methods.

A number of persuasive arguments in the field of language education underscore the necessity for constant innovation in instructional procedures and approaches. First, the understanding of the dynamic character of language itself serves as one main justification. Language, according to Baugh and Cable (1993), is a living thing that changes through time as a result of social, technological, and communication trends. To remain relevant and sensitive to the current linguistic landscape, language instruction must alter to reflect these changes. Second, the recognition of the various learning preferences and styles among language learners serves as another essential justification. Educators may foster a more inclusive and productive learning environment by combining effective educational practices (Richards & Rodgers, 2014). The development of technology, in particular, opens up possibilities for multimodal learning experiences that accommodate visual, aural, and kinesthetic learners. Additionally, the need to prepare language learners for communication in a world that is becoming more networked is highlighted by globalization and interconnection. According to Byram (1997), language instruction improvements should foster linguistic and intercultural communicative ability. This instruction entails giving students the know-how to successfully navigate cross-cultural dialogue, encouraging a better comprehension of various viewpoints, and promoting global citizenship. Another justification for innovation is the requirement for higher levels of learner motivation and engagement. Modern language learners react well to interactive and dynamic learning experiences because they are frequently engaged in a digital and multimedia-rich environment (Khamparia & Pandey, 2018). Teachers may build engaging language learning settings that pique students' attention and heighten their inherent drive to interact with the language by using effective technologies and approaches. This introductory chapter will provide an overview of language teaching in Vietnam and Cambodia, followed by a review of top-down and bottom-up innovations in language teaching in the two countries. The final section will summarize the ten chapters of this volume.

Overview of Language Teaching in Vietnam and Cambodia

The complex and dynamic nature of language teaching and learning in Vietnam and Cambodia reflects the historical, political, social, and economic situations of these two nations. With 54 ethnic groups and 110 languages, Vietnam is a multilingual and cosmopolitan nation (Nguyen & Nguyen, 2019). The majority of schools and institutions use Vietnamese as their primary language of instruction, although the government also supports and recognizes other languages spoken by ethnic minorities. English, in particular, is highly prized and pushed in school since it is seen to be crucial for global integration and advancement.

Over the last several decades, Vietnam and Cambodia's language education has experienced many changes and reforms as a result of numerous internal and external forces. The colonial legacies of French and Chinese languages and cultures have influenced the Vietnamese language and educational systems. Additionally, wars and disputes with other nations, including France, the US, and China, have influenced Vietnam's national identity and ideology (Nguyen & Nguyen, 2019). In the case of Cambodia, language learning and instruction have a long and varied history. Thai language (in the seventh century), French (between 1863 and 1954), Vietnamese and Russian (after the 1970s) all had an impact on the country (Hum, 2021).

Implementing and assessing language education in Vietnam confronts several obstacles, including a shortage of trained instructors, authentic materials, multimedia technologies, and internet connection (Nguyen & Nguyen, 2019; Giao & Nguyen, 2021; Nguyen et al., 2021) Second, there needs to be better understanding and preparedness to accept new language teaching and learning approaches and innovations, such as communicative language teaching (CLT), learner autonomy, learner-centeredness, and EMI (Giao & Nguyen, 2021; Nguyen et al., 2021). Third, there is a lack of coordination and coherence between the teaching and learning of languages and other facets of the educational system, such as the curriculum, syllabus, textbook, and assessment system (Nguyen & Nguyen, 2019; Nguyen et al., 2021). Last but not least, ineffectiveness in language assessment and language teaching and learning has been widely reported (Nguyen & Nguyen, 2019; Nguyen et al., 2021). In the case of Cambodia, some significant challenges and issues that affect the quality and effectiveness of language education include the lack of qualified and trained teachers, the low proficiency and motivation of learners, the inadequate resources and facilities, the outdated curriculum and assessment methods, the influence of traditional teaching culture, and the impact of social and political factors (Doeur, 2022; Heng et al., 2022).

The history and development of language teaching and learning in Vietnam and Cambodia are closely related to the political, economic, and social changes. In Vietnam, since the Doi Moi (Renovation) policy in 1986 (Nguyen, 2017a) has marked a significant difference in the country. This policy led to significant achievements in terms of GDP growth and foreign direct investment, which in turn influenced the demand and supply of English as a foreign language (EFL) instruction in Vietnam. In Cambodia, various initiatives and reforms have been implemented by the government, educational institutions, and other stakeholders to improve the situation of ELT in the country. First, the introduction of a new curriculum framework for general education in 2015, which emphasizes communicative language teaching and learner-centered approaches (MoEYS, 2015); the collaboration with international organizations and donors, such as UNESCO, UNICEF, USAID, British Council, and Australian Aid, to support various projects and programs related to ELT in Cambodia. There has also been a growth of exchange opportunities and funding programs for teachers and students in Cambodia to study abroad or attend regional seminars and conferences.

TOP-DOWN INNOVATION IN LANGUAGE TEACHING

Language policy is a set of decisions and actions that aim to regulate, manage, and promote the use and development of languages in a given context (Ricento, 2006). Various actors and agencies can initiate and implement language policy, such as governments, institutions, communities, or individuals. Depending on the source and direction of the policy, language policy can be classified into two types: top-down and bottom-up (Kaplan & Baldauf, 2008). Top-down language policy is a type of policy formulated and imposed by a central authority, such as a government or an institution, on the target population or group. On the contrary, bottom-up language policy is initiated and developed at the grassroots level, such as a community or an individual, based on their needs and interests.

In Cambodia, top-down innovation in language teaching refers to the changes and reforms initiated by the government and other authorities to improve the quality and effectiveness of language education. First, a new curriculum framework for general education was introduced in 2005, emphasizing communicative language teaching and learner-centered approaches (Kosonen, 2019). The second top-down innovation referred to expanding scholarship programs and exchange opportunities for Cambodian teachers and students to study abroad or attend regional workshops and conferences (Igawa, 2008). Third, the collaboration with international organizations and donors has supported various projects and programs related to language education in Cambodia (Dy & Ninomiya, 2003).

In Vietnam, there has also been a top-down innovation, particularly the government-issued Project 2020, relating to the teaching and learning of the English language. Project 2020, also known as the National Foreign Language Project 2020 (Chinhphu.vn, 2008), aims to improve the English proficiency of Vietnamese learners and teachers by 2020 (Bui, 2022; Nguyen, 2017b; Van, 2015). The project was launched in 2008 by the Ministry of Education and Training (MOET) with the approval of the prime minister. The project has five main goals. The first is to create a national framework for foreign language proficiency that is compatible with the Common European Framework of Reference (CEFR), the second is to make English language instruction mandatory from Grades 3 through 12, the third is to introduce English as a medium of instruction (EMI) for mathematics and science subjects in upper secondary schools, the fourth is to enhance English teachers' English language proficiency (ELP) and pedagogical knowledge, and the fifth goal is to develop a model for teaching English as a second language at selected universities.

As it demonstrates the government's acknowledgment of the significance and function of English as an international language in the context of globalization and integration, the initiative is seen as a breakthrough and an innovation in language policy and planning in Vietnam. The project also aims to address some of the problems and challenges currently plaguing English teaching and learning in Vietnam, such as the low ELP levels among students and teachers, the absence of coordination between the curriculum, assessment, and standards, and the dominance of traditional teaching methods and rote learning (Nguyen & Nguyen, 2019).

Bottom-up Innovations in Language Teaching

Bottom-up innovations are initiatives and actions that originate from the grassroots level, such as teachers, students, parents, or communities, to improve the quality and effectiveness of education (Kaplan & Baldauf, 2008). Bottom-up innovations can be seen as a response to the limitations and challenges of top-down policies and reforms that are imposed by a central authority, such as the government or the Ministry of Education. Bottom-up innovations can also be seen as a reflection of the needs and interests of the local context and culture.

In both Cambodia and Vietnam, the teachers and learners take the initiative to make changes and reforms to improve the quality and effectiveness of language education in the countries. Teachers have used online learning platforms and digital tools to facilitate language teaching and learning during the COVID-19 pandemic (Pham & Vo, 2021), creating professional learning communities and networks among language teachers and researchers to share experiences, resources, and best practices for language education (Doeur, 2022), involving learners in the design and implementation of language learning activities that suit their needs, interests, and goals.

In This Volume

Inspired by the top-down innovation policies, language teachers in both Vietnam and Cambodia implemented their innovative teaching methods into their professional contexts. In Chap. 2, Nguyen and Dinh examined how a public institution in Hanoi, Vietnam, adapted its curriculum to fit the demands of transnational undergraduate programs in Business Studies. The Intensive English Course track was initially targeted to meet the IELTS 5.5 admission criteria for an English as a Medium of Instruction (EMI) program. However, difficulties occurred when students had to grapple with subject-specific terminology and international academic standards. The authors and their team used Macalister and Nation's (2019) curriculum design method to improve the program, including environment and needs analyses relevant to EMI programs where students would later enroll. The backward design highlighted critical long-term outcomes, leading to the development of a more comprehensive English course. The innovation helps to enhance transnational education in Vietnam by bridging gaps across educational levels and providing a strong basis for students' following studies.

In Chap. 3, Eriko Yamato introduces the Vietnam-specific Bachelor Japanese language program of HCMC RMIT University Vietnam, which has been implementing participatory, active language learning since 2017. It emphasizes genuine assessment, interactive digital learning, and community participation to match the university's aims. The writer describes the program's framework to generate work-ready trilingual graduates. The unique use of hybrid-mode "flipped classrooms" and "authentic assessment" without textbooks preserves program integrity and signifies its core innovation. The merits and downsides of various techniques are discussed using student feedback, industry input, and teacher comments to inform language program development.

In Chap. 4, Louw and Reaksmey reported the launch of Siem Reap's first trilingual K-12 curriculum in 2016, including Khmer, English, and Chinese. The curriculum used the transitional immersion program design to blend content instruction and language acquisition. The authors then used interpretative phenomenology to assess the program from English, Khmer, and Chinese department heads' viewpoints. Results showed differing views of achievements and failures, suggesting a lack of interdepartmental collaboration due to rivalry for students' classroom time and school resources. This perspective is essential for comprehending the challenges in implementing innovation from administrators' perspectives.

In Chap. 5, Ng and Mannion present details of the development of a new MA in English program in Sihanoukville, Cambodia. The authors discuss their participation in curriculum creation and execution against the backdrop of a city undergoing fast expansion and an institution with limited or diminishing finances and support. The quest for alternate sources of assistance, the utilization of technology, and the fortunate collaboration of key stakeholders are highlighted. The difficulties encountered are also documented, which is instructional to similar endeavors.

In Chap. 6, through developing and piloting a Grade 5 Vietnamese practice book, Do et al. provide an innovative way to teach Vietnamese to ethnic minority primary children in Vietnam. The project employed a culturally and linguistically responsive technique to create pedagogically sound resources for effectively acquiring Vietnamese as a second language (L2). Materials, such as texts and visuals, were carefully chosen to reflect students' cultural beliefs and traditions while also promoting language acquisition through familiarity with their home language. Teachers have responded positively to the book's culturally relevant visual components, role models, texts, and learning activities. Following a review of the material pilot and teacher comments, the writers underline the need for continuing efforts to offer varied and comprehensive resources that appeal to all ethnic minority groups.

In Chap. 7, T. L. Nguyen suggests that pronunciation instruction be revised to go beyond an ad hoc approach, typically consisting of incidental recasts and/or prompts, despite empirical data demonstrating the effectiveness of communicative pronunciation training on second language learners' comprehension and/or intelligibility. This may be due to the fact that instructors often need more training on how to incorporate communicative pronunciation training into their language programs successfully. The chapter reports a project in which a group of six Vietnamese tertiary EFL instructors introduced communicative pronunciation instruction into their English courses. A detailed review of successes and challenges helps to inform other efforts in implementing pronunciation instruction in Vietnam and beyond.

In Chap. 8, Nguyen Thi Nhu Ngoc presents a mock conference (MC) that has been introduced into the graduate internship course for final year English translation students at a member university of Vietnam National University, Ho Chi Minh City. This novel technique gives seniors hands-on experience in the professional preparatory processes for successive conference interpretation. The MC design comprises research articles provided by Vietnamese teachers and administrators from multiple university faculties, as well as an authentic situated-learning environment. A poll completed in the school year 2022–2023 reviews the innovation after four years of deployment. The writer examines mock conferences, discusses the design and organization process, and evaluates students' input on organization, lecturer assistance, advantages, obstacles, and performance variables. The findings have significance for preparing translation majors with professional knowledge and abilities.

In Chap. 9, Vu Thi Thanh Nha discusses how Vietnamese English Language Teaching (ELT) teachers dealt with the COVID-19 pandemic, particularly group work and online student interaction. Online group collaboration (FCOG) and locally accessible technology were used in the action research project with 25 postgraduate students in an English-medium course. Students worked in asynchronous and synchronous groups for 12 online sessions. Results included improved communication and collaboration, academic advancements in critical thinking and knowledge, and peer support. Time management, technological difficulties, involvement, group dynamics, work distribution, and complexity were challenges. The study emphasizes the need for novel online learning solutions for future education and research.

In Chap. 10, Nghi Tin Tran et al. examine how mobile applications are used to teach English at a Vietnamese university to improve students' language abilities, engagement, and motivation. The study assesses these applications' effects on student perceptions and instructor expectations. Mobile apps may motivate and engage students in student-centered education. Interactive learning experiences through these applications boost attitudes and English learning engagement, suggesting its role in innovating language education. The writers strongly advise language instructors and policymakers to use modern teaching methods and technology to build dynamic and effective learning settings that meet today's language learners' diversified needs.

In Chap. 11, Thi Nguyet Le examines blended learning (BL) in Vietnamese university EFL programs and its confusion and ineffectiveness. The study of 20 EFL professors from ten institutions found that personal, institutional, and socio-cultural/economic variables affect BL integration. Personal elements include instructors' views, pedagogies, and agency. Policy, technology, and professional assistance are institutional elements. Confucian teachings and Vietnam's economy are socio-cultural and economic variables. Personal and institutional variables align for effective BL implementation, but socio-cultural and economic considerations typically provide hurdles. The chapter presents conceptual implications for efficient BL implementation in Vietnamese EFL instruction.

CONCLUSION

In conclusion, this introductory chapter has explored various innovations in language teaching and learning in Vietnam and Cambodia. These innovations have emerged from both top-down policies and bottom-up classroom practices, aiming to enhance language education and meet the evolving needs of learners. At the policy level in Vietnam, the government's implementation of Project 2020 has been a significant top-down innovation. In Cambodia, the government has implemented a new curriculum framework for general education to promote communicative language teaching and learner-centered approaches and provide a wide range of scholarship programs and collaboration with international partners to support various projects and programs related to language education in Cambodia. Furthermore, bottom-up innovations have emerged within classrooms, with teachers implementing various approaches and methods to enhance language learning. The employment of English as a Medium of Instruction (EMI), flipped classrooms, backward design in curriculum development, linguistically and culturally responsive pedagogy, communicative pronunciation teaching, mock conferences for translation classes, virtual classrooms, MALL, and blended learning have opened up new possibilities for language teaching and learning in Vietnam and Cambodia.

Looking ahead, the development of language teaching and learning in Vietnam and Cambodia will continue to evolve. Future innovations may focus on further integrating technology, such as ChatGPT and AI Tools, addressing the needs of specific learner groups, and fostering intercultural communicative competence. Policymakers, educators, and stakeholders must collaborate and provide ongoing support to ensure the success and sustainability of these innovations, ultimately contributing to the overall advancement of language education in these two countries.

REFERENCES

Baugh, A., & Cable, T. (1993). *A history of the English language*. Routledge.

Bui, T. H. (2022). A theoretical evaluation of the English textbooks for Grade 12 students under the National Foreign Language Project 2008–2020. *TESOL Communications, 1*(2), 34–64. https://doi.org/10.46451/tc.20220203

Byram, M. (1997). 'Cultural awareness' as vocabulary learning. *Language Learning Journal, 16*(1), 51–57.

Chinhphu.vn (2008). Decision No. 1400/QĐ-TTg of the Prime Minister for 'Teaching and Learning Foreign Languages in the National Education System, Period 2008 to 2020'. Retrieved from https://chinhphu.vn/default.aspx?pageid=27160&docid=78437

Doeur, B. (2022). Implementation of communicative language teaching: Cambodian EFL teachers' attitudes toward communicative language teaching. *International Journal of Instruction, 15*(2), 155–170. https://doi.org/10.29333/iji.2022.1529a

Dy, S. S., & Ninomiya, A. (2003). Basic education in Cambodia: The impact of UNESCO on policies in the 1990s. *Education Policy Analysis Archives, 11*, 48–48. https://doi.org/10.14507/epaa.v11n48.2003

Giao, L. T. C., & Nguyen, B. D. (2021). Project-based learning in an EFL setting—A case study at a university in Vietnam. *International Journal of*

Education, Psychology and Counseling, 6(38), 225–236. https://doi.org/10.35631/IJEPC.6380018

Heng, K., Hamid, M. O., & Khan, A. (2022). Research engagement of academics in the Global South: the case of Cambodian academics. *Globalisation, Societies and Education*, 1–16. https://doi.org/10.1080/14767724.2022.2040355

Hum, C. (2021). Investigating conference feedback in Cambodian EFL class: Students' writing accuracy improvement and their views of the feedback. *Journal on English as a Foreign Language, 11*(1), 104–124. https://doi.org/10.23971/jefl.v11i1.2314

Igawa, K. (2008). English language and its education in Cambodia, a country in transition. *Shitennoji University Bulletin, 46*(1), 343–369.

Kaplan, R. B., & Baldauf, R. B. (Eds.). (2008). *Language planning and policy in Asia: Japan, Nepal, Taiwan and Chinese characters.* Multilingual Matters.

Khamparia, A., & Pandey, B. (2018). Impact of interactive multimedia in E-learning technologies: Role of multimedia in E-learning. In *Digital multimedia: Concepts, methodologies, tools, and applications* (pp. 1087–1110). IGI Global.

Kosonen, K. (2019). Language education policy in Cambodia. In W. M. Chan, A. B. M. Tsui, & S. Kaur (Eds.), *The Routledge international handbook of language education policy in Asia* (pp. 213–225). Routledge.

Macalister, J., & Nation, I. P. (2019). *Language curriculum design.* Routledge.

MoEYS. (2015). *Curriculum framework of general education and technical education.* MoEYS.

Nguyen, N. T. (2017a). Thirty years of English language and English education in Vietnam. *English Today, 33*(1), 33–35. https://doi.org/10.1017/S0266078416000262

Nguyen, T. (2017b). Vietnam's National Foreign Language 2020 Project after 9 years: A difficult stage. In *The Asian conference on education & international development* (pp. 443–464). National Chengchi University, Taiwan.

Nguyen, X. N. C. M., & Nguyen, V. H. (2019). Language education policy in Vietnam. In *The Routledge international handbook of language education policy in Asia* (pp. 185–201). Routledge.

Nguyen, H. T. T., Sivapalan, S., Hiep, P. H., Van Anh, P. T., & Lan, N. T. M. (2021). Teaching English as a second language in Vietnam: Transitioning from the traditional learning approach to the blended learning approach. In *SHS Web of Conferences* (Vol. 124, p. 01003). EDP Sciences. https://doi.org/10.1051/shsconf/202112401003

Pham, V. P. H., & Vo, N. D. T. (2021). CALL in Asia during Covid-19 and models of E-learning. In *Proceedings of the 17th International Conference of the Asia Association of Computer-Assisted Language Learning (AsiaCALL 2021).* Vol. 533, pp. 1–10. Atlantis Press. https://doi.org/10.2991/assehr.k.210226.001

Ricento, T. (2006). Language policy: Theory and practice–An introduction. In *An introduction to language policy: Theory and method, 10*, 23. Wiley & Sons.

Richards, J. C., & Rodgers, T. S. (2014). *Approaches and methods in language teaching.* Cambridge University Press.

Thornbury, S. (2006). *An AZ of ELT: A dictionary of terms and concepts used in English language teaching.* Macmillan.

Van, H. V. (2015). The development of the ten-year English textbook series for Vietnamese schools under the National Foreign Language 2020 Project: A cross-cultural collaborative experience. *VNU Journal of Foreign Studies, 31*(3) Retrieved from https://jfs.ulis.vnu.edu.vn/index.php/fs/article/view/15

PART I

Program and Curriculum Developoment

CHAPTER 2

Using Environment and Needs Analyses to Innovate an Intensive English Course in Transnational Bachelor's Programs

Tuan Nhat Nguyen and Huong Thi Bao Dinh

INTRODUCTION

Internationalization has been considered a strategic approach to improving and reforming the Vietnamese higher education system (Tran & Nguyen, 2018). To achieve this goal, English as a Medium of Instruction (EMI) programs at Vietnamese universities have been promoted as a key player. EMI programs are seen as a modality to enrich the curriculum, improve international collaboration, and improve institutional ranking and reputation (ibid., p. 94). The implementation of EMI programs has received considerable support from the government as well as the

T. N. Nguyen
International Education Center, Hanoi University, Hanoi, Vietnam
e-mail: tuannn@hanu.edu.vn

H. T. D. Dinh (✉)
Postgraduate Studies Department, Hanoi University, Hanoi, Vietnam
e-mail: huongdtb@hanu.edu.vn

© The Author(s), under exclusive license to Springer Nature Switzerland AG 2024
L. Phung et al. (eds.), *Innovation in Language Learning and Teaching*, New Language Learning and Teaching Environments, https://doi.org/10.1007/978-3-031-46080-7_2

universities themselves. The number of both foreign and domestic EMI programs in the country has increased dramatically over the last two decades.

At the same time, there have been numerous discussions related to students' English language proficiency (ELP) and their ability to study in an EMI environment. EMI programs are the second choice for a large number of students in Vietnam when selecting a university program. Consequently, most students enrolling in EMI programs have low entry requirements and lack preparation for attending EMI courses. Subsequently, students in many EMI programs struggle with lectures, reading materials, assignments, or in-class discussions (Nguyen et al., 2017). Even students with a high level of English proficiency face the challenge of adapting to an international environment where the academic culture and requirements are completely different from those of Vietnamese universities. Such a situation highlights the importance of establishing a language course that not only enhances students' ELP to meet the essential entry level but also prepares them for the academic requirements of international universities. This issue needs to be addressed in a serious and thorough manner, particularly when more and more universities are offering EMI degrees (Nguyen et al., 2016). This is the focus of the chapter, which explores the redesign of learning activities in an English intensive course in a transnational EMI bachelor's program at a public university in Vietnam.

Regarding the structure of the chapter, first, we review the role of English in EMI programs. The chapter then gives information on outcome-based learning and Macalister and Nation's (2012) curriculum design model. The major part of the chapter focuses on a project conducted at a public university in Hanoi, Vietnam, to redesign the syllabus of an intensive English course in transnational programs following the outcome-based learning approach with a focus on environment and need analyses.

The Role of English in EMI Programs

Dafouz et al. (2016) argue that the implementation of EMI programs has changed the function of English, from a subject to study to a tool of knowledge acquisition in tertiary education. Firstly, it can be used as a gatekeeper in the admissions process. The first and foremost requirement for admission to the majority of EMI programs in most countries, whether

Anglophone or non-Anglophone, is English proficiency, which is often demonstrated by either internationally standardized English tests such as IELTS or TOEFL or equivalent institutional tests. Secondly, English is used as the medium of instruction for both teaching and learning activities. The role of English in an EMI environment varies according to the amount of English use, and it can be categorized into three types (Alexander, 2008, p. 82). The first is *replacement programming*, in which the local language is replaced by English, which serves as the sole medium of instruction from the beginning to the completion of a degree program. Staff and students are, therefore, supposed to have sufficient English proficiency to perform effectively in this environment. The second type is *cumulative programs*, which refers to a teaching environment where the amount of English use goes up as students' English proficiency levels up. Finally, the *additional type* is used to describe situations in which English is used as an assisting language to help international students transition smoothly into academic environments where the local language is used as the medium of instruction.

In brief, the implementation of EMI programs has led to a significant shift in the way the role of English is seen in higher education. The paradigm switched from the idea that English is a language that is taught and learned in foreign language lessons to the viewpoint that English is a lingua franca that can be used for both pedagogical and social purposes (Dafouz, 2017). From a language teaching perspective, it means that teaching should not only focus on training students to become successful English learners who master all the rules and achieve proper results in locally and internationally standardized tests but also assisting them in becoming "highly skilled communicators" who can use their language competence effectively for the sake of their interactions in the relevant environment (Jenkins et al., 2011).

OUTCOME-BASED LEARNING

As part of the Bologna Process, which aimed to establish an accessible and united European Higher Education Area, Outcome-Based Learning (OBL) was hailed as a novel method for rethinking the educational experience at the university level in the European Union (Kennedy, 2009). According to Driscoll and Wood (2007), an outcome-based approach to education is one that encourages institutions to be held accountable for their impact on students' learning and fosters a culture of constant focus on that impact. In their view, outcome-based learning is a method of teaching in which the goals of instruction and evaluation both focus on improving students' ability to learn. As a matter of fact, learning is prioritized through the promotion of OBL which aims at "structuring everything in an educational system around what is needed for all students to be able to accomplish successfully at the end of their learning experiences" (Spady, 1994, p. 1).

Kudlas (1994) argues that OBL is a method that centers on learning outcomes. This approach entails continuing to work with students until the desired result is achieved. In other words, what matters is "not the score, label, grade, or percentage that someone adds to the performance, but the improvement of students' knowledge, competence and qualities after they exit the educational system" (Spady, 1998, p. 25). For example, the focus of an intensive English course in the preparatory stage for university study should not only be the IELTS 5.5 but also that students who complete the course can perform successfully in an academic environment where English is used as a tool to express their critical thinking and understanding of a subject. Therefore, outcomes should be attainable, evaluable, and transparent. Outcomes should also identify what learners have not accomplished, and reflect the result of learning, not process (Tavner, 2005). Consequently, curriculum, instruction, and evaluation are all guided by learning objectives, or explicit expectations of what a student will have learned. These elements are designed to help students of any level learn more efficiently (Driscoll & Wood, 2007).

In other words, OBL is a backward design approach to curriculum development (Spady, 1994). The implementation of OBL involves determining learning objectives, then creating learning contents and activities that will help students to achieve the desired results, and finally evaluating the learning results through different forms of assessment.

The design of a syllabus following this philosophy is distinguished by the fact that course contents are described in terms of what students should be able to do when they complete their study, which are referred to as "intended learning outcomes—ILOs," which according to Baume (2005) must be: (1) attractive—students want to achieve them, (2) comprehensible—students know the meaning, (3) attainable—students can learn to achieve them, and (4) coherent—they clearly fit into their program.

In a nutshell, outcome based approach focuses on increasing students' learning and ultimate performance abilities to highest possible levels when students complete a course or a study program.

MACALISTER AND NATION'S (2012) CURRICULUM DESIGN FRAMEWORK

Curriculum design can be considered as both a product and a process (Macalister & Nation, 2012). As a product, it is what a teacher can use as a guideline for their daily classes, and as a process, it is a series of steps one should take in order to create the final product. These curriculum design steps are very similar to the writing process, which includes gathering ideas, organizing them, converting them to text, reviewing, and editing. According to Macalister and Nation (2012), the curriculum design model is made up of three outer circles and a subdivided inner circle. The outer circles consist of principles, situation analysis, and needs analysis, which are directly related to factors that will have significant impacts on the processes of curriculum development and course operation. These factors are the learners' existing level of language proficiency and what they lack, the resources available, including course duration, the professional knowledge and pedagogical skills of the teachers, and the principles of teaching and learning. If these factors are not well-considered, the product of curriculum design may appear to be unsuited to the context, and the learning and teaching process may then be ineffective and inefficient. Findings from situation analysis can be ranked in accordance with the effect that each element in the investigated context has on the learning situation. On the other hand, the outcome of a needs analysis is a practical list of essential language items and skills that learners need to achieve upon completion of the designed course based on their current level of language proficiency and their future needs and wants. The development of a curriculum, therefore, comprises both choosing the most remarkable factors to implement and monitoring their implementation through the whole design process.

Situation Analysis

'Situation analysis' (Richards, 2001) or "environment analysis" (Tessmer, 1990) investigates factors that may influence decisions related to goals, contents, delivery, and assessment of a course. These factors can be accounted for by the learners, the teachers, and the teaching and learning environment. There are many factors that could have strong effects on curriculum design, so the curriculum designer should be able to classify and give priority to factors that play key roles (Macalister & Nation, 2012). To identify the importance of a factor, two questions should be asked: (1) whether the course will still be useful if the factor is not taken into account and (2) how large and pervasive the effect of the factor is on the course.

The following table provides a checklist to help sort out the few that curriculum developers should pay attention to during the curriculum design process. The following checklist describes factors and their possible effects (Table 2.1).

Needs Analysis

Needs analysis is directly related to the goals and content of a course. It analyzes the current level of language proficiency among learners and the gap between the existing level and the expected goals. The needs analysis ensures that the course contains relevant and useful content for students. According to Hutchinson and Waters (1987), learning needs can be categorized as *target needs* (the context beyond the classroom where language will be used and the learners need to perform effectively) and *learning needs* (what learners need to learn effectively). The analysis of target needs investigates the following:

1. Necessities: Target situations in which language is used, its stylistic and pragmatic features. For example, do the learners have to paraphrase what they understand when writing answers to exam questions, or do they just need to recite everything accurately?
2. Lacks: What do the learners lack and need to learn? For example, are there aspects of writing that students have not mastered?
3. Wants: What do the learners wish to learn, and what are their expectations?

In short, lacks are about present knowledge, needs are about required knowledge, and wants are about subjective needs (Macalister & Nation, 2012). A good needs analysis thus covers a range of needs utilizing a range of data collection tools. More importantly, needs should be analyzed from various perspectives such as the gap between existing level of language

Table 2.1 Checklist for situation (environment) analysis

	Factors	Description	Possible effect
Learners	Age	Are the learners interested in all kinds of topics? Can the learners do all kinds of learning activities?	Take account of learners' interests. Use appropriate activities
	Background	Do they share a (first) language? Can their first language be used to help learning?	Use teacher-centered activities. Use some translation. Use first language prereading activities
	Learning motivation	Will they use English for a wide range of purposes? Do they expect to learn certain things from the course? Do they have expectations about what the course will be like? Are they interested in learning English? Can they attend class regularly?	Set general purpose goals. Include expected material. Allow learners to negotiate the nature of the course Use highly motivating activities Recycle activities. Use a spiral curriculum
Teachers	Background	Can they provide good models? Can they produce their own spoken or written material? Can they correct spoken or written work?	Provide taped materials. Provide a complete set of course material. Use activities that do not require feedback
	Experience	Can they prepare some of their own material? Can they handle group work, individualized learning?	Provide ready-made activities. Use group work activities
	Time	Can the course include homework? Can the course include work which has to be marked?	Provide homework activities. Provide answer keys

(*continued*)

22   T. N. NGUYEN AND H. T. B. DINH

Table 2.1 (continued)

	Factors	Description	Possible effect
Learning & teaching environment	Facilities	Can the arrangement of the desks be changed for groupwork? Is the blackboard big enoughand easily seen?	Use group work activities. Use material that does not require the students to have a course book
	Course duration	Can the learners reach the goals in the available time? Is the course intensive? Can the learners give all their time to the course?	Set staged goals. Provide plenty of material. Set limited goals
	Resources	Can material be photocopied? Can each learner have a copy of the course book? Is there plenty of supplementary material	Provide individualized material. Use teacher-focused material. Match the content to available supplementary material

Source: Macalister and Nation (2012)

proficiency and the expected level, context where language will be used after the course, or interest of learners. A thorough needs analysis should be able to collect information related to learners' learning experience, their existing level of language proficiency, future tasks and materials that learners may come into contact with, type of texts they should read or produce, communication discourse where they will perform. Needs analysis can be conducted before the initial stages of a course, and during the running of the course and at the end of a course. The before-course analysis can be used for designing a curriculum, the during-course analysis serves the purposes of making essential changes and the post-course analysis is used for reflection and innovation.

THE CURRICULUM DEVELOPMENT PROJECT

Context

The university where this research study was conducted is a public institution established in the 1950s in Hanoi, Vietnam. The university offers 40 bachelor's programs, including 16 EMI courses. Four of the EMI courses are joint degrees with international partner universities, and they are all related to the business field (University website). While the degrees are awarded by the partner universities from Australia, the United Kingdom, and Austria, the courses are instructed by Vietnamese lecturers who have to pass a strict process of selection, and the delivery is controlled by a system of quality assurance at partner universities. These programs recruit a total of around 200 students per academic year, most of whom go through an Intensive English Course (IEC) to reach IELTS 5.5 before commencing their official study in EMI programs.

The IEC is 18 weeks long with 30 contact hours per week. This course aims to provide students with essential language development to further their study in the chosen EMI program. Initially, the IEC focused solely on general English study skills in order for students to achieve IELTS 5.5. However, in their implementation of the course, the course designers, who were also the lecturers in the IEC came to realize that such a focus was too narrow because it did not provide students with sufficient academic skills and language items for their degree programs. Therefore, it was decided that the learning outcome-based approach was employed to revise the syllabus to better prepare the students so they would not only pass the language entry requirements but also have the academic skills needed for the EMI programs for their bachelor's degrees in business-related fields. The first priority in this process was to undertake a detailed analysis of the academic environment of the EMI program (environment analysis), the academic requirements of the program, and the students' current level of language proficiency and academic skills (needs analysis).

Curriculum Design Process

Environment and Needs Analysis

The following tasks were performed to conduct the essential analyses:

Task 1   A focus group interview with 12 language instructors of IEC programs who had been instructed at the program for at least three years. This meeting focused on identifying strengths and weaknesses of the existing curriculum, issues with students' learning, suggestions for improvement from the instructors. This meeting lasted for three hours.

Task 2   A focus group with eight lecturers who had been lecturing at different EMI programs at the university in the research context. This meeting aimed to identify types of assignments and their requirements, popular classroom activities and lecturers' expectation of students' performance. This meeting was also held for about three hours.

Task 3   Obtaining results of language proficiency tests in IELTS format from a sample of 100 students who were nearing the end of their IEC course.

Task 4   A focus group interview with 20 students who were in the first and second year of the business-related degree courses to discuss challenges they faced after completing the IEC course and starting their major program. This interview lasted for approximately three hours.

Task 5   Gathering course outlines from the first-year degree courses.

The data collection revealed the following major environment-, instructor-, and student-related factors:

Environment Factors

Learners' English proficiency levels on admission to the IEC program ranged from IELTS 3 to 5, and they had to achieve IELTS 5.5 before starting their degree programs. At the beginning of the course, it was difficult for them to get used to the communicative language teaching approach of university lecturers as they were more accustomed to the grammar-vocabulary approach and test preparation at high school. Besides, they were overwhelmed by the workload and assignments. It took them about five to six weeks to get used to the new environment and their oral literacy often developed faster than their written literacy. Students, who were in the first and second year of their business-related degree programs reported that the IEC should provide more contents related to the future subjects of degree programs and more guidelines related to academic writing skills so that they could perform better in the first semester. It is also noted that students often perceived that course work in their subject majors was more motivating and valuable than English language courses.

In terms of the learning organization and resources, class sizes varied from 16 to 22 students for the IEC courses and 25 to 30 for EMI programs. Students typically had access to printed textbook or electronic learning resources beyond the class time but they were not used to self-directed independent learning. In both programs, English was used as the medium of instruction, however, some lecturers used Vietnamese in classes to make the content more accessible. In the degree program, there were a considerable number of required assignments and presentations in a semester with strict academic requirements including the use of APA 7th reference and citing, updated resources of reference, the use of Turnitin plagiarism checker and length of at least 2000 words and beyond. It is also reported that critical thinking and the ability to explain what is learnt with concrete examples were of importance in the degree programs. Memorization of exact words was not encouraged and may lead to a failure in the written examination.

When it comes to language instructors and lecturers, the results were as follows. In the 2019–2020 academic year, approximately 20 English instructors were employed at IEC. They had a minimum qualification of a master's degree in TESOL and an IELTS certificate at 8.0. All instructors either graduated from Vietnamese universities or from universities abroad. Instructors were assigned to teach a specific set of language skills in a semester, and they were encouraged to use extra material while teaching. In their opinion, they believed that the combination of both assigned learning resources and teacher-made materials gave them sufficient space to direct students' learning process. They were all aware of the fact that their teaching should not only focus on IELTS preparation but also on implementing language into practice. However, they had difficulties designing extra materials to enhance students' language competence for degree programs as they had little idea of learning activities used at those programs.

Similarly, lecturers from degree programs had a minimum qualification of a master's in different areas of business and an IELTS certificate of at least 7.0. All instructors either graduated from EMI programs or universities abroad. In their opinion, they were satisfied with students' language skills, especially presentation skills. However, they claimed that students should be introduced to critical readings during the IEC as it would help students to read more effectively later on. Additionally, they suggested that students should have more opportunities to conduct research on some basic business, accounting, management, and marketing terms so that they would be less overwhelmed in the first semester of the degree programs.

Needs Analysis
The first consideration in necessities is the demands of the target tasks that students must complete in an EMI environment. An analysis of the course outlines of the EMI programs showed that the main tasks included listening to lectures, participating in tutorials, writing assignments and tasks, and doing written exams. In order to fulfill the course requirements, students should possess a wide range of both academic vocabulary and academic terms, together with appropriate grammatical accuracy. Furthermore, they should be able to write assignments in the form of descriptions, analyses, and comparisons. The interview with eight EMI lecturers who were involved in delivering course contents and marking such assignments provided insights into what they expected in a good assignment. In fact, they were not concerned with the grammatical accuracy of the writing but more concerned that the students show their understanding of academic writing rules and demonstrate their knowledge of the subject.

A crucial part of needs analysis involves investigating students' understanding of academic requirements and their existing academic skills, as well as what they thought would be beneficial for their study. This was done through interviews with 20 students in the first and second year of degree courses. It was discovered that there was a significant academic gap between what was taught in school and the academic expectations in the EMI environment. While at Vietnamese school memorization was prioritized, in EMI programs critical thinking and the ability to apply what was taught into practice were of great importance.

Revising the Syllabus Following a Learning Outcome-based Approach
Before the intended learning outcomes for the course were redesigned, the IEC's Program Learning Outcomes (PLOs) were identified based on needs analysis. Previously, IEC objectives were described based on the materials to be covered. The goals for learning were written in terms of what the teacher would teach the students. Before redesigning the IEC course using OBL, the previous course outline was reviewed and converted to OBL format. This helped language instructors to have a better understanding of their teaching outcomes. Below are some examples (Table 2.2):

Table 2.2 Examples of learning outcomes

Language objectives	Course intended language learning outcomes
1. Develop competence in academic reading skills.	Demonstrate a high level of understanding of English academic literacy in written contexts and subject knowledge.
2. Understand academic texts related to various topic	Demonstrate their understanding of academic texts by summarizing the key ideas and arguments, selecting related examples to illustrate a specific point/idea.
3. Write full academic essay of various length	Apply academic writing rules and styles into writing essays of length from 500 to 3000 words, using proper reading resources and referencing styles.
4. Understand some basic ESP terms	Demonstrate their understanding of terms related to business management by being able to explain and provide related examples.

The Final Curriculum Product

After analyzing the environment, needs and redesigning the learning objectives in accordance with the outcome-based approach, the next step centered on working within and against them to achieve the objectives of developing students' language and academic skills. In order to organize the necessary time for language proficiency and to explore topics of interest related to the subject majors in the EMI programs on business studies, the course designers followed two separate phases, with each phase aiming at providing students with the necessary knowledge and skills to both pass the language entry requirements into the EMI programs, and to be able to do the required academic tasks in the EMI programs.

Phase 1: Developing and Enhancing Language and Study Skills through the Use of IELTS-Oriented and Content based Textbooks
In this phase, extensive development was needed in all four language skills in order to access important concepts covered in the future study. For this reason, 80% of the teaching time is used for intensive language training and 20% for academic skills. The same topics appeared in each unit of the respective listening, speaking, reading, and writing materials, which were developed and compiled based on a number of existing textbooks in the market. The instructors were also required to design additional tasks to target students' weaknesses.

To maximize opportunities to recycle language form, meaning, and use on familiar topics, additional receptive and productive tasks are added. For example, 200-word dictation passages were designed based on previously encountered texts. Some texts were designed for extensive reading or fluency development with a controlled range of vocabulary, meaning that 50 to 60% of the words were derived from course material or the first and second thousand most common English words. By creating repeated opportunities to consolidate and extend language use in multiple contexts, low-proficiency learners would have time to comprehend texts, recognize language forms, and practice using them in meaningful contexts. Guided independent language learning was the final element that instructors were encouraged to include in their teaching process. Primarily, this entailed assigning homework as preparation for the upcoming class. However, instead of focusing on practicing language items, the given homework aimed to develop students' self-learning and research skills. Students were asked to either select an article or audio from given resources and summarize their content in the form of a mini presentation or to conduct a mini research on current news or events.

Phase 2: Developing Content-Specific Language and Improving Language Proficiency in Relation to Specific Business Disciplines through Project Work and Integrated Skills Tasks
While Phase 1 focused on improving academic language development, Phase 2 gave students the chance to work on integrated skills, issue-based projects to address motivational issues related to the relevance of future course contents or the chance to review and direct their own learning. The course developers added English for Specific Purposes and English for Academic Purposes lessons in the new curriculum with a frequency of six hours per week. With this introduction, students had opportunities to explore a variety of topics related to their future study in business fields. They were also introduced to basic research skills and rules of academic writing, as well as steps to approach different kinds of academic assignments. Such an approach was expected to help students gain greater confidence in using language productively. For their part, the instructors were required to support productive language use and increase awareness of appropriate academic discourse and academic conventions through a read-to-write model.

Phase 2 set a platform to develop students' independent research skills and experience in directing their own learning, which help them to develop their personal project work. Such an approach was based on the suggestion of lecturers from degree programs. Additionally, language instructors could contribute to students' learning development thanks to their roles as project coaches. This gave students opportunities to work under supervision and to enhance not only their academic skills but also social skills.

Course Piloting

In the academic year 2020–2021, the new IEC curriculum was piloted. The course structure and goals were thoroughly presented to both language instructors and students at the start of the semester, emphasizing the intended outcomes. During the implementation process, mid-course and end-of-course feedback from instructors and students was collected. Additionally, regular feedback from all parties shed light on timely changes, and it all benefited the learning and teaching processes. Nearly **200** students and **20** English language instructors took part in the pilot.

When asked to fill out a survey form anonymously, almost all of the students (93%) stated that the outcomes were clear to them and that motivated them to study. Besides, they quite enjoyed the learning activities of courses and felt confident when doing simulated tasks and assignments, which indicated that the changes in the approach and the learning content brought positive feedback. Additionally, all students agreed that the outcomes of the course helped them develop better academic skills for their future degree programs, and their confidence was boosted as they had a clearer understanding of what studying in an EMI environment would be like. It was also reported by the instructors that students appeared to be more engaged in classroom activities, and there was a positive teacher-student relationship.

On the other hand, a number of challenges were also identified. As for students, a number of them felt overburdened with the number of tasks and assignments they had to complete. When compared to the language-only learning environment, learners of the new curriculum had to take more risks and try harder to master challenging academic work than before. As for the language instructors, the changes in the curriculum design approach meant changes in their teaching methods and material development. It was reported that designing lesson plans and activities appeared to be challenging since there should be a strong connection between what teachers wanted to teach and the intended learning outcomes. It was also recorded that it took time and effort to be well prepared, and language instructors had to pay considerable attention to structuring learning experiences to help learners learn effectively and achieve the intended outcomes. Sometimes, the instructors found it difficult due to the limited resources and time. Finally, it was of great responsibility and pressure for the course designers in determining what things were "essential for all students to be able to do," which was often a contentious issue, and it was not always an easy task to clarify the intended learning outcomes to language instructors so that they could use the outcomes to guide their lesson planning and instructional practices.

REFLECTION AND CONCLUSION

The experience of analyzing the environment and needs while designing a program to meet the needs of various stakeholders has revealed the dynamic nature of the curriculum design process. It also reveals that when learning needs have been identified, outcome-based learning will help learners focus on their intended learning outcomes so that they can enhance both their knowledge and skills upon completion of a course. Such an approach also makes learning more student-centered and redefines the instructor's role. In an OBL context, instructors need to think from the learners' perspectives and pay attention to how they can help learners achieve the intended learning outcomes and be able to transfer what they have achieved into a more challenging environment. It is also noted that to implement OBL successfully in an intensive English course for EMI degree programs, it is essential to first come up with a set of generic outcomes at the degree program level and then develop a set of IEC learning outcomes that must be based on the generic outcomes in a specific manner. It is, therefore, critical to design realistic, comprehensible, achievable, and transferable intended learning outcomes based on the specific requirements of a degree program, and to ensure that teaching and learning activities are directly related to the future degree program outcomes. Finally, feedback from students and instructors is important for further adjustment and improvement of the entire practice of curriculum design.

In the final note, this chapter, in spite of its small scale, has contributed to research in curriculum design, especially in EMI in transnational programs, a current trend in education internationalization in Vietnam.

References

Alexander, R. J. (2008). 'International' programmes in the German speaking world and Englishization: A critical analysis. In R. Wilkinson & V. Zegers (Eds.), *Realizing content and language integration in higher education* (pp. 77–95). Maastricht University.

Baume, D. (2005). *Outcomes-based approaches to teaching, learning & curriculum.* Powerpoint presentation on 15 December 2005 for Hong Kong Polytechnic University, Hong Kong.

Dafouz, E. (2017). English-medium instruction in multilingual university settings: An opportunity for developing language awareness. In P. Garrett & J. M. Cots (Eds.), *The Routledge handbook of language awareness (Routledge handbooks in linguistics)* (pp. 170–185). Routledge.

Dafouz, E., Hüttner, J., & Smit, U. (2016). University teachers' beliefs of language and content integration in English-Medium Education in multilingual university settings. In T. Nikula, E. Dafouz, P. Moore, & U. Smit (Eds.), *Conceptualising integration in CLIL and multilingual education.* Multilingual Matters.

Driscoll, A., & Wood, S. (2007). *Developing outcomes-based assessment for learner-centered education: A faculty introduction.* Stylus Publishing, LLC.

Hutchinson, T., & Waters, A. (1987). *English for specific purposes.* Cambridge University Press.

Jenkins, J., Cogo, A., & Dewey, M. (2011). State-of-the-art article: Review of developments in research into English as a lingua franca. *Language Teaching, 44*(3), 281–315. https://doi.org/10.1017/S0261444811000115

Kennedy, K. (2009). *Outcomes based learning: Concepts, issues and action.* http://www.ied.edu.hk/obl/files/OBLConcepts%20Issues%20and%20Action_Kennedy.doc

Kudlas, J. M. (1994). Implications of OBE: What you should know about outcomes-based education. *The Science Educator, 61*(5), 32–35.

Macalister, J., & Nation, I. S. P. (2012). *Language curriculum design.* Routledge.

Nguyen, T. H., Hamid, M. O., & Moni, K. (2016). English-medium instruction and self-governance in higher education: The journey of a Vietnamese university through the institutional autonomy regime. *High Education, 72.* https://doi.org/10.1007/s10734-015-9970-y

Nguyen, T. H., Walkinshaw, I., & Pham, H. H. (2017). EMI programs in a Vietnamese University: Language, pedagogy and policy issues. In B. Fenton-Smith, P. Humphreys, & I. Walkinshaw (Eds.), *English medium instruction in higher education in Asia-Pacific: From policy to pedagogy* (pp. 37–52). Springer.

Richards, J. C. (2001). *Curriculum development in language teaching.* Cambridge University Press.

Spady, W. D. (1994). *Outcomes based education: Critical issues and answers.* American Association of School Administration.

Spady, W. D. (1998). Outcomes based education: An international perspective. In J. Gultig, C. Lubisi, B. Parker, & U. Wedekind (Eds.), *Understanding outcomes based education: Teaching and assessment in South Africa.* SAIDE & Oxford University Press.

Tavner, A. (2005). Outcomes-based education in a university setting. *Australian Journal of Engineering Education, 02,* 1–14.

Tessmer, M. (1990). Environment analysis: A neglected stage of instructional design. *Educational Technology Research and Development, 38*(1), 55–64.

Tran, L. T., & Nguyen, H. T. (2018). Internationalisation of higher education in Vietnam through English Medium Instruction (EMI): Practices, tensions and implications for local language policies. In I. Liyanage (Ed.), *Multilingual education yearbook 2018* (pp. 91–106). Springer International Publishing AG.

CHAPTER 3

Out of the Ordinary: Implementation of a New Japanese Language Program in Higher Education in Vietnam

Eriko Yamato

INTRODUCTION

RMIT University Vietnam is one of the foreign university campuses in Ho Chi Minh City. It has played an important role in leading tertiary education in the region as an international institution since 2000. In line with higher education programs offered at the main campus in Melbourne, Australia, all programs of the Vietnam campus are designed to supply an industry-led and student-centered learning experience. Apart from the common educational goals that are shared with the other campuses, the Vietnam campus has implemented learning and teaching strategies where single-source textbooks and traditional end of semester examinations have been replaced by authentic assessment tasks and online resources

E. Yamato (✉)
School of Communication and Design, RMIT University Vietnam,
Ho Chi Minh City, Vietnam
e-mail: eriko.yamato@rmit.edu.vn

© The Author(s), under exclusive license to Springer Nature Switzerland AG 2024
L. Phung et al. (eds.), *Innovation in Language Learning and Teaching*, New Language Learning and Teaching Environments,
https://doi.org/10.1007/978-3-031-46080-7_3

across all programs to realize the educational goals of preparing students for life and work. To support this move, the campus has organized a number of learning and teaching workshops for both lecturers and students. Innovative methods of self-directed and interactive learning with engaging digital learning materials and authentic assessments have been encouraged. Industry engagement is also incorporated in every program, including industry field trips and guest speaker sessions as well as industry-led projects and internships (RMIT University, 2022; Brown et al., 2022).

Coming from over 20 years of teaching experience in public tertiary education in Southeast Asia, where the process of curriculum reform was rather slow and learning and teaching innovations were limited, I was excited to be a part of the journey to execute educational policies at RMIT University Vietnam. Contrary to the expectations I had of the institutions and students in socialist societies, I saw interactive English classrooms with group work and active students engaging enthusiastically in class and sitting on sofas with their laptops in on-campus spaces. These sights gave me an incentive to learn more about the underpinning pedagogical philosophies, and I was exhilarated by the new challenges. The Vietnam campus was small enough to have individual induction sessions about the university's learning and teaching policies for new staff at the time I was onboarded in 2017. Furthermore, when I started my work to prepare to launch the new undergraduate program, the Bachelor of Languages in the School of English, the School had an open atmosphere for innovation, and I had opportunities to explore novel ideas through both workshops and invitations to observe classes.

In addition to these unexpected new environments I encountered, the initial inspiration for designing the Japanese courses for a Bachelor of Languages program was met with skepticism about the fixed structural syllabus approach that has been common in Japanese language education, especially outside Japan. In Noda's, 2012 book on research in Japanese education, the widely held pro-textbook sentiment, which has a strong influence on the structural syllabus in Japanese language education, is questioned by some Japanese scholars. They also called for research on authentic Japanese materials and real communication among native speakers, as well as between native and non-native speakers of Japanese. In her 2009 book chapter on research and pedagogy in Japanese grammar, Kobayashi, a leading scholar in Japanese language education in Japan, pointed out the huge gap between real communication and communication in the Japanese language classroom. In everyday life, we never have conversations for the purpose of using specific grammatical forms and rules. Instead, we communicate with others and use the language to deliver specific intended content. While rethinking the syllabus of Japanese courses, I ended up changing the assessments to fit the campus policies first and then gradually, while delivering courses every semester, got ideas for another course at one level higher. The word "authentic" in authentic assessment prompted me to move away from grammar-centric learning content. If knowing the sentence structures were the core learning outcome of the courses, testing knowledge of grammar in a written examination would be appropriate, but RMIT's learning outcomes for courses did not stop at the lower-order learning level. So asking what was "authentic" in authentic assessment for language learning is the first step for me in beginning to develop the Japanese courses within the Bachelor of Languages program.

This chapter begins with an introduction and overview of the Japanese major along with its underpinning core concepts aimed at producing work-ready graduates equipped with the necessary trilingual language and soft skills. Secondly, it explains the efforts to develop a quality higher education program utilizing hybrid-mode based on the concept of "flipped classroom" and "authentic assessment" at every level in the language learning process. Finally, the pros and cons of these approaches are discussed featuring three different views: students, stakeholders, and course instructors.

Bachelor of Languages: Japanese Major

The Bachelor of Languages degree program consists of two majors: the Translating and Interpreting major, which focuses on the Vietnamese–English language pair, and the Japanese major. The core framework of this program was designed by the School of English Language, RMIT Vietnam, in cooperation with executives and language experts at the Melbourne campus. The Japanese major program is based on the model of successful pre-university-level English language programs with participatory active language learning as its fundamental pedagogical approach. While consolidating students' language skills in both English and their native language and/or the third language, the program also aims to guide students in developing soft skills such as critical thinking, problem-solving, and adaptability. In 2019, the Bachelor of Languages program was shifted to be managed by the School of Communication and Design and has continued to evolve as a higher education program that reflects the university's learning and teaching strategies, including authentic assessment, digitalized learning, and industry and community engagement.

Each course of the Japanese major is designed to contribute to cultivating various aspects of the learning outcomes of the Bachelor of Languages program. The program's learning outcomes aim to develop the attributes expected of RMIT undergraduate program graduates as work-ready, global in outlook and competent, culturally and socially aware, active and lifelong learners, and innovative. The six levels of Japanese language proficiency courses cover fundamental to intermediate knowledge of the Japanese language, provide formative, hands-on practice in productive skills, and enhance sociocultural awareness as well as soft skills throughout the integrated activities, which are performed by students outside of face-to-face class hours. Each course includes a recommended total of 120 learning hours with 36 hours of face-to-face classes and self-directed learning using online materials provided in the university's Learning Management System (LMS).

To enable students to engage in authentic communication at the beginner level, the main topic of each course is related to life in Vietnam. The scope of topics is then gradually expanded to wider surrounding phenomena, events, and issues in higher-level courses. Weekly face-to-face classes are divided into two sessions focusing on helping students practice speaking and writing, respectively. By referring to traditional Japanese language textbooks that are structured based on simple to sophisticated grammatical aspects in progression, Japanese 1 introduces simple sentence patterns and Japanese 2, 3 and 4 bring in some compound sentences and clauses involving aspects and modalities. From Japanese 3, weekly course content is framed by topics that allow students to select grammatical points that are necessary to express their content. Even though Japanese 1 to 3 supply vocabulary lists in the LMS, students are encouraged to use the open-source online dictionary (Ahlström et al., n.d.) developed to search for the words needed to deliver their intended meanings in their own contexts.

The Vietnam campus' "no single textbook" policy directs us to make use of the LMS for each course. Each course coordinator or lecturer is responsible for creating and updating the LMS content, which consists of modules and assessment guidelines. As for language courses, the "no single textbook" policy was apparently too ambitious, because publishing one series of textbooks takes a lot of effort and time, and it is almost impossible to produce the same quality of content in a short time.

Nevertheless, while teaching one semester with one textbook, I realized that there were open-source supplemental materials available for well-known textbooks as well as some websites and videos that individual Japanese language educators and enthusiasts had created and shared online. I started to select and compile some of those, and I restructured the syllabus. During this process for the first two levels, I also realized that we should not rely solely on a printed textbook, which easily becomes outdated, in order to maintain "authenticity" in the courses in terms of vocabulary use.

The top-down policies that were introduced at the beginning not only freed us from limiting vocabulary but also allowed us to roll out a new initiative on the *Kanji* writing system, which is one of the most difficult aspects of Japanese language learning. The Kanji writing system hinders the learning of reading and writing in the Japanese language as it includes over 2,000 symbolic characters. To initially reduce this complexity, the approach used for Japanese school children is commonly applied in Japanese language education. Introducing some simple Kanji characters according to the number of strokes for beginner learners leads to odd spellings of some nouns that are supposed to consist of two Kanji characters. To avoid going through this children's writing stage with adult learners, we introduce typing skills from the very beginning of the first course. Students are also exposed to authentic writing materials in the second-level curriculum and learn to convert words using the prediction candidates that pop up while typing texts with a computer in Japanese input mode. This reflects the current situation where handwriting skills are not much needed in authentic written communications in both private and work settings.

Every Japanese course also includes a range of integrated activities that immerse students in authentic communication. These activities require students to apply speaking, writing, listening, and reading language skills, regardless of their level of language proficiency. The authenticity of each activity is defined by using "authentic language," which means the language is not altered according to course content such as introduced vocabulary and sentence patterns. From Japanese 1 to 3, students make use of English as a learning medium to complete Japanese tasks. From Japanese 4, they engage with native speakers of Japanese through different activities such as teaching Vietnamese to Japanese residents, conducting language and cultural games for Japanese children, and interviewing industry partners. These activities were initiated and developed according to the university's learning and teaching strategies and policies such as authentic assessment and industry and community engagement.

INSTITUTION-DRIVEN INNOVATION

This section highlights the efforts to realize hybrid-mode "flipped classrooms" without the use of printed textbooks and the implementation of "authentic assessment" at every level in the language learning process while maintaining the integrity of the university's higher education program.

Flipped Classroom

Since the use of the LMS was fundamental to the new courses from the designing stage of the Japanese major courses, approximately three years were spent developing the first flipped classroom content for ten courses. According to the broad definition of a flipped classroom, "events that have typically and traditionally happened inside the classroom" take place "outside the classroom" (McNally et al., 2017, p. 282). In language learning, the knowledge of vocabulary and grammar can be considered lower order but essential learning content so that students should be self-prepared before engaging in higher-order learning activities that need an instructor's guidance as Jong (2019, p. 393) explained in relation to Bloom's Taxonomy. When a course is designed based on a single textbook, introducing knowledge of a language, such as vocabulary and grammar, and assigning exercises to consolidate students' understanding of sentence patterns are essential classroom activities, especially for the beginner levels. Now, this knowledge-based content is all included in the LMS and accessible to students outside the classroom setting.

The year we started developing Japanese course content in the LMS, the English program was also developing its online content and incorporating technological learning tools in their face-to-face teaching. There were a few experts in language learning and technology at the university, and the campus also had support staff who were familiar with educational technology and assessment processes in general as well as staff whose expertise was purely in the use of specific functions of the LMS. In addition to the skilled workforce assistance provided by the university, we used students' feedback after each delivery to determine the suitability of the course in terms of both amount and content. Official course experience surveys conducted by the university and interviews with program representatives were the main source of feedback from inaugural students. The direction of course development was discussed and decided at the program level in reference to the feedback. Since students were generally inactive in giving individual qualitative feedback in the official survey despite its anonymity, the instructor also conducted self-administrative surveys after the course assessment ended. These consisted of more course-specific questions in order to understand students' experiences in language learning in the pre-intermediate to advanced courses. Although updating pre-class preparation content and formats has been a continuous challenge because the instructors had limited technical knowledge and spare time to enhance the online environment, assistance with this issue has been provided at the campus level by online learning support experts and through workshops and individual consultations for lecturers as needed.

In the past five years, however, what we have experienced is that having all enrolled students engage in self-directed, non-assessed pre-class learning activities is a never-ending challenge in implementing the flipped classroom format. Since the flipped classroom is a university-driven policy, every course is supposed to have basic content utilizing standard format, including pre-class pages in the module section, regardless of delivery format. The Vietnam campus also has a quality assurance process at the beginning of every semester to ensure each course fulfils standard requirements in line with the learning and teaching policies of the campus. All new students have opportunities to explore successful learning strategies specific to this university and to attend hands-on sessions to use the LMS at the beginning of their study journey. That means that every senior student is anticipated to be familiar with the LMS and its learning style. The lecturers are optimistic about gaining the "students' endorsement" of the delivery format and learning style before their course enrollment. However, these campus-level efforts have not successfully increased every student's engagement in their learning, and how to create stimulating and encouraging non-assessed pre-class tasks is an area for improvement during the process of updating the LMS content across the programs.

In the macro view of the students' background, Vietnamese students are accustomed to the teacher-led and knowledge-based learning style, and that cannot be changed overnight. This is, in fact, similar to the results of McNally et al.'s (2017) study on the flipped classroom approach, where only the students who endorsed the concept had positive attitudes toward all course activities regardless of whether they were conducted online or face-to-face. For recent Japanese courses, therefore, to guide students in managing their pre-class learning, 30 minutes to 1 hour have been allocated to interactive brainstorming sessions about the course format, with the instructors acting as facilitators and navigators for their learning. Yet, it has been more difficult to achieve full acceptance of this learning format by beginner-level students than those at higher levels because of their attitudes and expectations regarding the course. For instance, in 2019, students of Japanese 1 occasionally left unfavorable comments in the section of the official course experience survey regarding the expectation of self-study before coming to the class. In 2022, after more emphasis was put on the flipped classroom format, one wrote that they wanted improvements to "the teaching style. We are left to learn the content on our own and go to class to practice." This implies the student's knowledge of the learning style but lack of understanding of the reason for its implementation. More obviously, Japanese instructors have only seen a few students who engage in the pre-class tasks, despite receiving mostly positive comments about the modules.

Despite resistance from some students regarding the flipped classroom approach, obvious differences in the students' outcomes were witnessed over the past five years between students who engaged well in pre-class preparation and those who started looking at pre-class materials when physically coming into the classes. These challenging aspects of the flipped classroom approach are, in fact, similar to those Nunez and Monsivais (2020) pointed out in relation to nursing education. They observed that since pre-class engagement is a student-centered process, an instructor cannot do much without changing the mindset of the students. However, one of the challenging aspects highlighted in the research, the heavy course preparation workload of setting up all courses in the flipped classroom format, has at least been overcome by now. With a sufficient volume of online course content ready, making further changes from time to time is a manageable task in between semesters. Regular discussions at the course level and cyclical reflections at the program level are a platform to initiate any change in the course content. Recently we started documenting changes to be able to track what we have done and to analyze students' performance reflectively.

Another element related to the flipped classroom approach in the Japanese major program is that, from Japanese 3 onwards, formative weekly assessments are designed to be directly tied to pre-class and in-class activities. This means that content could not be merely "flipped" from its in class use to pre-class platforms. Applying this approach requires that major course content and delivery format revisions be made to established, pre-existing course content as well as related methods of assessment. The pre-class content, which was selected lower-order knowledge, was centered around broad topics, yet too open-ended for students to be able to select what they want to deliver. The in-class content was, therefore, adjusted according to their pre-class tasks as formative assessments to help students learn what they are lacking and improve their work. The formulation of ideas to design the course creating pre-class tasks, in-class activities, and post-class assessments was stimulated by following the workshops organized by the university's learning and teaching department. There were also sharing and discussion sessions about the other lecturers' practices for higher-level courses across the schools. Another recent positive phenomenon is that the strict COVID-19 lockdown situation in Vietnam made most students familiar with online learning and its environment. The instructors also adapted to the latest online tools, such as online meeting/sharing applications and online whiteboards to enhance both pre-class and face-to-face learning methods with support from the university through online information sessions and hands-on workshops across the campuses. After parting from the School of English, the key conceptual input came from the content courses, and the language courses provide ideas to consider such aspects as what resources and what activities to be applied.

Authentic Assessment

Authentic assessment is a core concept included in the design of each Japanese course in the program. We were under pressure to make our program consistent with the other programs offered on the same campus and fit the fundamental educational goal of achieving the learning outcomes of each course as well as the program learning outcomes, including skills such as communication, intercultural competence, life-long learning, teamwork, and critical thinking. Gulikers et al. (2004) defined authentic assessment as "an assessment requiring students to use the same competence, or combinations of knowledge, skills, and attitudes, that they need to apply in the criterion situation in professional life" (p. 69). The concept of "professional life" in the context of the Japanese program encompasses any type of work utilizing the Japanese language, and everyday life themes cannot be excluded from the context of professional life since we need the ability to deliver everyday topics in professional contexts as well. The beginner-level course, Japanese 1, thus begins with "Self and Students," which relates to the immediate surroundings and everyday lives of the students. Subsequently, the topics of each course are gradually extended to the wider surroundings of both Vietnam and Japan.

As authentic assessment was a top-down initiative, when we designed the online passage-writing tasks as the summative assessment for Japanese 1 in the first semester, we received an inquiry from the campus' learning and teaching department and were required to explain the reason for having a kind of "test" at the end of the semester for the newly launched course. By getting support from the English language program, we insisted on the necessity of testing productive skills on-site at the end of the course, and our assessment tasks have some critical elements to make the assessment authentic for the specific proficiency level. According to Sokhanvar et al.'s (2021) systematic literature review of authentic assessment in higher education, the main formats and tools of the assessment tasks are presentations, mini projects, case studies, reflective journals, and interviews, while paper examinations are excluded. Our format of the summative assessment did not fit the expectations of the general framework of authentic assessment that the department had at that time.

Japanese 1 to 6, nonetheless, have summative assessment tasks at the end of the course to indicate whether students achieved the learning outcomes of each course which reflect certain levels of language proficiency. Because the focus of each course is to support students in developing productive skills in the Japanese language that are difficult to achieve without the presence of others. Thus, each assessment task assesses their productive skills while the use of receptive skills is incorporated to complete the task. When course assessments are designed as "authentic" for students, their learning experiences differ from those of courses specifically designed for knowledge-based traditional examinations. Even though students are supposed to acquire the target language and enhance their communication skills in the language, without developing essential soft skills such as collaboration skills, critical thinking and problem-solving skills, self-awareness, and self-confidence, they would not be ready for professional life when completing the undergraduate program. A decade ago, Ashford-Rowe et al. (2014) determined the critical elements of authenticity in assessment tasks, and found eight critical elements: challenge, performance, or product (outcome), transfer of knowledge, metacognition, accuracy, fidelity, discussion, and collaboration.

3 OUT OF THE ORDINARY: IMPLEMENTATION OF A NEW JAPANESE...

To apply the authentic assessment principle, we have designed each assessment task by considering aspects that are close to what Villarroel et al. (2020) highlighted in their discussion on redesigning traditional examinations. These are "injecting realism into tests" (p. 42) and "assessing complex thinking" (p. 43). For instance, Japanese 1 and 2 cover basic vocabulary and simple sentence patterns, although to complete each assessment task, students need to make use of transfer skills such as judging and deciding as well as the lower-level analytical skills of comparing and relating in order to complete whole tasks. In terms of the format of the tasks, images or videos are used to contextualize each task in a realistic situation, and the task questions are open ended so as to elicit innovative original ideas from the students' perspectives.

At the campus level, in-class and summative assessment tasks utilizing online tools in the LMS are not eliminated even after the final examination weeks in the academic calendar and the campus did not have a final examination department to collect question papers and conduct the examination following the university guideline. Overall, the campus was gifted with strong leadership to put authentic assessments in place, and their approach was successful because each coordinator and lecturer had a chance to voice and share their issues in the transition process. As for the Bachelor of Languages program, we were on board in this process from the beginning of the program and we continue to adjust the assessment format of each course by considering both the nature of the subject and what is authentic for the context of the course.

DISCUSSION

By expanding what was presented in the earlier sections, this section discusses the pros and cons of the approaches based on the feedback of students about their beliefs about language learning, the expectations and feedback of industry participants, and the heuristic reflections of course instructors in the program.

Recognition and Resistance by Students

The activity-based, face-to-face classes and the number of authentic elements in language use generally allowed students to engage well in their courses, and thus the general feedback on the course experience survey was positive among the Japanese major students over the past five years.

The response rate of the survey has been statistically insufficient for most semesters. Still, we have occasionally received intuitive comments and taken action if it is reasonable and affordable to do so. For instance, available online sources were apparently adequate to assist students' analytical tasks on colloquial Japanese, on which Japanese 5 deliberately focuses. However, one student pointed out the lack of references in the University Library to support their assessment tasks. This feedback made us realize that there were students who wanted to learn Japanese but did not have an interest in Japanese popular cultural products such as films and animation, so they needed more assistance in exposure to colloquial Japanese. Some first-cohort students, who understood the fact that the Bachelor of Languages was a developing program in the context of Vietnam, were cooperative in expressing their thoughts after completing each course. As for the whole program, we maintained an attitude of learning from the students and judging feedback fairly, and we reacted accordingly despite occasionally receiving unconstructive feedback. Most students' feedback was not explicitly directed towards the educational policies and pedagogy fundamental to the courses. The students often referred to the flipped classroom concept as "self-study," and authentic assessment as "no paper final examination." As far as I know, there were no calls for a final examination in place of authentic assessment, even though some students were struggling to meet the assessment due dates that fell around the end of the semester.

At the same time, students' resistance was observable through their reactions. Some students who registered for Japanese 1 as an elective quit the course early in the semester because of overwhelming online content and constant assessment tasks that needed to be handed in every week. The elective students enrolled in Japanese 3 and above gave both positive and negative responses about the self-study component. The students who could cope with formative assessments had good academic performance overall and they appreciated our efforts to give constant feedback and opportunities to improve their productive skills despite the challenging timeline. Those who expressed their dissatisfaction were confused by the flipped classroom approach and by the instructors' roles, which did not involve teaching the grammar points in face-to-face classes as they had experienced in the other language classes outside the university. There were also students who valued real experiences in Japanese and the courses, in fact, improved their productive skills.

One of the alumni of this program confessed after completing eight courses of Japanese that she relied on software that shows Kanji written in syllabic letters called *Furigana*. The software assisted her to read online materials and make presentations in Japanese throughout the intermediate to advanced courses. She also added that she could comprehend spoken Japanese based on each context and could convey her ideas even though she lacked grammatical accuracy. This student was one who accepted and made efforts to adapt to our approaches in language learning. When she had the opportunity to write about her journey of learning Japanese at RMIT in an online Japanese magazine, she praised the student-centered learning even though it was more challenging than she had expected. Her suggestion for the program was to include testing or a scale to monitor Kanji learning for every course at that time. She was concerned that she would not feel confident if she could not see quantifiable achievement in her language learning from an examination with scores. At any rate, she took the Japanese Language Proficiency Test (JLPT) and passed the intermediate level without much test preparation.

The students who progress to higher-level Japanese courses might struggle and feel overwhelmed because all the materials used for Japanese 6 and above are authentic materials on specific topics or from academic fields that Japanese natives read and listen to, and every course includes authentic communication with classmates and instructors as well as other native speakers for specific purposes which are not usually associated with general everyday discourse. Nevertheless, some Vietnamese students became interested in Kanji because the formation of the words is similar to the Vietnamese language, since both languages were influenced by the Chinese language, and they started making efforts to learn the characters by heart even though they were not imposed as course assessments.

Benchmark of Japanese Proficiency and Stakeholders

At the campus level, one department in charge of building and expanding industry relations supports lecturers by contacting both global and Vietnamese companies. With the assistance of this department, the Japanese program has established relations with Japanese companies in Vietnam. Some visit the campus and hold meetings, and some have become partners to engage with our students in the course activities. The Bachelor of Languages program also formed an industry advisory committee that consists of Japanese expatriates in Vietnam. The most useful input we had for developing our program came from personal meetings and informal conversations during functions organized by the Japanese Chamber of Commerce in Ho Chi Minh City, especially about the JLPT.

The JLPT is an instrument used as part of an internationally recognized Japanese language certification system. When applying for posts in Japanese companies and roles requiring Japanese language skills, learners of the Japanese language are classified according to their JLPT results. In our program, we encourage students to prepare for and take the JLPT N3, which is the middle of the five levels of the JLPT, before their internship even though our program is not designed according to the JLPT levels. One of the reasons for this is the feedback from industry stakeholders, especially from recruitment agencies that support both companies and Vietnamese Japanese speakers to find better employment opportunities. On the other hand, we also heard from many sources that job applicants who passed the N3 and higher did not really have sufficient productive skills in Japanese. Most recruitment agencies said that the JLPT result is a benchmark used to reduce the number of candidates for bigger companies to interview, which is the main process for selecting final candidates with adequate levels of language proficiency. They did not blindly rely on the JLPT results to hire any personnel.

When our students interacted with Japanese native speakers as part of the course assessments, industry people and Japanese residents complimented their achievements in productive skills. In fact, there were also alumni who gained internship positions that required N2, which is the pre-advanced level, without having any JLPT official result. I do not deny the importance of having a benchmark and certificate to prove one's language skills; however, we accepted some students who passed the N3 or N2 before enrolling in our program/courses and found that they could not write comprehensive essays/reports with a logical flow and could not demonstrate mature ideas in oral presentations because of a lack of practice in formulating ideas and conveying them in the target language even though they have the knowledge of grammar and vocabulary to be benchmarked at an intermediate or advanced level.

Test results and certificates show clear achievement in learning the target language and provide self-satisfaction to learners from the proof that their efforts have been beneficial. Clear indicators such as the number of recognizable Kanji characters and vocabulary and understandable grammatical points ease our anxiety and uncertainty in the language learning process. However, the reality is that native speakers have various levels of knowledge in terms of Kanji characters and vocabulary, and have familiar topics that they can easily talk or write about but also encounter unfamiliar language that needs to be checked in a dictionary. The authentic assessment approach allowed us to be free from the ideas of having fixed and ready-made frameworks and indicators in designing our Japanese program at RMIT. We have observed some students realizing their improvement in speaking and writing skills throughout the courses and extending whatever knowledge they have outside of the course. Some of them also realized that second and third language acquisition is a never-ending lifelong process. Even though some students may be confused and a few of them lose confidence in their learning journey, without developing abilities to use the target language in authentic situations, they will not be able to communicate their messages and engage in real communication especially in professional contexts.

Concluding Remarks

Compared to the pre-university English program at RMIT Vietnam, which has 200 hours of face-to-face class hours for its seven levels, the success of the Bachelor of Languages, Japanese Major program has been uncertain since the planning stage as it depends on whether students are prepared for life and work with adequate Japanese language proficiency upon completion. Since the Japanese courses were designed to be embedded in the higher education program offered by an international university in Vietnam, other program components such as culture and language-related courses were included as they are irrefutably effective in the acquisition of fundamental linguistics knowledge and intercultural communication skills while learning a third language as an adult. The actual hours required for learning the Japanese language have been limited and very much dependent on students' motivation and engagement levels with the target language, which is not under the direct control of the course designer and instructors.

Nevertheless, these flipped classroom and authentic assessment policies work well in adjusting the usual syllabus and learning methods. The cultivation of innovative thinking starts with a reflection on the thinking that currently exists. We have not abandoned the previous efforts, including the structural syllabus that Japanese language education worldwide has relied on for more than three decades. On top of that, throughout the designing, delivering, and revising process, we also learnt several important lessons about realizing changes as an institution. The educational policies of the university are crucial when implementing drastic changes in educational practices. Due to a number of constraints, such as finances, workload, and resources, we could not have accomplished what we did without the strong conviction of the campus leadership team. To add one online software/application, we need a license, a workforce to support both instructors and students, and devices to be able to run it and make it accessible to all, as well as space to store the devices. The executing teams must also have flexible mindsets even though the policies are implemented from the top down. Different courses have different characteristics, and the lecturers should agree on what they are delivering.

It's also worth highlighting the fact that the words we use in the policies can be interpreted differently. Without an understanding of the broad sense of "authenticity" in the authentic assessment policy, the Japanese program could not fit into this framework. In the course of second and third language acquisition, students have limited proficiency to carry out authentic communication, especially at the beginner levels. This means that if "authenticity" is only for carrying out real work projects, it is not possible for students to have an authentic assessment until they have achieved a workable level in Japanese. It is also important not to limit ourselves to sharing practices and issues only within our own field of study when looking for the best assessment and delivery formats. Opening to all possibilities and hearing about what others are doing helps us to have new ideas for each course.

To be confident in what you have decided to do, opening our mind to students' feedback is essential. Negative feedback can be heartbreaking at the surface level of the words used, but if we think about the reasons why students choose particular expressions in their feedback, it leads to insightful understanding or changes being made to existing practices. Qualitative input by students and external stakeholders should be reflected within a particular program background and the learning outcomes of each program.

Finally, the mindsets of both instructors and students are key to making any innovation effective. For higher education especially, students should be informed as to why they are learning in ways that differ from what they have been accustomed to. Even though they may have been exposed to similar methods before, as adult learners they should be guided to understand the reason for the learning methods used. Institutional policies are a driving force for innovation, but the people involved in learning and teaching are key players in ensuring that new educational practices are fruitful.

REFERENCES

Ahlström, K., Ahlström, M., & Plummer, A. (n.d.). *Jisho*. [Open-source online dictionary]. https://jisho.org/

Ashford-Rowe, K., Herrington, J., & Brown, C. (2014). Establishing the critical elements that determine authentic assessment. *Assessment & Evaluation in Higher Education, 39*(2), 205–222.

Brown, M., Nomikoudis, M., Bouilheres, F., Nkhoma, C., & Akbari, M. (2022). Implementing a strategic campus-wide approach to authentic assessment: Considerations and recommendations for implementation. *Higher Education, Skills, and Work-Based Learning, 12*(5), 914–927. https://doi.org/10.1108/HESWBL-05-2021-0100

Gulikers, J., Bastiaens, T. J., & Kirschner, P. A. (2004). A five-dimensional framework for authentic assessment. *Educational Technology Research and Development, 52*(3), 67–86.

Jong, M. S. Y. (2019). To flip or not to flip: Social science faculty members' concerns about flipping the classroom. *Journal of Computing in Higher Education, 31*(2), 391–407.

Kobayashi, M. (2009). Research and pedagogy in grammar teaching [Bunpou kenkyu to bunpou kyouiku]. In O. Mizutani, M. Kobayashi, & J. Hibiya (Eds.), *Past, present, future of Japanese language education [Nihongo kyoiku no Kako, genza, mirai]* (pp. 117–138). Bonjinsha.

McNally, B., Chipperfield, J., Dorsett, P., Fabbro, L., Frommolt, V., Goetz, S., Lewoh, J., Molineux, M., Pearson, A., Reddan, G., Roiko, A., & Rung, A. (2017). Flipped classroom experiences: Student preferences and flip strategy in a higher education context. *Higher Education, 73*(2), 281–298. https://doi.org/10.1007/s10734-016-0014-z

Noda, H. (Ed.). (2012). *Nihongo kyoiku no tameno komunikeishon kenkyu* [Communication research for Japanese language education]. Koroshio Publishing.

Nunez, F. L., & Monsivais, D. B. (2020). It takes more than one somersault to flip a classroom. *Nurse Educator, 45*(3), 116–118.

RMIT University (2022). *Learning and teaching.* RMIT Vietnam. Retrieved December 12, 2022, from https://www.rmit.edu.vn/about-us/who-we-are/our-commitments/learning-and-teaching

Sokhanvar, Z., Salehi, K., & Sokhanvar, F. (2021). Advantages of authentic assessment for improving the learning experience and employability skills of higher education students: A systematic literature review. *Studies in Educational Evaluation, 70.* https://doi.org/10.1016/j.stueduc.2021.101030

Villarroel, V., Boud, D., Bloxham, S., Bruna, D., & Bruna, C. (2020). Using principles of authentic assessment to redesign written examinations and tests. *Innovations in Education and Teaching International, 57*(1), 38–49. https://doi.org/10.1080/14703297.2018.1564882

CHAPTER 4

A Trilingual K-12 Program in Siem Reap: Reflecting on Successes and Failures

Stephen Louw, Raksmey Rath, and Wenwen Tian

In 2016, the authors of this chapter established a trilingual K-12 program in Siem Reap, Cambodia. This was the first trilingual program in the city, offering Khmer, English, and Chinese, and was innovative in its attempt to integrate content and language learning utilizing an adapted transitional immersion framework. The program was designed by the first two authors, but its implementation has since fallen to the head of the English, Khmer,

---

S. Louw (✉)
Faculty of Liberal Arts, King Mongkut's University of Technology Thonburi, Bangkok, Thailand
e-mail: stephen.louw@kmutt.ac.th

R. Rath
Westgate International School, Siem Reap, Cambodia
e-mail: raksmey@western-international.edu.kh

W. Tian
School of Foreign Studies, Northwestern Polytechnical University, Xi'an, People's Republic of China
e-mail: wenwen.tian@nwpu.edu.cn

© The Author(s), under exclusive license to Springer Nature Switzerland AG 2024
L. Phung et al. (eds.), *Innovation in Language Learning and Teaching*, New Language Learning and Teaching Environments, https://doi.org/10.1007/978-3-031-46080-7_4

51

and Chinese departments at the school. In this chapter, we report an evaluation of the program. Taking an interpretive phenomenological approach, we aimed to explore the perspectives of these three leaders on the program's successes and failures thus far. Interviews of the department heads were analyzed to identify stories and anecdotes that give expression to their lived experience as leaders of their teaching teams. The findings indicate the three heads perceived the program's success and failures in distinct ways, expressing dissimilar concerns about the functioning of their departments in the school. One important insight emerging from the data is a lack of interdepartmental collaboration, possibly a result of rivalry over students' classroom time and school resources. These findings are useful to understand the concerns and challenges of academic managers as they work to fulfill their departments' goals.

INTRODUCTION

Siem Reap is a small city in northeast Cambodia with a population of less than 200,000. As the gateway to the UNESCO world heritage site of Angkor, it attracts large numbers of tourists, over 2.2 million in 2019 (Khmer Times, 8 June 2022). This tremendous tourist traffic in a relatively small city means that many residents are heavily reliant on tourism-based incomes, either directly as tour guides, or indirectly through the tourism service industry. Success in this environment requires confidence in English, traditionally the tourists' lingua franca. A recent increase in the number of tourist arrivals from China, however, has added to the city's linguistic landscape. Around 35% of 2019 arrivals were from mainland China (Ministry of Tourism, 2019), many of them not conversant in English. There is an increasing awareness of the importance of both English and Mandarin Chinese as keys to future success (Dahles et al., 2020), which in turn has placed pressure on parents to ensure their children obtain a multilingual education.

Education in Cambodia is compulsory for the six years of primary and three years of lower-secondary grades. The final three years of upper secondary are non-compulsory. The national curriculum stipulates 30 hours of classroom time a week in primary grades, and 40 hours in secondary grades (Em, 2022), though not all state schools achieve this number of hours. English is one of the ten mandated subjects at the secondary level (Au Yong Lyn & Greco, 2022).

State schooling in Siem Reap faces several issues. A primary problem is the lack of classrooms and facilities, so schools offer classes on a shift basis. One group of students attend classes for four hours in the morning, and a second group in the afternoon. This arrangement leaves individual students free for a large portion of the day, and also means classroom time falls below the stipulated number of hours per week. The lack of classrooms also means class sizes are large, officially up to 50 students (MoEYS, 2018), but in some cases far more, leading to challenges with classroom management and learner engagement (Watson Todd, 2012). A second problem is a shadow education program endemic in many state schools (Bray, 2010; Marshall & Fukao, 2019). While ostensibly free, children in state schools are encouraged to attend fee-based extra classes, often taught by their own classroom teachers. Those who do not attend are at risk of suffering negative consequences during regular school hours. Together, these problems have created some mistrust in the state education system and parents with means choose, instead, to enroll their children in private schools.

Private Education in Siem Reap

Private schools offer students smaller class sizes, a more exclusive circle of classmates, and greater accountability on the part of the school's administration. Traditionally, private schools specialize in either English or Chinese courses. This specialization has led to children being enrolled in multiple schools, each with its own focus. A child may study Khmer at a state school in the morning, an intensive English course in the afternoon at a second school, a Chinese class at a third school, and finally attend extra classes for content subjects in Khmer in the evening. This imposes various challenges on parents and students: the necessity for multiple uniforms, the logistics of transporting the children to different locations, and the need for children to acculturate to different schooling systems and juggle demands from teachers who are unable to coordinate their efforts.

Increasing availability of private primary and secondary schools offering the national curriculum now allows children to be enrolled in a single school for Khmer, English, and Chinese. As an example, authors of this chapter started to offer such a program, which we refer to as Campus 1. The program at Campus 1 mirrors the already familiar system of a Khmer program for half the day, English for the other half, and Chinese as an

54   S. LOUW ET AL.

optional extra. Parents can, therefore, select from a Khmer curriculum, an English one, or both so their child attends a single school all day.

This buffet-style approach to education at Campus 1 can best be described as a dual language bilingual program, which aims for a balance of languages, close to 50%:50% (Baker, 2001). Central to a dual language bilingual approach is the separation and compartmentalization of the languages. This facilitates using specialist teachers for each language and ensures maximal language use in each time block. One problem with this separation of languages was the disconnect between the two groups of teachers and content in the different blocks. The Khmer teachers follow the national Cambodian curriculum, the English teachers follow another (in our case, an adapted version of Singaporean curriculum), and neither group coordinates with the other to ensure continuity. As a result, subjects may be taught twice in a single day by two different subject teachers in two languages. Another problem has been that the two programs run their own placement tests, meaning a child may need to change classes according to their level for each language. For example, a student in Grade 8 in Khmer may be placed in Grade 2 in English.

Establishment of Campus 2

When planning our second campus, our aim was to ameliorate these problems by creating an integrated program which would avoid the duplication of material by separating content areas by language and allowing students to study with the same group of classmates all day. To do so, we made a move away from a dual-language bilingual approach to an immersion-style program (Baker, 2001).

The immersion bilingual system was first implemented in Canada in 1965. It has been shown to lead to literacy in L2 without hindering achievement in the students' L1 and has been implemented in schools across the globe (Cenoz, 2013). Immersion programs are characterized by six assumptions:

1. Both languages are prestigious.
2. Entry into the immersion program is voluntary.
3. Both languages are respected and allowed.
4. The teachers are bilingual. This facilitates communication that is meaningful and authentic rather than contrived and repetitive.

5. All students start as monolinguals, creating a group of relatively homogenous language users in which language development is unthreatening and uniform.
6. The immersion program follows the mainstream curriculum.

In our new school, the languages involved are prestigious, entry into the school is not compulsory, the students are (upon registration in kindergarten) monolingual Khmers, and the content would follow the Cambodian national curriculum. This met assumptions 1, 2, 5 and 6.

However, with assumptions 3 and 4 we were constrained by the local context. As with other Asian countries, parents in Cambodia expect English to be taught by native English-speaking teachers (Walkinshaw & Oanh, 2014), who, almost as a rule, cannot speak Khmer. Similarly, many Khmer content teachers do not have confidence in their English skills. Because teachers would not be able to communicate, it would be impossible to implement a fully integrated immersion program. Our solution was to appoint a head for each language department who could cooperate with one another to achieve some of the benefits of an immersion-style bilingual program.

In designing the new program, we needed to decide how the languages would be introduced and used across the 15-year span of the children's school career. This necessitated deciding when to introduce English medium instruction. Immersion into the L2 can be early (kindergarten), delayed (at around 9 or 10 years old), or late (at the secondary level). Among studies supporting late commencement immersion is that of Muñoz (2007), who found that late commencement, at 14 years old, resulted in faster language learning progress. Similarly, Snow and Hoefnagel-Höhle (1978) reported that younger learners (3–5 years old) achieved lower success than a late commencement group (12–15 years old). The Maldives, for instance, has successfully implemented a late commencement bilingual system, opting to focus on L1 literacy in primary and early middle school (Hameed, 2020).

There is, however, a substantial body of research showing that early commencement leads to better learning outcomes. One argument put forward for this is underpinned by the critical theory hypothesis (Penfield & Roberts, 1959), which posits that children can acquire language to native levels only if it is introduced before a certain age. Evidence supporting the success of early commencement includes studies of French immersion programs in Canada (e.g., Johnson & Newport, 1989). Muñoz

(2007) suggests that early commencement is likely to be more effective for aspects of the language best learned implicitly.

Notwithstanding the evidence on this issue, the decision about the age of commencement for English in Campus 2 was dictated, again, by local constraints. The first of these was parents' expectations of quick results in their children's acquisition of English, preferably as early as kindergarten. Late commencement immersion would not satisfy these parental expectations. A second constraint on age of commencement was the national policy on entry into Cambodian universities. Tertiary institutions in Cambodia require applicants to submit a Cambodian national school-leaving certificate. Foreign high-school diplomas are not accepted. For our future Grade 12 students, we would expect there to be substantial pressure on the students as they worked towards their final school-leaving examination. Having a greater focus on Khmer language in the latter stages of the program would facilitate this. Based on these two constraints, the decision was made to adopt an early commencement approach to English immersion.

Our next decision was to separate the content across languages. Immersion programs use the immersion language as a medium of instruction for content subjects like mathematics and physical education. Since we needed English to be the focus in the early years, and Khmer for later years, we decided on a transitional system. Transitional bilingual education programs prioritize one language and gradually transition to a prioritization of the other (Baker, 2001). These programs are more commonly associated with minority language speakers being eased into a majority language learning environment (e.g., Slavin & Cheung, 2005). For our purposes, we wished to transition from English medium instruction to Khmer to promote uptake of English in the early years, and then facilitate preparation for the high-stake national examinations in Khmer at the secondary level.

Finally, we needed to decide how Chinese would fit. Our goal with Chinese was basic communicative competence and literacy. As a result, Chinese would be treated as a foreign language, with a limited number of hours fixed across the children's entire school career.

The program initially approved by the school board is summarized in Fig. 4.1. It might be described as an inverted transitional immersion program, with English (L2) the language of immersion in the lower grades, transitioning to Khmer (L1) in the upper grades, and Chinese (FL) given constant limited exposure. In the initial iteration, all content subjects were

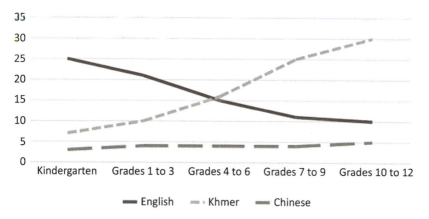

Fig. 4.1 Summary of the trilingual transitional immersion curriculum

distributed between English and Khmer as the medium of instruction. For example, mathematics was allocated to English medium in the early grades and then Khmer medium from grade 6.

Our announcement of the plan to the academic teams led to vigorous opposition from the Khmer department. It was felt that a poor foundation in the early years would lead to difficulties at the higher levels in the crucial period before the final Grade 12 examination. A second concern was the allocation of core curricular subjects like mathematics to English teachers. The curriculum was to follow the national Cambodian curriculum, but the English teachers would not be following the prescribed national textbooks, and the delivery of any content subjects in English may undermine students' uptake of necessary skills and key terminology. Students would have insufficient knowledge of the content material that forms the foundation for the senior secondary years. To address these concerns, changes were made to accommodate a greater presence of the Khmer teachers in the early years, somewhat reducing the number of contact hours with the English team.

The school is currently in its eighth year of operation. Children starting in Grade 1 are now in the lower secondary phase. The highest grade offered is Grade 11 and preparations are underway for the school's first Grade 12 group. It was timely, then, to explore the effectiveness of the program. There is a rich literature on curriculum and program evaluation (Klenowski, 2010; McCormick & James, 2018) often based on quantitative metrics like student performance in tests (e.g., Faubert, 2009). In this chapter, however, we wished to explore the program's effectiveness through a more qualitative lens, eliciting the perspectives of the three key stakeholders tasked with implementing it.

Phenomenology

To gain access to the perspectives of the three department heads, we made use of an interpretive phenomenological approach. Phenomenology aims to give access to an individual's lived experiences and the personal meanings attached to them. Interpretive phenomenology, based on the work of Martin Heidegger, studies 'how something appears' (King, 2001, p 109), thereby guiding a researcher's exploration of a particular phenomenon. From a Heideggerian perspective, a phenomenon is something that is taken for granted but concealed because it is ubiquitous (Heidegger, 1996). The focus of interest in this chapter was the experience and meaning of managing a department, a daily, taken-for-granted experience and therefore hidden from view by those engaged in it. Interpretive phenomenology aims to bring such hidden experiences to light and can be characterized as follows (Van der Mescht, 2004):

1. It is an interpretive methodology where emphasis is on accessing the lived experience of the participants through interviews.
2. Participants are purposively selected on the basis of their experience of the phenomenon.
3. The researcher adopts a naïve position, ignoring a priori theories or suppositions. This characteristic sets interpretive phenomenology apart from Husserlian phenomenology, which includes researchers' reflections (Schweitzer, 2002).
4. Analysis is based on natural meaning units, which focus on meanings as they are expressed in the words of the participant.
5. The researcher describes what is presented, attempting to capture the lived world of the participant.

Phenomenology has previously been used in investigation of educational leadership (e.g., Handford & Leithwood, 2013) and in school program evaluation (Isobel et al., 2016). It is a powerful way of making sense of leaders' experience and can provide useful insights into the complex process of implementing educational programs.

METHOD

Interviews were arranged with the head teachers of the three language departments, Khmer, English, and Chinese. These three heads are responsible for achieving the program goals set out for their language and the subjects taught through that medium of instruction. In addition, given that the immersion program assumes some level of cooperation between the departments, these heads are expected to work together to create a coherent school-wide program for the students. The three participants were informed of the goals of the study and that any findings would not constitute an evaluation of their performance.

As school directors, we felt it would not be appropriate to conduct the interviews ourselves. We, therefore, recruited three colleagues, one for each language, to conduct the interviews. Following the principle of the naïve researcher, such third-party interviewers are justified in interpretive phenomenological studies (Wright-St Clair 2015). To ensure consistency in the data collection, interviewers were instructed in the use of an active listening approach to draw out anecdotes (Louw et al., 2011) and given an interview protocol based around the program evaluation framework proposed by Tsou and Chen (2014).

The interviews were transcribed and translated into English. The three participants were asked to read the transcripts as a member check. No changes were requested, but each elaborated somewhat on the content. These elaborations were added to the data. The data were then arranged into natural meaning units (Van der Mescht, 2004) which were used to explore participants' anecdotes and stories. In the description of the findings below, we have attempted to capture the essence of the leaders' experiences of managing a department. All names are pseudonyms.

FINDINGS

English

The head of the English Department, *Mandy*, has led the department since the school opened, and had some part in the initial design of the program. She is a native English-speaking South African who started her career as a kindergarten teacher but was promoted to the position of head of English on the school's opening. As the longest serving member of the academic team, she has witnessed the various iterations as the program was adapted in response to the Khmer team's concerns over the number of hours allocated to Khmer medium instruction.

In her professional experience as a teacher, Mandy prides herself on the success she has achieved with her classes and expresses trust and affection for the individual students. She knows the names of each of the 260 children in the school and has taught all 17 classes. Her judgment of the success of the students in the school comes, then, from her personal interaction with the students and their work.

Mandy's experience of the program is overwhelmingly positive. She sees the students as succeeding in terms of its goals of getting students speaking and writing English confidently. In her view, the program '*has just proven that it works because their English is so strong. It's unreal.*' Her view is that the children in the lower levels who have been at the school since kindergarten are likely to surpass the success evident with the current upper grades, '*the younger ones are going to definitely surpass the older ones right now.*' She feels confident that the program's goal of an IELTS 6.5 score for each child at the end of Grade 12, once seemingly over-optimistic, is unquestioningly achievable.

Mandy believes that the students are well-informed through their involvement on social media, a result of their online learning during the Covid lockdowns. The students enjoy studying in English and have responded well to the project-based activities that have been introduced over the years. That this Western-style education has been embraced by students is evidenced by their wish for even more American-style innovations in the school: '*They want a lot more of what we're offering. They want a student council, and they also want Prom.*' According to Mandy, students show responsibility and initiative. For instance, the secondary students started a chess club and have made a noticeable effort to be more punctual for school in the mornings. Mandy sees the success of her department indicated through students' participation in cultural activities such as the Christmas Day party, and their willingness to act as translators at teacher-parent meetings for parents unable to interact with the English and Chinese teachers.

Mandy admits that there are some problems. In response to a small group of students in each class having notably weaker English, she started a pull-out program which temporarily allows weak students access to a support teacher. This intervention affects two or three students per class, or around 20% of the student population. Mandy feels this has made a real difference: '*You can see their attitude has completely changed ... They're getting better results.*' She worries about the entire Grade 7 group, which is unaccountably weaker than the other classes, possibly a result of being a very small group who do not get along well.

Several practical problems face the department. One is the extraordinary workload imposed on the students by the Khmer department. English teachers, therefore, avoid assigning time-consuming homework or large out-of-class projects. Another problem is that the Khmer teachers *brush aside* English as unimportant in favor of Khmer-medium subjects. Children's failure to achieve high scores in Khmer subjects leads to punishment by both the school and the parents, forcing students to prioritize Khmer even though they report to prefer studying with the international teachers. In terms of a working relationship with the other departments, Mandy describes the head of the Khmer department (Dara) as *amazing* because he is *very modern*. The Khmer teaching team, however, are *still so traditional* and use techniques which, she feels, prioritize politeness rather than interpersonal relationships. She laments that the Khmer teachers avoid participating in school events (like the Christmas party), and that their poor English impedes bonding between the Khmer and international teams. As the number of hours allocated to English dwindles in the higher-level grades and students become more removed from the English teachers, Mandy feels that they miss their English lessons, probably *'because it's fun. They get to be themselves. It's where they want to be.'*

In terms of her own teaching team, a major obstacle to further success is the quality of some of the teachers. To deal with teacher inexperience and lack of expertise, Mandy runs regular in-service teacher workshops. However, not all teachers implement the new ideas, nor do they explore lesson materials beyond the textbook. *'They're just doing it as a job. And even with training, you'll see things don't change.'* Mandy feels teachers like these undermine the team's success with the students.

Khmer

The head of the Khmer department, Dara, has over 18 years' experience in the Khmer national school system. He has been head of the Khmer department for three years and is the third department head since the school opened. He has a reputation as forward thinking and modern, having implemented a variety of innovations such as a Khmer reading competition and Khmer language computer courses. He aims to be relaxed and personable with the students, but his job demands preclude the possibility of frequent classroom instruction. As a result, much of his interaction with students is in morning assemblies or in his role as disciplinarian.

As a relative newcomer to the team, Dara has inherited a system which he had no part in developing. He is aware that there have been lengthy negotiations with the other departments over the number of hours allocated to Khmer since the school started, and he is sensitive to the claims of the other departments over student time. Occasional discussions over students' classroom hours still form a focus in his dealings with the other department heads. This, however, is marginal to the more serious issue of getting students ready for the national examinations, the results of which affect the students' futures but are also used as a yardstick for the success of the entire school. In preparing for these exams, the department needs as much time with the students as possible and more resources from the school. For instance, he points out that the English Department has a library in which students can read and explore texts at their leisure, but no such space has been allocated for a Khmer library.

Since the students spend much of their time with the English Department when they are in the lower grades, Dara largely concerns himself with the secondary-level students who are working towards their national Grade 9 and 12 examinations. In secondary school, the Khmer language dominates the students' schedule, and weaknesses in their learning and knowledge become worryingly evident.

Dara's primary concern is that students lack *the basics*. In Grade 7, when the number of Khmer-medium instruction hours first exceeds English, he feels it necessary to check students' basic Khmer literacy. Students need to function in the Khmer medium with complex content and jargon in subjects like mathematics, physics, and chemistry, for which they need a firm foundation. Since students have largely studied this content material in English to this point, there is the threat that gaps in their knowledge will impinge on their success. Dara's guess is that '*between 70 and 90 percent*' of the students coming into secondary school have the ability to succeed. He takes this to be a worrying number since a great deal of work is necessary with those who cannot meet the minimum requirements. Since the end of the Covid lockdowns, he has instituted extra lessons and additional work for the low-achieving students. It is unclear, however, how successful this intervention has been at this stage.

There are further barriers to success. Students do not voluntarily participate in extra-curricular activities organized by the department. For example, the Khmer reading competition attracted relatively few students.

This may be, Dara believes, a result of students' lack of confidence. A second barrier to success is the lack of parental support for the school's efforts. An example Dara gives is the school's policy with mobile phones. In the classrooms, phones are banned because they distract students and interrupt the lesson. However, parents put pressure on the school to allow students to keep their phones with them. Dara feels that this lack of trust from parents for school policy undermines the school's efforts. A third barrier to success is the attitude of some of the students, especially in terms of willingness to put in effort. A lazy approach to study, he believes, coupled with poor routines at home, are detrimental to the department's work in readying students for the high-stake examinations.

Despite these problems, there are successes of which Dara is proud. The school is constantly developing its facilities to improve the range of courses that can be made available to the students. The department has recently introduced a robotics program, as well as an innovative life orientation course, both of which students seem to really enjoy. The life orientation course incorporates '*various disciplines such as Sociology, Psychology, Political Science, Human Movement Science, Labor Studies and Industrial Studies,*' and has been helpful in getting students to '*know more about life's realities.*' The results from this course indicate that '*students can be more competitive to achieve their personal goals.*' There are also instances where students have surprised Dara with their enthusiasm. He cites two examples where students have really excelled beyond all expectations: the school fair, an open day for parents to inspect student work, and in inter-school sports competitions which students have taken very seriously although they have not yet succeeded in beating rival schools. These extra-curricular activities have led to students '*building teamwork and tenacity.*'

Chinese

Lee, the head of the Chinese department, is a Khmer national fully bilingual in Khmer and Mandarin. He took over the position of department head during the Covid lockdowns when the previous Chinese-teaching team returned to mainland China. In the years before his arrival, those teachers worked with minimal supervision, deciding for themselves what to teach. The Chinese department has now increased to five full-time teachers: three expatriates from Taiwan and China, and two Khmers. Lee leads this team, manages course material and content, and tries to standardize the teachers' classroom practice. He is a passionate teacher and enjoys getting into the classroom when he can. He believes in prioritizing student learning, which is an ongoing struggle since students themselves lack awareness of strategies for learning and the long-term benefits of hard work and effort.

Lee understands that the school's Chinese program is *small scale* in that the time allocated to Chinese language is limited: four hours a week for all grades. This severely restricts what can be realistically achieved. Given these constraints, his goal for the department is to simply '*teach students some very foundational Chinese*,' including Chinese Pinyin, simple Chinese character strokes, and basic conversation.

A barrier to achieving these very modest goals is the demanding workload imposed on students by the school program in general. Content subjects taught in English and Khmer dominate students' attention, who therefore fail to focus on Chinese as a purposeful goal. With the limited time available in the school schedule and the distracted attitude of the students, even very simple language learning goals seem to be unachievable. Lee's solution is to prioritize homework, thereby extending learning beyond what can be scheduled during school hours. Students are frequently assigned homework based on classroom instruction. This works particularly well for mechanical aspects of the language, like character strokes. He has found, however, that students are not easily motivated to do this homework and he has had to use various strategies to both encourage and force students to do so. One strategy is to '*include a behavior score*' on the Chinese score sheet which reflects students' completion of homework, and also their conduct both in class and on the school campus, which Lee believes reflects their moral values.

Lee has a strong conviction about the development of students' morals and ethics. Chinese cannot be learned without the cultural and moral elements that are built into the language. It is the Chinese teacher's job not only to teach the language, but to incorporate the essence of Chinese moral values. '*I believe that giving students moral instruction is more important than teaching them language skills only*.' To do so, he has regular conversations with individual students on issues like punctuality, respecting teachers' time, and completing homework. He finds students' tardiness in the mornings unacceptable and feels the five-minute grace period given by the school to late students encourages bad habits. With China a growing influence in the country, learning the language and culture is increasingly important for the students' future. To Lee, students appear to be unaware of the importance of learning and using Chinese, and also of the cultural values that the Chinese hold to be important. Dealing with this will take time, but he aims to build a '*culture of Chinese*' in the school through activities like preparing gifts for parents and grandparents.

The students' success at Chinese is poorer than might be expected. Currently, Lee estimates around 30% of students are reaching the course targets. In each class, there are a few students who excel, and the teachers can use these to motivate and help the others in the class. Despite this low success, Lee '*can see the progress of the students*' and does not feel unduly concerned by the limited proficiency of the students.

In addition to the severe limitations on the time and students' apparent lack of awareness of the importance of Chinese and Chinese cultural values, Lee feels there are two further challenges to achieving the Chinese department's goals of schoolwide basic Chinese literacy. The first is the negative influence of parents, who are insensitive to the demands placed on the students and have unreasonable expectations for their children's success. Lee feels they do not give their children the right emotional support and their heavy-handed techniques pressure students unnecessarily. What students need from parents and teachers is care and support to see them through their learning journey.

A final challenge comes from the poor quality of some of the members of the Chinese teaching team. Lee asks that his teachers provide weekly lesson plans, samples of their classroom worksheets, and records of the students' performance. In his experience, the three foreign Chinese teachers fulfill these requirements easily, possibly a result of their language proficiency. The Khmer Chinese teachers, however, are late and slovenly with their teaching records. They need constant assistance with their teaching load and are prone to giving inadequate feedback on students' work. This lack of timely and useful feedback means students are not aware of their errors. Unprofessional teachers risk making students lose their trust in Chinese. There is then, a need for professional development, which Lee has not yet found a way of scheduling into the teachers' busy routines.

DISCUSSION

In designing the program for our new school, our proposal had been to create an environment in which students could develop confidence in three languages. Our broader aims were threefold: a Khmer national school-leaver's certificate, an IELTS score of 6.5, and competence in conversational Chinese. We saw an integration of these goals into a single program to be an improvement on the multiple-school arrangement popular in Siem Reap, in which content and language programs are not coherently coordinated. Since its opening, the school has attracted a strong following, now with a student population of over 250. As a metric, student enrollment indicates a measure of the program's success in the community. The focus of this chapter is on whether the school program is achieving the various goals we set out when designing the program.

Using a phenomenological lens, we aimed to make known the lived experiences of the three department heads to get an insider's view on the successes and failures of their respective departments. The value of a phenomenological approach has been demonstrated in previous studies on school leadership (Smith, 2019; van der Mescht, 2004). What is striking from the data is the disparity of the opinions on the program's success, and the differences they identify as the cause for its problems. Only Mandy is positive about what has been achieved. Dara and Lee are preoccupied by the perceived failures. Dara focuses on student deficiencies, such as their laziness, and Lee feels the problem is the students' lack of awareness of Chinese culture. Both indicate a lack of parental support. These findings are useful for us, as directors, to understand the motivations and preoccupations that drive the department heads' decisions about handling students and managing the teachers in their departments.

A rare point of consensus across the interviews is the enormous pressure on students although different opinions are expressed on the sources of pressure. Lee sees it as a result of parental expectations, Mandy from the demands from the Khmer department, and Dara from the upcoming high-stake final examinations. There is also no consensus on the effects of this pressure on students and the program. For Lee, students are distracted and unwilling to complete Chinese homework, and for Mandy it means fewer opportunities to do out-of-class projects. That each leader identifies different causes and effects suggests this has not formed a focus of joint reflection by the three as a team, and perhaps a lack of coordinated response to the issue. Looking at these findings, we wondered whether it would be possible for the three departments to work together to mitigate students' workload, for example, by rotating homework assignments or examination dates.

A second point of consensus across all three heads is the limited number of classroom learning hours. Lee sees the Chinese program as *small scale* and, therefore, needs to make compromises on what can be feasibly achieved. Similarly, Mandy believes that the Khmer teachers 'brush aside'

English lessons as unimportant, as do parents and the school administration, who prioritize success in Khmer. Since the opening of the school, the English and Khmer departments have regularly negotiated, both in formal meetings and casual discussions, the distribution of hours between the two languages. This competition over the limited resource of student time has become the focus for some interdepartmental rivalry. Such rivalry has been widely reported elsewhere in business and school settings (e.g., Sykes, 2015). Conflict between the departments is not explicitly stated in the data, but there's also no mention of cooperation. Moreover, explicit comments on the other departments are sometimes disparaging. For instance, Mandy comments on the poor teaching methods of the Khmer teachers, and Dara laments that his department's resources are inferior to those of the English Department. Again, we interpret this as a lack of a systematic effort for the departments to work together. Since the school's aim is to offer an integrated program with three languages, greater interdepartmental efforts are a crucial area of focus for the future of the school and similar educational innovation. Finding a strategy to encourage such cooperation is an issue we will need to focus on in the years ahead, but we suspect that such a change in culture will require careful consideration and intervention (Tichnor-Wagner et al., 2016).

In terms of student success, opinion is divided. Mandy believes strongly that the program is *working* and praises the students on their English levels and their success in their uptake of American school customs, like prom. Furthermore, the small number of weak students in each grade, which Mandy estimates to be around 10% of the school population, are being successfully handled. The Chinese and Khmer departments are less positive about the success of the program in terms of student learning. In Chinese, only '30%' of the students are showing success, but because they are *making good progress*, this figure appears not to be a source of distress. Dara estimates the success rate of students in the Khmer department at between 70 and 90%. It is noteworthy that Mandy and Dara estimate similar statistics for student success, but their interpretations are distinctly different. While Mandy sees this as a resounding success, Dara feels the figure indicates serious problems. The source of this difference in perception may be a result of the negative washback that drives the Khmer department's efforts. Since the focus of attention for the Khmers is the final school exit examinations, failure is a serious issue. On the contrary, the English Department's goal of an IELTS 6.5 for Grade 12 students is likely to be considered less pressing, especially by the Khmers. Unlike the national school examinations, students have the option of retaking the IELTS multiple times.

A second area of disagreement among department heads is a description of student behavior. Dara describes students as lazy and showing poor attitudes, and Lee describes them as unmotivated and lacking morals. By contrast, Mandy's experience is that the students are responsible and respectful. These disparate perspectives on students' character may be explained by differences in teacher expectations, the dissimilar approaches to classroom methodologies, and different perceptions of classroom management. Having had so much time with the foreign teaching staff in the early years of their schooling, the students may have become familiar with the interactive classroom styles and open communication that the international language teachers encourage. In the Khmer and Chinese classrooms, teachers may prefer a more hierarchical classroom congruent with high-power distance (de Jong et al., 2013). Mandy's comments that the Khmer teachers are *still so traditional* supports this explanation.

The different perceptions of student attitude may also explain inconsistencies in the three accounts of student involvement in extracurricular activities. To Mandy, students are highly involved in school activities, as seen in the Christmas festival. Dara, however, states the students' involvement is poor and refers to the low turnout in the reading competition. As with classroom methods, Mandy reasons that the hierarchical and traditional approach taken by Khmer teachers may be a reason why students appear to embrace English activities more readily.

Conclusion

This chapter of the lived experiences of the department heads has provided valuable insights into their perceptions of the program's success. Each of the heads provided a distinct perspective, reflecting their different preoccupations that inform their understanding of their experience of managing a team and fulfilling their departments' goals. Some findings from the study were predictable, such as the competition between the three departments over student learning time, an issue which arose even before the school opened. The data has, however, shone light on the meanings attributed to these challenges from each department head. To some extent, what was not expressed by the three managers, particularly the absence of any evidence of interdepartmental cooperation, is of greater interest to us as school directors, and a worthwhile focus for attention as we work to develop the program. With these findings in mind, we are looking to build strategies for increasing collaboration between the departments in the upcoming academic year.

The relevance of our experience with the planning and development of the school may be limited to our particular context (Burdick-Will et al., 2013). Immersion and transitional bilingual programs are common across the globe (Cenoz, 2013) but have different characteristics (Polanco & Luft de Baker, 2018). We have not encountered an immersion program in the literature which initially prioritizes a foreign or second language and later transitions to first language literacy. Nevertheless, these findings may be useful to the bilingual community, and to schools considering setting up a program in similar communities. That Mandy feels the students in the school have been able to achieve excellent levels of English by early secondary levels indicates the possible effectiveness of this kind of early commencement immersion. Despite Dara's concern about students' lack of basics, we would argue that a 70 to 90% success in Khmer indicates that early immersion has not severely affected the students' L1 literacy. In fact, Dara's guess that 10–30% of our student population can be considered low achievers may represent the proportion of low-achieving students in any student body (OECD, 2016).

Less clear is the result of our decision to include Chinese as a foreign language. Lee's estimate at 30% success is worrying. With students, parents, and the school prioritizing the English and Khmer programs, there are credible reasons for students' lack of motivation to study Chinese. Though useful for marketing the school, the effectiveness of this entire department is in question and needs careful reconsideration. It is possible that such shoehorning of the third language into the program, and the resulting poor performance of the department, is a reason why schools may be unwilling to introduce trilingual education. We believe that Chinese literacy is a worthwhile goal given the probable future directions of the tourism industry. However, its status in the school as *small scale* may be inhibiting students' focus on it. In the wake of these findings, the academic director and Lee have begun auditing the Chinese department to explore ways to increase its exposure in the school.

There is no doubt that the implementation of this innovative program constituted a major risk. Eight years on, we personally believe it is a success. The students speak English with confidence, are on track to success in their Khmer examinations, and Chinese is an accepted, though marginal, part of school life. Perhaps some of this success has been the result of the willingness of the department heads to negotiate and compromise with one another on the initial program design, and the dedication of each head to the success of their respective departments. The data shows, however, that there is more work to be done to strengthen and develop the school leadership, particularly with inter-department collaboration. As directors, this empirical approach to investigating the school's leadership has provided a fascinating set of insights which have created a focus for developing the academic department in the years ahead. In another eight years, we believe it will be worth revisiting these findings, and re-evaluating the school's progress through the lens of its academic leaders.

References

Au Yong Lyn, A., & Greco, G. (2022). Factbook education system: Cambodia. *CES Factbook Education Systems, 19.*

Baker, C. (2001). *Foundations of bilingual education and bilingualism* (3rd ed.). Multilingual matters.

Bray, M. (2010). Researching shadow education: methodological challenges and directions. *Asia Pacific Educational. Review, 11,* 3–13. https://doi.org/10.1007/s12564-009-9056-6

Burdick-Will, J., Keels, M., & Schuble, T. (2013). Closing and opening schools: The association between neighborhood characteristics and the location of new educational opportunities in a large urban district. *Journal of Urban Affairs, 35*(1), 59–80.

Cenoz, J. (2013). Bilingual and multilingual education: Overview. In C. A. Chapelle (Ed.), *The encyclopedia of applied linguistics* (pp. 425–429). Wiley-Blackwell.

Dahles, H., Khieng, S., Verver, M., & Manders, I. (2020). Social entrepreneurship and tourism in Cambodia: Advancing community engagement. *Journal of Sustainable Tourism, 28*(6), 816–833.

de Jong, R., van Tartwijk, J., Wubbels, T., Veldman, I., & Verloop, N. (2013). Student teachers' discipline strategies: relations with self-images, anticipated student responses and control orientation. *Educational Studies, 39*(5), 582–597.

Em, S. (2022). Challenges of English language learning and teaching in Cambodia: A case study of Kith Meng Brasat High School. *Cambodian Journal of Educational Research, 2*(1), 62–80.

Faubert, V. (2009). School evaluation: current practices in OECD countries and a literature review. *OECD Education Working Papers,* No. 42, OECD Publishing. https://doi.org/10.1787/218816547156.

Hameed, H. (2020). Bilingualism and the medium of instruction. *The Maldives National Journal of Research, 8*(2), 89–100.

Handford, V., & Leithwood, K. (2013). Why teachers trust school leaders. *Journal of Educational Administration. Journal of Educational Administration, 51*(2), 194–212. https://doi.org/10.1108/09578231311304706

Heidegger, M. (1996). *Being and time* (J. Stambaugh, Trans.). Albany, NY: State University of New York Press.

Isobel, S., Pretty, D., & Meehan, F. (2016). 'They are the children of our clients, they are our responsibility': a phenomenological evaluation of a school holiday program for children of adult clients of a mental health service. *Advances in Mental Health, 15*(2), 132–146. https://doi.org/10.1080/18387357.2016.1251827

Johnson, J. S., & Newport, E. L. (1989). Critical period effects in second language learning: The influence of maturational state on the acquisition of English as a second language. *Cognitive Psychology, 21*(1), 60–99.

Khmer Times. (2022). Retrieved April 14, 2023, from https://tinyurl.com/4rrkah7v.

King, M. (2001). *A guide to Heidegger's being and time.* State University of New York Press.

Klenowski, V. (2010). Curriculum evaluation: Approaches and methodologies. *International Encyclopedia of Education [3rd edition], 1,* 335–341.

Louw, S., Todd, R. W., & Jimarkon, P. (2011). Active listening in qualitative research interviews. In *Proceedings of the International Conference: Research in Applied Linguistics, April.*

Marshall, J. H., & Fukao, T. (2019). Shadow education and inequality in lower secondary schooling in Cambodia: Understanding the dynamics of private tutoring participation and provision. *Comparative Education Review, 63*(1), 98–120.

McCormick, R., & James, M. (2018). *Curriculum evaluation in schools.* Routledge.

Ministry of Tourism of Cambodia. (2019). *Tourisom statistics report.* Retrieved April 17, 2023, from https://www.nagacorp.com/eng/ir/tourism/tourism_statistics_201912.pdf

MOEYS. (2018). Education in Cambodia: Findings from Cambodia's experience in PISA for Development, Phnom Penh. Retrieved April 17, 2023, from https://tinyurl.com/5x843p8/

Muñoz, C. (2007). The effects of age on foreign language learning: The BAF Project. In C. Muñoz (Ed.), *Age and rate of foreign language learning* (pp. 1–40). Multilingual Matters.

OECD. (2016). Low-performing students: Why they fall behind and how to help them succeed. PISA, OECD Publishing, Paris, https://doi.org/10.1787/9789264250246-en.

Penfield, W., & Roberts, L. (1959). *Speech and brain mechanisms.* Atheneum Press.

Polanco, P., & Luft de Baker, D. (2018). Transitional bilingual education and two-way immersion programs: Comparison of reading outcomes for english learners in the united states. *Athens Journal of Education, 5*(4), 423–444.

Schweitzer, R. (2002). *Editorial. Indo-Pacific Journal of Phenomenology, 2*(2), 1–2. https://doi.org/10.1080/20797222.2002.11433874

Slavin, R. E., & Cheung, A. (2005). A synthesis of research on language of reading instruction for English language learners. *Review of Educational Research, 75*(2), 247–284.

Smith, P. A. (2019). *Leading while Black and male: A phenomenology of Black male school leadership.* Doctoral dissertation,. Columbia University.

Snow, C., & Hoefnagel-Höhle, M. (1978). The critical period for language acquisition: Evidence from second language learning. *Child Development, 49*(4), 1114–1128. https://doi.org/10.2307/1128751

Sykes, A. H. (2015). Models of educational management: The case of a language teaching institute. *Journal of Teaching and Education, 4*(01), 1–23.

Tichnor-Wagner, A., Harrison, C., & Cohen-Vogel, L. (2016). Cultures of learning in effective high schools. *Educational Administration Quarterly, 52*(4), 602–642. https://doi.org/10.1177/0013161X16644957

Tsou, W., & Chen, F. (2014). ESP program evaluation framework: Description and application to a Taiwanese university ESP program. *English for Specific Purposes, 33,* 39–53.

Van der Mescht, H. (2004). Phenomenology in education: A case study in educational leadership. *Indo-Pacific Journal of Phenomenology, 4*(1), 1–16.

Walkinshaw, I., & Oanh, D. H. (2014). Native and non-native English language teachers: Student perceptions in Vietnam and Japan. *Sage Open, 4*(2), 2158244014534451.

Watson Todd, R. (2012). The effects of class size on English learning at a Thai university. *ELT Research Journal, 1*(1), 80–88.

Wright-St Clair, V. (2015). Doing (interpretive) phenomenology. In S. Nayar & M. Stanley (Eds.), *Qualitative research methodologies for occupational science and therapy* (pp. 53–69). Routledge.

CHAPTER 5

Harnessing Partnerships and Technology to Establish a New Language Program in Cambodia

Joseph Ng and Patrick Mannion

INTRODUCTION

Starting a new English program at a private university in Cambodia's port city of Sihanoukville seems almost counterintuitive. This city's spectacular transformation is no secret, amply reported in Southeast Asian media over the past five years (e.g., Lim, 2022). A former haven for Western backpackers soaked in temple itineraries to detox on the long white beaches of Cambodia's southwest outcrop, Sihanoukville is now craggily crowned with a skyline of skyscrapers and skeleton infrastructure from an explosive but abandoned infusion of Chinese capital from around 2017 (Maliszewska

J. Ng (✉)
Department of English, Life University, Sihanoukville, Cambodia
e-mail: biblicist@gmail.com

P. Mannion
Faculty of Foreign Studies, Kansai Gaidai University, Osaka, Japan
e-mail: mannionp@kansaigaidai.ac.jp

© The Author(s), under exclusive license to Springer Nature
Switzerland AG 2024
L. Phung et al. (eds.), *Innovation in Language Learning and Teaching*, New Language Learning and Teaching Environments,
https://doi.org/10.1007/978-3-031-46080-7_5

& van der Mensbruggh, 2019; The Organisation for Economic Co-operation and Development, 2018). Linguistically, the battle for second language prominence has shifted from French in colonial times to English to Mandarin. Add to this the advent of the coronavirus pandemic, the public affairs response of Western diplomatic missions, and the vicissitudes of student recruitment at local universities, and you get some unique challenges to establishing a postgrad English enclave in the port city.

Facing declining enrollment, most critically in the English Department, the university in focus in this chapter (henceforth *the university*) pivoted to try some new initiatives, including the innovative exploitation of strategic partnerships and technologies to establish a new degree program. Under the adverse circumstances already mentioned, decades-long "unassailable" objections to tech applications suddenly melted and morphed into brilliant imperatives as school lockdowns took effect. PDF textbooks, Zoom classes, a whole succession of learning management systems (LMSs), automated assessments, and even asynchronous classes took root. The challenge was to select and cobble together as optimal a solution as possible for the survival and possible success of all stakeholders.

Besides technology, strategic partnerships also played a significant role in the survival. Most notably, the American Embassy in Phnom Penh from March 2021 helped avail the university with two PhD teaching fellows from the US State Department's English Language Fellow Program, which is administered by Georgetown University (US Department of State, n.d.), to complement the pool of eight volunteer teachers at the university. This would happen virtually over Zoom initially and then, with the lifting of Covid travel advisories, onsite. Additionally, social connections to the international schools in the vicinity created teacher recruitment opportunities with foreign teachers unable to travel to their home countries due to international lockdowns. Yet, with the start-up successes came mixed results and outright disappointments. But an unlikely MA in English program had been born in a Mandarin-ascendant enclave in Cambodia, with teething challenges still attendant.

This chapter primarily surveys, from the head of English Department's (Joseph's) point of view, what transpired, both positively and negatively, and the slightly innovative if serendipitous efforts to make redemptive lemonade from the unhappy postsecondary lemon. Joseph, who has lived and worked in Sihanoukville since 2017, has spent much of his life in Southeast Asia. Through strategic partnerships and technology adoption, he was able to witness the birth of a postgraduate English degree program in an otherwise hopeless situation in Sihanoukville. Patrick contributes to this chapter from his experiences being an online instructor for the university from March through August 2022, and from being physically present on campus from then until June 2023.

Harnessing Partnerships and Technology to Establish a New Language Program in Cambodia

As one of the anticipated engines of economic growth for the Kingdom of Cambodia, the southwestern port city of Sihanoukville has been carrying the hopes of the entire nation (Khmer Times, 2022). Overlaying these hopes were the global developments of China's Belt and Road Initiative (BRI) (Maliszewska & van der Mensbruggh, 2019) and the global coronavirus pandemic (World Health Organization, 2022). The result was a massive transformation of an idyllic Westerner backpacker's beachside refuge to something quite unrelated (Sorkhean, 2020), including a virtual emptying out of students at the English Department at the university, which was a major tertiary institution in the city.

The Stunning Shenzhenization of Sihanoukville City

Problematizing the degradation of the postsecondary English language education situation in Sihanoukville requires a bit of depiction of its recent history for those not already tracking it on sources such as Channelnewsasia and Aljazeera news, besides *Khmer Times* locally. Much of this description is based on personal experiences and knowledge Joseph obtained from living for years in Sihanoukville. That history may be observed in the name change from *Kampong Som* (Chhang, 2021), whence its airport code KOS, to *Sihanoukville*, in honor of the current monarch's father, and finally, as the Chinese investors inundated its streets and shops, to *Xigang*, literally "West Port" in Mandarin. It is the third and last christening that is representative of the radical and rapid transformation of the city, with devastating consequences on the learning and teaching of English. English would no longer be the language of promise and prestige. The choice of Shenzhen (Hui, 2020; Khmer Times, 2022) over Singapore (Joseph's erstwhile hometown) as an urban development model may be prophetic. Shenzhen and Singapore grew out of small fishing villages into the large metropolises they are today. But they took different paths, driven by political, economic, environmental, social, and linguistic choices (Yamada, 2019).

Meteoric Wealth Trajectory

Fueling the dramatic changes was the flood of foreign direct investment evidenced in a changed skyline and loss of the sea view, clogged streets with Rolls Royce and Lexus SUVs juxtaposed with gleaming Bajaj tuk-tuks and legacy motorcycles, and real estate and rental prices ballooning to ten times of what they were within the space of three years. Eighty new casinos sprouted up all over the city (GGR Asia, 2022), with hotels and restaurants associated with each one. Planeloads of Chinese tourists would arrive at KOS airport and board coaches to their luxurious gambling destinations. Many would invest in shops, mainly business-to-business, for advertising, food, transport, financial services, for their compatriots.

In addition, I (Joseph) witnessed the appearance of mysterious building complexes, some named "Chinatown," situated beyond the city center, seemingly dissociated from the rest of the metropolis. Difficult to access and well guarded by private security, these veritable fortresses would be ablaze with lighting at night against their dark semi-rural backdrop. It would later emerge that beyond in-person and online gambling, these would be scam operations with sophisticated slave-like conditions for "pig slaughter" and honeypot strikes on the lonely and naive from Chinese, English, and other language populations, raking in unknown amounts of money (Ford & Vimonsuknopparat, 2022). What is clear was their ability to attract and retain young people with salaries multiple times of what their teachers were earning, and those with some facility in Mandarin could command an additional premium.

While the Chinese Department at the university became the premier choice of incoming freshmen, some of whom were said to be already earning in excess of their teachers, the English Department saw a significant decline in intake, down to zero for the 2020 cohort.

Language and Power Shift

With the arrival of the new "mandarins" of power came new signboards and a new name for the city, Xihanuke (西哈努克), which became in shorthand Xigang (西港), to reflect the port status. Irate locals petitioned municipal officials to make sure that the big bold Chinese characters in public did not outshine the letters of their native language, Khmer (Voun, 2019) (see an example in the photo below). Signs reflecting French, Korean, Japanese, and other languages—including English—became scarce, in tandem with the exodus of pizzerias and boulangeries, leaving restaurants in the city with a uniform *mala* flavor.

A building in the city

To fully support the rapid urban development, the Cambodian government plowed in USD 300 million to upgrade the roadways and drainage, the latter a huge problem with flooding blamed on land reclamation of ponds for new real estates (Khmer Times, 2021). A spectacular esplanade was built over a quiet beach in the heart of the city. New Chinese shopping centers and supermarkets popped up. But nothing approached the impact of the new expressway linking the capital Phnom Penh to Sihanoukville, reducing travel times to just two hours, a third of the time needed on the old roadway (Ministry of Economy and Finance, General Department of Public-Private Partnerships, n.d.; Ratha Chan, 2022; Xinhua, 2022). From October 2022, day trips to the sea became possible for the capital dwellers, who hitherto may not have thought much of the Chinese investment in the highway or its strategic role in its global BRI.

Things might have gone down swimmingly had the Cambodian government not rather abruptly announced the end of its permission for online gambling (Samean, 2021). In a matter of months, blooming businesses were shuttered and droves of investors obediently headed back to China, pulling their kids out of school and bringing their families with them (Sorkhean, 2020). Any prospect for a medium-term return after a couple of years evaporated with the onset of the coronavirus pandemic (World Health Organization, 2022). The remaining Chinese who headed back north were greeted with new Zero Covid policies (Gan, 2022) that stanched what regularly scheduled flights remained between the two countries (Office of the Council of Ministers, 2020).

All over Cambodia, schools were closed, and the university was no exception. If not for prior connections via Facebook and Messenger, later augmented by Telegram, we might have lost contact for good. Things were not looking up at the English Department. Enrollment was three in Year 2, five in Year 3, and six in Year 4, at the end of 2020. At the end of 2021, it was down to zero Year 2 students, three Year 3 students, and four Year 4 students. To round out the situation, the department's largely volunteer lecturers from India, China, and Korea had returned to their homelands.

Surveying and Addressing the Postsecondary Wasteland

Founded in the mid-2000s as a community outreach ministry of a Christian church, the university hosted a resident faculty comprised of over 30 volunteer lecturers from overseas, who taught subjects spanning nursing and midwifery, business management and accountancy, architecture and civil engineering, tourism and hospitality, computer science and math, and Korean, Chinese, and English. The English Department looked like it was heading for a suspension, as was what eventually happened to architecture and tourism and hospitality. From a high of over a thousand students, the student body had dwindled to just over 200 by 2020. All teachers received early vaccinations and booster shots during the pandemic, thanks to government insistence, but with no end to the lockdowns in sight, speculation was rife as to the next pivot. Should the university reinvent itself to become a vocational institute specializing in HVAC (Heating, Ventilation, and Air Conditioning) and auto repair? Or perhaps become a hospital, given the pandemic's healthcare needs? Or go online as much as possible?

For the English Department, the question was downright existential. Was it better to drag on through online classes or shut down for a season? Would the first option even be possible?

Softened Resistance to Ed Tech

Having co-invented BLORMS as a bifurcated ePortfolio LMS in Canada, I (Joseph) was eager to sing and share the benefits of online tools, formative assessment, and community of practice (Wenger-Trayner & Wenger-Trayner, 2015) and peer-scaffolding pedagogical techniques upon first arrival at the university in 2017. Little did I expect the pushback to these ideas as wireless data access seemed affordable at USD 1 a week for 6GB, iPhones and Androids apparently on every student, and everyone was ostensibly smiling and eager to learn. As it turned out, the reality beneath first blush was very different. Nothing could be done about the exam and summative assessment-based grading scheme, due to the Ministry of Education, Youth, and Sports' policy. Pen and paper exams, twice a semester, reigned inviolate. Yet, shortly after school lockdowns were announced, word had come down from the same authorities that LMSes and Zoom were now acceptable, nay, compulsory.

Luddite cynicism and rejection melted away as faculty training courses in LMSes were hurriedly organized for Edmodo, Google Classroom, Canvas, and then back to Google Classroom. Previously heretical practices like exams on Google Forms now became heralded as superior, with ranks of faculty proctors staring into notebook screens acting as invigilators. To be concise and charitable, we shall not discuss the proctoring outcomes at this juncture.

Dormant Drawbridges: Pre-approved Programs

Right about this time, a visionary project to convert all curricula, textbooks, and course syllabi into a "Cyber University" was mandated for all departments, and the English Department was able to pull it off through an able assistant head who had, most serendipitously, just been hired and who stayed for a few months, just long enough to complete the project, before resigning. Even though only undergraduate classes were in operation with no foreseeable plans to start a postgraduate program, the Cyber University conversion for the English Department forged ahead to cover the MA in English portion as well. This covered the online curriculum and the syllabi, PDF textbooks, and supplemental materials for every course. The program had been approved by the Education Ministry and university accreditation agency, and now they wanted to pre-approve the online version as part of pandemic preparedness. As long as the door was open to cyber anything, regardless of any future likelihoods, we might as well put some postgraduate planes on the runway.

SWEETS DOWN SERENDIPITY STREET

Often, divine providence appears in the most secular of garbs, not unlike the pedestrian "coincidental" events in the biblical Book of Esther that ultimately saved the lives of an ethnic diaspora. The street branching out from the iconic two-lion statuary at the heart of the city to the now-defunct tourist jetty, lined with backpacker inns and eateries before the great casino advent, is dubiously named Serendipity Street. In the bleak pandemic midwinter, strategic partnerships seemed to lurk where none seem to have existed. And this was exactly what complemented the sudden openness to the deployment of technology at a critical moment.

Still Small Voices: Volunteer Partners

Résumés in by Sunday, May 24th [2020], please!
Anyone want to teach English over Zoom as a volunteer university lecturer?

Out went the call on Joseph's Facebook page on May 19, 2020, and to the rescue came four unpaid volunteer lecturers from Tokyo, Taipei, and Singapore. There were two others, from Ipoh, Malaysia, and Sihanoukville itself, sponsored by a generous patron in Singapore. The lecturer from Tokyo had just finished her master's degree and was awaiting her graduation day in locked-down conditions. Rather than sit around, she jumped in to teach four courses! One Singapore volunteer was a Bible college lecturer who was a Facebook friend of a friend of Joseph's. So was the other Singapore lecturer, an author and university lecturer, who volunteered only when satisfied with a background check of Joseph's LinkedIn profile recommendations, as she would later divulge. And Taipei's

5 HARNESSING PARTNERSHIPS AND TECHNOLOGY TO ESTABLISH A NEW... 81

volunteer was an ex-colleague of mine (Joseph's) who had left Cambodia for good. Several of them had a paid subscription to Zoom and were willing to use it to avoid the 40-minute cutoff on the free accounts. So, through volunteer help alone and at no financial cost to the university, we fulfilled our end of the contract to our undergraduate English majors.

Most of the Year 4 students served out their internships at an international school associated with the university. One of them, though, was confined to company housing as part of a football-betting syndicate. So I (Joseph) got her to assist all the overseas lecturers in administrative work, especially the corralling of students by phone to get on Zoom and taking attendance.

Timely Transformers: Foreign Assistance Programs

In March 2021, the international PreK-12 school associated with the university suggested that the university apply to the US State Department's English Language Fellow Program (US Department of State, n.d.), which is administered by Georgetown University, to have an English Language Fellow (ELF) teach at their school. As it turned out, the opportunity was golden. Due to rampant and byzantine airport protocols around the world, the U.S. State Department had issued travel advisories against unnecessary flights overseas. And so our bid for an ELF to help teach English and explain culture became one for a VELF (US Department of State, n.d.), a Virtual Fellow who would teach over Zoom.

With the success of the bid, an instructor with a doctorate degree was assigned to teach three courses a week, comprising two weekday sessions and a Saturday morning session on business English attended by civil engineering students besides our three English Y2s. In addition, a weeknight conversation session was set up to provide cultural exchange and conversational practice to exclusive, private-island resort workers in the Koh Rong Archipelago just off the coast of Sihanoukville. As it turned out, the English Y2s dropped out, and the VELF found himself teaching into a recording for much of the semester.

The mixed success of the VELF semester with the undergrads triggered the idea of finally launching our pre-approved MA program, pending approval for another VELF or even an in-person ELF. In March 2022, such an approval was obtained, and a second instructor possessing a doctorate degree (Patrick) joined the inaugural postgraduate faculty, first as a VELF and then, in August, as an ELF. Given the limited period of Patrick's fellowship tenure, courses had to be tightly stacked within policy but with little downtime to ensure timely completion of the 45-credit curriculum. What existed as a pipedream on paper had become, quite unexpectedly, not just a Cyber University curriculum but an actual on-Canvas series of courses.

Scouring the Highways and Byways: Student Recruitment

Student recruitment took place on several fronts. Onsite discussions and projections in the university predicted that the greatest interest would come from educational institutions with English teachers and customer-facing government and commercial offices. So the university vice-president for graduate studies wrote invitation letters to seven secondary schools in the surrounding Preah Sihanouk Province, made follow-up calls, and waited. The waiting continues. He and I (Joseph) also spent a couple of days marching up and down Ekareach Street, the main thoroughfare of Sihanoukville, hitting up the managers at the dozen banks and offices along that stretch. This was augmented by car rides to the tourist, port, and religion/cults bureaus. Polite smiles and name card exchanges done, it was time to wait. And wait.

Internal advertising went on in parallel, with teachers in the international and local schools associated with the university. Likewise, a call went out to the university's alumni on Facebook, and one responded, from Kampot, a smaller coastal town just east of Sihanoukville. And then something started humming, among the Filipino teachers on campus and then their larger community beyond, and interest turned into enrollments. Classes were initially scheduled for 5:30 p.m. on weekdays. Audit students were welcome, a first for the university, to foster greater classroom and online interactivity. To cater to the diverse work schedules represented, synchronous in-person or online sessions were recorded for later viewing, and the Canvas assignments and assessments allowed for asynchronous participation.

Rearview Mirror on the First Couple of Blocks

By the end of 2022, the master's program had four credit-seeking students moving into the thesis-writing phase, one going into the second semester, and two audits. About five prospective students awaited the new January intake. To say that surviving the pandemic and birthing a postgrad English program on the buckle of the Chinese BRI brought some level of satisfaction is to state the obvious. But that sense of satisfaction was complex and deserves some critical consideration. What lessons might one draw?

What Has Gone Well

Challenges caused by the pandemic, along with the university's responses to them, have resulted in some positive developments. To begin with, using online and hybrid courses has had, in some cases, a positive impact on student enrollment and attendance. Switching to online course delivery has made it possible for students who may not have been able to commute to the campus for face-to-face lessons to enroll in programs and attend courses. Some students in the MA in English program, who live too far from the campus to attend classes face to face (e.g., on offshore islands), join classes through Zoom. In addition, because we record the courses on Zoom, students who are busy or have unreliable internet connections have the option of watching recordings of classes and completing course assignments in Canvas, an LMS.

The option of teaching online has also improved the availability of course instructors. Instructors can now teach from remote locations, including other countries. This has enlarged the potential pool of instructors, and made it possible for instructors to cover for each other when unable to make it to campus to conduct face-to-face classes.

Online and hybrid teaching have also made it possible to employ a variety of resources and tools in classes that instructors may not have otherwise been able or inclined to use in face-to-face classes on campus. These digital tools, in our opinion, have scaffolded learning and made it more student-centered, and have elevated levels of student motivation and engagement. Online tools and materials and mobile device apps we have employed include YouTube videos and game and quiz apps. The use of tools such as Google Apps have also made it possible for synchronous and asynchronous online students to collaborate on assignments and engage in peer feedback.

The university's response to the exigencies caused by the pandemic led them to adopt the use of LMS. The university currently employs Canvas. We consider this a positive development because LMSes make course management, even for face-to-face or hybrid classes, much more convenient. Students can easily find class resources (e.g., presentation slides, articles) and know when assignments are due. We have also found it convenient to create and employ quizzes and exams in Canvas, which students may take online from their own homes.

To deal with frequent internet and power outages, instructors and students have shifted to using mobile phones and mobile phone hotspots to keep lessons going. Many people own mobile phones in Cambodia and subscription rates are relatively cheap (Phong et al., 2016). During the autumn semester in 2022, the university added ethernet cable connections to the internet in the classrooms we use for MA in English courses, which has improved the overall quality of internet connections, when that service is uninterrupted.

The online environment has also enabled students to share their knowledge of educational technology with students and instructors. For example, students helped me (Patrick) with Zoom, which I was initially unfamiliar with using as an instructor. A student also introduced me to EdPuzzle, an online tool which enables users to embed notes or quizzes in extant YouTube videos.

What Hasn't Worked Well

While many improvements occurred as a result of responses to the Covid pandemic, the university, the English Department, and their faculty and students faced multiple technology-related challenges.

Some students found adapting to hybrid or online courses to be challenging. For some, using necessary technology, such as video-conferencing platforms (e.g., Zoom), was difficult. I (Patrick) also found using Zoom for teaching, instead of for learning as a student, to be challenging at first. However, students more familiar with this type of technology helped their classmates and me, making classes go smoother.

Other challenges have been related to physical and internet infrastructure. There have been frequent power and internet outages interrupting classes. Poor internet connections have led to students and instructors being unable to understand each other during course meetings. When internet connections are poor, both students and instructors often resort to connecting their computers to the internet through their mobile phones' hotspots. While internet service interruptions may frequently occur, mobile phone connection quality tends to remain better. And as mobile phone service charges are relatively inexpensive in Cambodia

(Phong et al. 2016), students and institutions often switch to mobile phone use instead of using Internet connections.

On one occasion, because internet interruptions frequently occurred, interrupting the class repeatedly, I (Patrick) gave up on conducting the class synchronously, and recorded a lecture with screen-recording software. The various technology-related challenges seemed to be never-ending. At a later time, after updating the operating system on his laptop computer, I (Patrick) discovered I could no longer record audio with that screen-recording software.

Student and Homework Attrition and Stamina

While still in its first year of existence, a number of students withdrew from the MA in English program. In addition, submission of student course-work also steadily decreased as the initial terms progressed. Most of the students were part-time or full-time teachers, and some explained that they were busy with their jobs and lacked the time and stamina to attend classes and complete coursework. These are issues which we still need to address.

Pedagogical Limitations, Administrative Rigidity, and Class Size

Other challenges with developing a new MA in English Program related to bureaucratic resistance. Expectations have been to conduct lessons and assessments in traditional ways, including the use of end-of-term high-stakes exams instead of alternative means of assessment, such as ePortfolios, that might have more practical use for students (Lam, 2022). There has also been institutional preference to continue enrolling students in cohorts at the start of the school year rather than employing rolling enrollment and admissions throughout the school term, which may help counter the dwindling number of students in the MA in English program. However, one student was admitted to the program between cohorts so there does appear to be some flexibility. Small class sizes during the pandemic years at the university have limited the types of learning activities teachers can conduct. For example, it has been challenging to conduct anonymous peer review on Canvas and small-group activities because classes have had as few as three to five students.

RECOMMENDATIONS

In this section, we offer suggestions to other instructors and program administrators based on what worked and did not work for us.

Instructors who have to deal with poor internet connections in their universities, such as those at the university, may wish to consider being prepared to use mobile phones to conduct their classes. For example, when WiFi or wired connections and LED projections are interrupted, as happens during blackouts, teachers and students can continue to access the internet through their mobile phones. When we lost WiFi or LAN internet connections during classes, we reconnected our computers to the internet and Zoom with mobile phone hotspots, and students rejoined our course Zoom meetings with their mobile phones. The mobile phone plans available in Cambodia are relatively cheap (Phong et al., 2016), and most, if not all, instructors and students in the MA in English program have mobile phones. Faculty and students in similar situations may wish to plan and prepare for using mobile phones when internet connections become unstable. Being prepared for internet interruptions may help lessons go much smoother. With a SIM card and a powerbank in hand and cell towers functioning, the place of mobile-assisted language learning (MALL) is unassailable.

From our experiences, preparing students to engage in hybrid or online courses is important. In hindsight, I (Patrick) believe my classes might have gone smoother, particularly in the beginning, if I had concentrated earlier and more on educational technology involved in the courses. In particular, initial course delivery would have involved fewer interruptions if the class had been more familiar with Zoom from the beginning. Programs such as the MA in English program may wish to offer tutorials to instructors and students on video conferencing tools so that they can make effective use of them.

The university's implementation of an LMS in its courses, as a response to COVID-19, presented challenges. Programs in circumstances similar to the MA in English may benefit from ensuring both instructors and students are familiar with LMS to ensure smooth course delivery. While I (Patrick) had used my university's chosen LMS, Canvas (Instructure, 2022), as a student, I had never employed it before as an instructor, and learning how to use it effectively took time. Training for both instructors and students in how to employ LMSes may make transitions from face-to-face to online or hybrid course delivery smoother.

Students more accustomed to face-to-face, or even synchronous, participation in courses may also be unfamiliar with expectations regarding how to participate in online or hybrid courses. Some of our students lacked knowledge about how to engage with other students (e.g., posting in discussion threads) and how to submit assignments in Canvas. Instructors may need to set aside time at the outset of courses to carefully explain course activities and expectations. Demonstrations of how to interact with classmates (e.g., write and respond to posts in Discussion threads), submit assignments, take assessments, and access files stored in the course page in the LMS may promote student success in online and hybrid courses.

Implementation of technology for course delivery and course activities also offers opportunities to adapt alternative approaches to teaching-learning and assessment. For example, the use of technology may better enable programs to employ goal- or product-oriented approaches to learning and assessment such as Task-Based Language Teaching (TBLT) (Nunan, 2004) and ePortfolios, the latter of which I (Joseph) had experience with in an adult ESL program for immigrants in Canada. TBLT, or similar approaches, may help motivate students by engaging them in goal-oriented learning activities. Students in programs similar to the university's MA in English may benefit professionally by developing an ePortfolio stocked with practical and useful items such as lesson plans, curriculums, papers, research projects, CVs, cover letters, and demonstrations of competence with languages or language education (e.g., videos of themselves communicating in target languages or teaching target languages).

Conclusion

The tumultuous changes in Sihanoukville over the last few years should have tanked a university English Department, but the advent of technology and availability of support networks saved it. The introduction of Chinese investment and construction (Alfram, 2020; Horton, 2020) and the impact of COVID-19 (World Health Organization, 2022) drove expatriate teachers back to their own countries and threatened to stymie students' educational prospects. Against this background, the university's English Department took steps to exploit technology to address student enrollment, instructor availability, and course delivery. While administrators, faculty, and students have negotiated some challenges (e.g., implementation of LMS to increase enrollment and class attendance), others have been more difficult to overcome (e.g., student unfamiliarity with LMS or expectations in hybrid courses). Stakeholder responses to these challenges have resulted in some positive outcomes. Faculty, students, and administrators became more familiar with technology as they negotiated the demands of conducting classes in digital environments. Implementing face-to-face, online and hybrid course delivery, including the option of watching recorded lessons, made it possible for busy students who were unable to attend classes to enroll in the MA in English program. The use of digital tools had the added bonus of improving student motivation and engagement. Challenges more difficult to overcome have included infrastructure issues (e.g., internet and power interruptions), net drops in student enrollment, and student unfamiliarity with hybrid lesson delivery. From our experiences, we recommend that instructors and administrators in similar situations anticipate and take proactive measures regarding potential infrastructure issues (e.g., being prepared to seamlessly switch to mobile phone use during classes when internet interruptions occur), preparing instructors and students to engage in online and hybrid course delivery (e.g., increasing familiarity with LMS), developing students' understandings of how to engage in online course activities (e.g., participating in discussions and submitting assignments in LMSes), and considering alternative approaches to teaching-learning activities and assessment (e.g., Task-Based Learning, use of ePortfolios instead of high-stakes learning). Because programs in similar situations may find it challenging to overcome all challenges resulting from the pandemic and exacerbated by infrastructure and budgetary constraints, employing locally available resources (e.g., cheap mobile phone service), harnessing existing and emerging partnerships and opportunities, and adapting approaches to education and assessment may help overcome the often catastrophic geopolitical developments on their doorstep.

REFERENCES

Alfram, M. (2020, May 9). Sihanoukville pays the price for heavy reliance on Chinese. *Bangkok Post*. https://www.bangkokpost.com/business/2306938/sihanoukville-pays-the-price-for-heavy-reliance-on-chinese

Chhang, Y. (2021, November 16). Cambodia's history, viewed through Sihanoukville. *The Diplomat*. https://thediplomat.com/2021/11/cambodias-history-viewed-through-sihanoukville/

Ford, M., & Vimonsuknopparat, S. (2022, December 29). Inside the call centre scam that lured vulnerable workers to Cambodia and trapped them in the murky world of human trafficking. *ABC News*. https://www.abc.net.au/news/2022-12-29/inside-call-centre-scams-in-cambodia-torture-fear-and-survival/101770352?utm_campaign=abc_news_web&utm_content=link&utm_medium=content_shared&utm_source=abc_news_web

Gan, N. (2022, November 7). No immediate end in sight for China's costly zero-Covid policy. *CNN*. https://edition.cnn.com/2022/11/07/china/china-zero-covid-disaffection-intl-hnk/index.html

GGR Asia. (2022, October 13). Over 80 Cambodia casinos pending permit renewal: Ros. *GGR Asia*. https://www.ggrasia.com/over-80-cambodia-casinos-pending-permit-renewal-ros/

Horton, C. (2020, January 9). The costs of China's Belt and Road Expansion. *The Atlantic*. https://www.theatlantic.com/international/archive/2020/01/china-belt-road-expansion-risks/604342/

Hui, L. (2020, February 24). Sihanoukville eyes a bright future to become 'Shenzhen of Cambodia'. *Global Times*. https://www.globaltimes.cn/content/1180622.shtml

Instructure. (2022). *Canvas* [Learning Management System]. https://www.instructure.com/canvas

Khmer Times. (2021, December 2). More than $300 million spent in infrastructure building project shouldered by Cambodian investments. *Khmer Times*. https://www.khmertimeskh.com/50981287/more-than-300-million-spent-in-infrastructure-building-project-shouldered-by-cambodian-investments/

Khmer Times. (2022, December 28). Sihanoukville's expectations can match the hype. *Khmer Times*. https://www.khmertimeskh.com/501209931/sihanoukvilles-expectations-can-match-the-hype/

Lam, R. (2022). E-Portfolios for self-regulated and co-regulated learning: A review. *Frontiers in Psychology*. https://doi.org/10.3389/fpsyg.2022.1079385

Lim, D. (2022, July 18). The revival of Sihanoukville, Cambodia's 'Gold Rush' city. *ThinkChina*. https://www.thinkchina.sg/revival-sihanoukville-cambodias-gold-rush-city

Maliszewska, M., & van der Mensbrugghe, D. (2019, April). The Belt and Road Initiative: Economic, Poverty and Environmental Impact. *Policy Research Working Paper 8814*, World Bank Group. https://documents1.worldbank.org/curated/en/126471554923176405/pdf/The-Belt-and-Road-Initiative-Economic-Poverty-and-Environmental-Impacts.pdf

Ministry of Economy and Finance, General Department of Public-Private Partnerships. (n.d.). Phnom Penh-Sihanoukville Expressway. https://ppp.mef.gov.kh/detail/phnom-penh-sihanoukville-expressway?currentProjectListPid=190&cHash=409720af9e57ba30cafc54786ddde24f

Ministry of Education, Youth, and Sports. (n.d.). http://www.moeys.gov.kh/

Nunan, D. (2004). *Task-based language teaching*. Cambridge University Press.

Office of the Council of Ministers. (2020, January 30). Cambodian PM: Ban of China flights to destroy Cambodian economy. https://pressocm.gov.kh/en/archives/62685

Phong, K., Srou, L., & Solá, J. (2016). *Mobile phones and internet use in Cambodia 2016*. http://ticambodia.org/library/wp-content/files_mf/1485747618MobilePhonesandInternetUseinCambodia2016.pdf

Ratha Chan, S. (2022, September 28). Phnom Penh-Sihanoukville Expressway opens to public on one-month trial. *Khmer Times*. https://www.khmertimeskh.com/501158467/phnom-penh-sihanoukville-expressway-opens-to-public-on-one-month-trial/

Samean, L. (2021, November 16). 79 online gambling sites in Cambodia shut down. *The Phnom Penh Post*. https://www.phnompenhpost.com/national/79-online-gambling-sites-cambodia-shut-down

Sorkhean, B. (2020, March 4). Aftermath of Chinese exodus from Sihanoukville. *Khmer Times*. https://www.khmertimeskh.com/697816/aftermath-of-chinese-exodus-from-sihanoukville

The Organisation for Economic Co-operation and Development. (2018). *China's Belt and Road Initiative in the global trade, investment and finance landscape*. https://www.oecd.org/finance/Chinas-Belt-and-Road-Initiative-in-the-global-trade-investment-and-finance-landscape.pdf

US Department of State. (n.d.). Fellow Program. https://elprograms.org/fellow-program/

Voun, Dara. (2019, May 28). Shop signs displaying poor Khmer translations removed. *The Phnom Penh Post*. https://www.phnompenhpost.com/national/shop-signs-displaying-poor-khmer-translations-removed

Wenger-Trayner, E., & Wenger-Trayner, B. (2015). Communities of practice: A brief introduction. http://wenger-trayner.com/introduction-to-communities-of-practice/

World Health Organization. (2022). *Coronavirus disease (COVID-19) pandemic*. https://www.who.int/emergencies/diseases/novel-coronavirus-2019

Xinhua. (2022, December 22).Cambodian PM says using Chinese-invested expressway saves both money, time. *ChinaDaily.com*. https://www.chinadaily.com.cn/a/202212/22/WS63a3f8eca31057c47eba5b20.html

Yamada, S. (2019, August 4). Shenzhen in pictures: A former fishing village is transformed. *Nikkei Asia*. https://asia.nikkei.com/Business/China-tech/Shenzhen-in-pictures-a-former-fishing-village-is-transformed#:~:text=Shenzhen%2C%20which%20was%20a%20small,reform%20and%20opening%20up%22%20policy

PART II

Materials Development and Teaching Methodology

CHAPTER 6

A Culturally and Linguistically Responsive Approach to Materials Development: Teaching Vietnamese as a Second Language to Ethnic Minority Primary School Students

Thao Phuong Do, Hoa Do, and Linh Phung

IMPETUS FOR INNOVATION

As a linguistically heterogeneous country with 54 ethnic groups speaking approximately 100 minority languages alongside Vietnamese, the official national language of the country, the teaching of Vietnamese to ethnic minority primary school-aged students in remote and mountainous areas

---

T. P. Do (✉)
Faculty of Vietnamese Studies, Hanoi National University of Education,
Hanoi, Vietnam
e-mail: thaodp@hnue.edu.vn

H. Do
Department of Languages and Cultures, La Trobe University,
Melbourne, VIC, Australia
e-mail: thixuanhoa.do@latrobe.edu.au

© The Author(s), under exclusive license to Springer Nature
Switzerland AG 2024
L. Phung et al. (eds.), *Innovation in Language Learning and
Teaching*, New Language Learning and Teaching Environments,
https://doi.org/10.1007/978-3-031-46080-7_6

93

have always been a topic of concern in the country's modern language policy (Nguyen & Nguyen, 2019; Phan et al., 2014). In line with the implementation of the "one curriculum, many textbooks" approach in the education system in Vietnam, a number of textbook sets to teach Vietnamese to primary school students have been designed. The majority of them were designed to teach Vietnamese as a first language (L1) and do not include contents and activities relevant to the students' daily life and experiences, a factor contributing to the poor performance of ethnic minority students in acquiring Vietnamese (Thanh, 2010).

The past few years have witnessed a number of programs and projects piloting bilingual education and new approaches to teaching Vietnamese as an L2 to ethnic minority primary school-aged students. Some of the most prominent ones include the School Education Quality Assurance Program (SEQAP) running from 2010 to 2016 (Ngo, 2016), the Improving Care and Education Quality for Ethnic Minority and Disadvantaged Children project in Tam Duong district, Lai Chau Province implemented from 2016 to 2018 (Aide et Action, 2016) and the Mother Tongue-based Bilingual Education (MTBBE) conducted from 2008 to 2015 (Nguyen & Nguyen, 2019). These projects have produced positive outcomes including heightening parents' and students' awareness of the importance of bilingualism, improving teachers' pedagogical practices, running extracurricular activities focusing on ethnic minority children's customs and traditions, developing bilingual materials, and extending class time for Vietnamese (Nguyen & Nguyen, 2019; Phan et al., 2014; Tran, 2016). However, these one-off projects target broader educational aims, rather than focusing on developing Vietnamese language abilities of this population. They are also not easy to be replicated on a big scale given the complex linguistic and geographic context in Vietnam where more than one minority language is spoken in an area. The shortage of competent bilingual teachers and the absence of a systematic bilingual teacher education and training program in the country makes it even harder to

---

L. Phung
Eduling International, Pittsburgh, PA, USA

implement such initiatives nationwide. These challenges are likely to require much time and effort to be adequately addressed.

In addition, to ethnic minority students, Vietnamese is neither their mother tongue nor a foreign language, but a second language (L2). This means the approach to curriculum design and instruction to teach Vietnamese to this group of learners should be informed by the literature on second language acquisition. Ethnic minority students have their own cultural capital and linguistic resources in their L1 which bears some similarities and differences with the L2 and can be helpful for their L2 acquisition (Anderson, 2018). In developing curricula and learning materials for this group of learners, their specific needs and learning environment should be thoroughly analyzed, and their educational, social, cultural and linguistic background should be taken into account (Morgan & Houghton, 2011 as cited in Hector-Alexander, 2019; Nation & Macalister, 2009). Sobel (2011) emphasizes that teachers need to "teach like their students' lives really do matter" (p. 3) as learning and teaching in general and language education in particular is directly impacted by cultural and linguistic factors. The argument is specially relevant to schools in rural areas where access to technology is limited and students are diverse in their cultural and linguistic background (Curtis, 2021; Kumi-Yeboah et al., 2021). Therefore, adopting a culturally and linguistically responsive approach to material development and pedagogy can be an answer to improving the teaching of Vietnamese to ethnic minority students.

This chapter reports on a material development project that incorporates a culturally and linguistically responsive approach to materials development to teach Vietnamese as a second language to ethnic minority students for the time being. The chapter continues with an overview of culturally and linguistically responsive material development in second language education of minority students. It will then problematize teaching Vietnamese as an L2 to ethnic minority students in Vietnam to set the scene for a report on the development and implementation of Vietnamese practice book for Grade 5 ethnic minority students.

Culturally and Linguistically Responsive Materials Development

Culturally and linguistically responsive pedagogy has garnered attention in the field of education and second/foreign language acquisition in recent decades, particularly in such migration countries as the USA, the UK, Australia and Canada where students of diverse cultural, religious, linguistic, and ethnic backgrounds and life experiences gather in one classroom (Sobel, 2011). The pedagogy highlights the importance of valuing and utilizing cultural and linguistic backgrounds of minority students and language learners and their prior knowledge to create an inclusive and supportive learning environment for their literacy and language acquisition (Gay, 2010; Hollie, 2018; Lucas & Villegas, 2013). In practicing culturally responsive teaching, it is crucial that teachers know their students and how they acquire knowledge in order to plan for and deliver effective lessons and assess and provide meaningful feedback for their learning (Wallace & Campbell, 2014). They further argue that to support culturally and linguistically diverse students in learning English as a second or an additional language and the medium of instruction, schools and teachers must ensure a culturally inclusive curriculum, support in and for L1, an awareness that literacy skills in L1 transfer to English, scaffolding for zone of proximal development, and interaction in English in social and academic contexts. The same argument can be applied in the case of teaching Vietnamese as a second language to ethnic minority students in Vietnam where support in and for the students' L1 would facilitate their acquisition of Vietnamese.

Lee et al. (2007) list seven common practices that culturally responsive teachers should execute, three of which directly involves optimizing students' prior knowledge and lived experiences, delivering culturally and linguistically meaningful and relevant instruction, and integrating local knowledge, language, and culture into the curriculum. Siwatu (2007) proposes four areas where teachers can apply culturally responsive teaching including curriculum and instruction, classroom management, student assessment and cultural enrichment, the focus of which is utilizing students' cultural experiences and background knowledge to create a culturally safe, compatible and supportive learning environment. In the same vein, Gay (2002, 2010) outlines five aspects of preparing teachers for culturally responsive teaching: forming a cultural diversity knowledge base, designing culturally relevant curricula, demonstrating cultural caring and a learning community, cross-cultural communication, and delivering instructions that promote cultural congruity. Regarding materials development specifically, Gay (2002, 2010) confirms that it is first and foremost important for teachers to know about their ethnic minority students' cultural values, relational patterns, learning styles and traditions to form a knowledge base for their culturally responsive teaching since this kind of knowledge and awareness exerts a direct influence on teaching and learning. Translating the knowledge base into instructional materials then requires a thorough analysis of the "quantity, quantity, accuracy, complexity, placement, purpose, variety, significance, and authenticity of the narrative texts, visual illustrations, learning activities, role models, and authorial sources" in the materials (p. 108). In their book on bilingual education, Johnson and Swain (1997) persuasively argue that a culturally and linguistically responsive approach to materials development can promote language learning by providing students with opportunities to use language in a meaningful way. They state that by incorporating authentic materials and relevant real-life situations and contexts, teachers can help make the language more authentic and useful for students. This develops students' language learning and intercultural competence at the same time.

Informed by culturally and linguistically responsive pedagogy, this chapter contributes to the scarce literature on the application of culturally and linguistically responsive materials development in teaching Vietnamese, a less studied language, in an understudied context.

Teaching Vietnamese as an L2 to Ethnic Minority Students

As stipulated in the Vietnam Education Law, the Vietnamese language is both a compulsory subject and the official medium of instruction across the country at all levels (Socialist Republic of Vietnam, 2005). To ethnic minority students whose first language is not Vietnamese, the load of learning Vietnamese as a second language and using it to acquire knowledge in other subjects puts them at a disadvantage, which partially explains the high dropout rate among this group of learners (Kosonen, 2006; Tran, 2020). The teaching of the language itself has been found to be insufficient in developing students' four language skills, including listening, speaking, reading, and writing, which suggests much room for improvement (Do, 2018). In fact, with a focus on reading and writing skills, students' communicative abilities in Vietnamese have generally been neglected. In addition, currently there are two curricula for teaching the Vietnamese language to primary school-aged students in Vietnam: Version 2006 and Version 2018, both of which were designed to teach Vietnamese as a L1. In both curricula, these materials are not familiar to ethnic minority students who are not the majority Vietnamese-speaking Kinh group and whose mother tongue is not Vietnamese. The lack of culturally and linguistically relevant materials in the curriculum for ethnic minority students is striking and requires change and innovation in this area.

In addition, when the materials and teaching approaches do not consider the learning needs of ethnic minority students from a second language acquisition (SLA) perspective, these students are placed into a "swim or sink" situation without adequate support to develop their Vietnamese literacy and competence. Although first language and second language acquisition shares some similarities in the developmental sequences (stages that learners go through as they acquire a new language) and acquisition order of grammatical structures (Ellis, 1994; Larsen-Freeman, 1976; Pienemann, 1995, 2007), they differ in not only cognitive and affective processes that are involved but also socio-cultural factors that affect their learning process (Ellis, 1994; Krashen, 1985). Specifically, learners need rich, meaningful, comprehensible input; opportunities to produce meaningful output; and opportunities for interaction and negotiation of meaning; and corrective feedback, among other factors, to develop their competence in the second language (Krashen, 1985; Long, 1996; Lyster, 2018; Swain, 1993). In addition, in the classroom, teachers need to be able to scaffold students' learning within their zone of proximal development through different instructional techniques including the integration of students' first language and culture in their lessons and as a resource in their students' learning process. In fact, the practice of using one language (i.e., the L1) in order to reinforce the other also known as "translanguaging" in education has gained support in bilingual and foreign language education in recent years (Baker, 2001). Therefore, using materials designed for the majority group and teaching Vietnamese without making adequate use of students' L1 does not provide optimal conditions for ethnic minority students' language and literacy development.

In fact, Do's (2018) project with 100 teachers at eight primary schools in Son La, Dien Bien, Dak Lak and Kien Giang, four economically disadvantaged provinces in Vietnam found that 88% of the teachers reported primarily using the conventional approach in teaching Vietnamese and the majority used the students' L1 only for classroom management as well as comprehension and explanation of the most challenging vocabulary. The teachers justified their modest use of their students' L1 by claiming that an overuse of the students' mother tongue would hinder their acquisition of Vietnamese. This belief is what Clyne (2005) terms "a monolingual mindset" where a single dominant societal language is favored, resulting in other minority languages being undervalued. It can be inferred that with their monolingual mindset, the teachers were less likely to make use of their students' cultural and linguistic resources that could have been of help in their language lessons. Do's (2018) findings brought to light the teachers' monolingual mindset and their misconceptions about the relationship between the L1 and L2 in second language acquisition, both of which directly dictate their classroom practice and influence their students' learning and progress.

Recognizing the need for culturally and linguistically responsive materials to teach Vietnamese as a second language to ethnic minority students, the first author of this chapter developed a Vietnamese Practice Book for Grade 5 to accompany Vietnamese for Grade 5 from the Ministry of Education. The next section of this chapter reports on this innovation by discussing the steps to develop and implement the textbook set with a reflection on challenges and recommendations for similar projects.

THE INNOVATION

The Vietnamese Practice Book for Grade 5 was developed by the first author of this chapter as a result of a large-scale research project from the Vietnamese Ministry of Education to investigate methods of teaching Vietnamese as a second language for ethnic minority primary students in Vietnam. This project was led by the first author and implemented from May 2016 to December 2017 under the administration of Hanoi National University of Education. The project was conducted in eight primary schools in four provinces in regions with a population of ethnic minority students. In the Northwest region, Son La and Dien Bien provinces are home to students of the Thái, H'mông, Mường, Dao, Khơ Mú, Tày, Giáy, Hà Nhì, Lao, Cống, and Si La group. There are many students of the Ê-đê, M'nông, Nùng, Tày, Thái, and Dao group in Dak lak Province in the Central Highlands region. Kien Giang Province in the Mekong River Delta region is known to have students of the Khmer and Chinese group.

The overall project goal is to conduct exploratory research and suggest models on teaching Vietnamese as a second language for ethnic minorities primary students. Specific objectives include (1) set up the scientific and practical basis of teaching Vietnamese as a second language for ethnic minority students; (2) establish the standards for language skills and competencies that need to be developed for ethnic minority pupils at primary level; (3) set up the teaching process and teaching methods of Vietnamese as a second language; (4) experiment on methods of teaching Vietnamese as a second language for ethnic minority pupils at primary level; and (5) suggest the methodology for teaching Vietnamese language as a second language for ethnic minority pupils at primary level (including a system of methods, specific measures of each method and criteria for the development of language teaching products that are modern and consistent with the proposed methodology).

Apart from findings reported in Do (2018), one of the outcomes of this project was a set of textbooks for teaching Vietnamese as a second language to ethnic minority primary students. The first textbook that the first author and her project team developed was titled Thực hành tiếng Việt lớp 5 or Vietnamese Practice Book for Grade 5. The reason why the authors chose to develop this book first is that Grade 5 is the last year in primary school when students' abilities to use Vietnamese in the four skills (listening, speaking, reading, and writing) are the highest. This made the selection of materials easier.

The next section will report the materials development process with the focus on selecting culturally and linguistically responsive materials suitable to teach Vietnamese as a second language to ethnic minority primary students in Vietnam.

Materials Development Process

These are the stages we followed in the project.

First, we clarified the users and goals of the project. Overall, the main goal is to develop materials to teach Vietnamese as an L2 to ethnic minority primary students. The users would be teachers and students in this context. The materials follow the "Tiếng Việt" (or Vietnamese) curriculum for primary schools from the Ministry of Education and Training (MOET). The general objectives of these materials include:

- To consolidate knowledge covered in the Vietnamese textbook for primary students and enlarge students' vocabulary, grammatical resources, and socio-cultural knowledge through more relevant materials that reflect societal changes, Vietnamese culture, and minority cultures. These new materials aim to better relate to the teaching and learning situations in the mountainous and remote areas of Vietnam.
- To put into practice principles and methods of teaching Vietnamese as an L2 with specific teaching techniques, instructional activities, and learning materials to develop students' four language skills, that is, listening, speaking, reading, and writing.

In the second stage, we examined the national curricular guidelines for Vietnamese for primary students from the Ministry of Education published in 2018. In addition, we reviewed the standards for all students as well as for minority students at each grade level.

In the third stage, we researched the available materials, which include three sets of textbooks published by the MOET, textbook sets developed for ethnic minority students that had been published, and multimodal materials (texts, images, and video clips) related to ethnic cultures.

In the fourth stage, we developed materials for Grade 5 with an overall emphasis on using students' L1 resources to facilitate L2 development. This process has several steps including the development of 35 units for a school year. Each unit develops students' vocabulary, grammar, and knowledge about culture and society around themes already covered in the Vietnamese 5 textbook. Another step in the materials development process was the design of each lesson, which includes selecting reading texts and illustrations suitable for the Vietnamese proficiency level of the target learners and developing practice activities to address the four language skills of listening, speaking, reading, and writing. Notably, the texts selected reflect the Vietnamese national values, culture, and characters as well as the cultures of ethnic minority groups in Vietnam. In addition, we adapted the texts to ensure that they are comprehensible and beneficial for the development of Vietnamese as a second language. Specifically, we shortened the text to 200–300 words. We also ensured that the vocabulary in the text is familiar or has been taught to the students and the text includes target vocabulary items and grammatical structures. Moreover, we included culturally relevant illustrations and examples from the students' first languages.

102   T. P. DO ET AL.

Activities to develop students' vocabulary and grammar consist of those aiming to expand students' vocabulary knowledge and use in context. Students also learn to form sentences to meet communicative objectives in various situations. Speaking activities include those associated with real-life situations as well as topics related to Vietnamese culture, society, and values. Furthermore, writing activities aim to develop students' abilities to write paragraphs and common genres. Finally, each unit also consists of suggestions to students on how to approach difficult tasks.

Incorporating Culturally and Linguistically Responsive Materials

The most innovative aspect of this project is the inclusion of language input and activities from the students' language and culture. This is one of the most important features of culturally and linguistically responsive teaching (Gay, 2010; Lee et al., 2007). For example, to develop materials to teach students idioms and proverbs in Vietnamese, we researched the similarities and differences between those used in Vietnamese and in the Tày-Thái language, including 465 proverbs about animals in the former and 289 in the latter. A difference includes more frequent reference to animals in the lowland in Vietnamese in comparison to reference to animals common in the mountainous living conditions in Tày-Thái (Le et al., 2018). Therefore, there are certain animals that only appear in Vietnamese idioms, such as animals from the coastal plain region, and others that only appear in Tày-Thái idioms. Even when an animal like the buffalo is common in both languages, each notices different dominant characteristics. Vietnamese sees the buffalo as strong and voracious in such idioms as "khỏe như trâu" (as strong as a buffalo) or "ăn như trâu" (eat like a buffalo) while Tày-Thái notices the buffalo's inability to make sounds and its big size in such idioms as "vài kin lịn" (trâu ăn lưỡi in Vietnamese or tongue-tied buffalo) and "vài cải khỉ cải" (trâu to phân to in Vietnamese or big buffalo, big poop). Similarly, the two languages use different animals to describe different phenomena, such as "ngu như lợn" (as stupid as a pig) in Vietnamese and đăm bặng bể bọt (tối như dê mù in Vietnamese or as dull as a blind goat) in Tày-Thái. It is natural that each ethnic group thinks about the world through objects and phenomena observable in their environment. The lenses through which they look at the world are different.

In our materials, we purposefully include idioms with animal names common in the students' L1 to make the materials more relevant and comprehensible to the students, thus facilitating the development of Vietnamese. We also ask students to compare Vietnamese idioms with those in their mother tongue by asking such questions as:

- Are there similar idioms in your language?
- When talking about buffaloes, what characteristics do you notice? Share some idioms from your language that refer to buffaloes.
- When talking about someone strong/ weak/ fast/ slow ... what animal do you compare him/ her with in your language? What animal is used in Vietnamese?

These comparisons do not only develop students' awareness of cultural differences but also help them to better acquire the Vietnamese language through relatable content.

Another example of the development of culturally and linguistically inclusive materials in our project can be seen in the practice activity in Table 6.1. Students are asked to match the proverb in Column A with a cultural value in Column B. The proverbs chosen come from various languages and ethnic groups, including Vân Kiều and Thái, not only from the Kinh group.

In addition, our materials include role models and historical figures from ethnic minority groups (e.g., Kim Đồng and Vừ A Dính—see the illustration below), cultural practices from various groups (e.g., brocade weaving as seen in the photo below, drum festival in Quảng Bình, and rice harvest festival in Sa Pa), and distinctive sceneries from the mountainous regions (peach blossoms in the northwest and kơ-nia trees in the Central Highlands area).

These familiar materials will help students better comprehend and connect with the content of their Vietnamese lessons.

Finally, in our teacher guide, we encourage teachers to incorporate students' language and culture by decorating with words and images from both languages and students' works. This way, the students will feel they are seen and their culture is appreciated.

Piloting the Materials

After the materials were developed and printed, we piloted them by having 100 teachers teaching 10 units to 400 fifth graders in the 8 schools from September 2016 to May 2017. The ten units covered similar main themes

Table 6.1 Example practice activity

A	B
1. Nhà rộng, lòng chật ta đừng thèm đến. Nhà chật, lòng rộng ta muốn lại chơi. *A big house with a small heart—I don't want to visit.* *A small house with a big heart—I do want to see.* (Vân Kiều folksong)	Tôn sư trọng đạo (Respect for teachers)
2. Năng nhặt chặt bị. *More saving, fuller sack.* Kiến tha lâu có ngày đầy tổ. *Patient ants, full nests.* (Kinh proverb)	b. Cần cù lao động (Diligence)
3. Uống nước phải xem nguồn. *Know the source of the water you drink.* (Kinh proverb) Lên dốc phải xem hướng. *Know the direction while climbing up hill.* (Thái proverb) Ăn quả nhớ kẻ trồng cây. *Remember the one planting the tree when you eat the fruit.* (Kinh proverb)	c. Trọng tình nghĩa (Appreciation of kindness)
4. Một chữ cũng là thầy, nửa chữ cũng là thầy. *One word is thanks to your teacher. Half a word is also thanks to your teacher.* (Kinh proverb) Biết chữ biết mọi việc. Biết nghĩa biết thành người. *Knowing words is having knowledge.* *Showing gratitude is having humanity.* (Thái proverb)	d. Nhớ ơn nguồn cội (Respect for our roots)

Vừ A Dính—A young hero of the H'mông group

A Black Thái woman weaving brocade. (Photo taken from http://tpdienbienphu.gov.vn)

106   T. P. DO ET AL.

and topics to those in the official curriculum which was developed by MOET and was currently used nationwide. Each unit in the set was taught in one to two periods of 35 minutes.

We collected feedback from 100 teachers who used the materials in their classes and observed lessons in which the new materials were used to evaluate the effectiveness of the materials. After teaching the ten units, participating teachers completed a questionnaire to assess whether they thought the materials met five criteria (i.e., being relevant, contemporary, pedagogically sound, interactive, and systematic) in developing students' knowledge and skills in four areas: pronunciation, vocabulary, grammar, and communication. They gave a 0 for "not satisfactory" or 1 for "satisfactory." Table 6.2 shows the percentages of teachers selecting 1.

As can be seen, the majority of the teachers (ranging from 69 to 88%) evaluated the materials as meeting the five criteria outlined in the survey in the four areas. This reflects a positive response to the materials.

In addition, we also surveyed teachers for their opinions on the necessity and feasibility of using these materials to teach Vietnamese to ethnic minority students. The results of this survey are shown in Tables 6.3 and 6.4.

Table 6.2 Percentage of teachers rating the materials as meeting criteria

	Pronunciation	*Vocabulary*	*Grammar*	*Communication*
Relevant	75	76	74	69
Contemporary	80	86	76	88
Pedagogically sound	82	86	80	81
Interactive	83	84	76	87
Systematic	73	77	88	76

Table 6.3 The necessity of the materials

No	*Location*	*Response (Percentage)*		
		Necessary	*Neutral*	*Not necessary*
1.	Điện Biên	88	11	1
2.	Sơn La	77	21	2
3.	Đắk Lắk	69	26	5
4.	Kiên Giang	90	10	0
Average		81	17	2

Table 6.4 Feasibility of materials use

No	Location	Response (%)		
		Feasible	Neutral	Not feasible
1.	Điện Biên	86	13	1
2.	Sơn La	87	11	2
3.	Đắk Lắk	79	15	6
4.	Kiên Giang	91	7	2
Average		85.75	11.5	2.75

The table shows that the vast majority of teachers (69 to 90% with an average of 81% for the four provinces) agreed that the materials were necessary for the development of Vietnamese to ethnic minority students in their context with only 2% rating them as not necessary.

As can be seen, an average of 85.75% teachers rated the materials as feasible, 11.5% were neutral, and only 2.75% rated them as not feasible to use in their context. Together with Table 6.3, these data show that the teachers saw these materials as necessary and feasible to implement to develop their students' Vietnamese knowledge and skills.

In their response to open-ended questions in the questionnaire, the teachers added more specific feedback on the materials. While they thought highly of and were interested in developing culturally and linguistically responsive materials, they admitted having a low level of proficiency in their students' mother tongue, making it challenging for them to provide support in the student's L1. One solution to this problem, they suggested, was to get community members and parents involved in the development of the learning materials. They could help proofread culture-specific contents and provide classroom language in the L1 so that teachers would have a handy L1 toolkit to support their students. This suggests the teachers' newly gained perspective and enthusiasm in further innovation in this area.

DISCUSSION

Adopting a culturally and linguistically responsive approach to design learning materials to teach Vietnamese as an L2 to primary school students from ethnic minority groups was an innovation to improve the learning outcomes of ethnic minority primary students in Vietnam. The main textbooks were developed for the majority Vietnamese-speaking Kinh group, which are not really suitable to develop Vietnamese as an L2 as far as the content and teaching methodology are concerned. The materials reported in this project address minority students' specific linguistic and cultural backgrounds as well as learning needs. We intentionally included contents closely related to and representative of the students' cultural practices and values. The inclusion of idioms and proverbs in the students' culture as well as images of local heroes and sceneries rather than widely used illustrations of those of the Kinh group was underpinned by Gay's (2010) guidelines in developing formal culturally relevant curricula. Another strength of the materials is the design of guiding questions that elicit students' prior knowledge and draw their attention to differences in perception in different languages. This helps learners understand the meaning and usage of Vietnamese and differentiate the similarities and differences with their mother tongue. By doing this not only can students acquire Vietnamese but they can also construct knowledge about the relationship between knowledge construction and languages, which heightens their awareness of the power of language learning and multilingualism. This approach, therefore, has the potential to support the retention and development of the students' mother tongue when it is not the dominant societal language.

In addition, teaching Vietnamese as an L2 requires an understanding of the process of second language acquisition (SLA), which is different from first language acquisition (Ellis, 1994), and a different instructional approach which takes into account principles of L2 development. Our materials started to address these principles by making texts comprehensible to students as well as providing students opportunities to produce meaningful output through writing and speaking activities. The pilot implementation of the textbook changed the participating teachers' mindset and perspective as they started to view and treat the teaching of Vietnamese to this group differently. The teachers' assessment of the materials and changes in instructional practices as satisfactory, necessary, and feasible suggested that we were moving in the right direction in meeting the students and teachers' needs but further progress was needed.

Apart from these successes, we acknowledge some limitations in our materials and challenges during the project. First, while we aimed to include multimodal contents to include videos and audios, we could only incorporate visual and textual materials, which limited the students' opportunities to be exposed to rich aural input. Secondly, we could only focus on Tày-Thái and were not able to design more inclusive materials representing more ethnic minority groups due to the scant availability of materials on the internet and libraries. Finally, our relatively limited command of ethnic minority languages prevented us from generating bilingual texts or glossaries to further support students and teachers.

With this reflection, we recommend further work in this area. Specifically, we recommend having materials that aim to cover more ethnic minority groups and languages by considering their linguistic backgrounds and cultures. While more needs to be done to improve the instructional practice and learning outcomes, offering culturally and linguistically materials that take into account principles of second language development is the starting point in making lasting changes.

Together with a set of suitable materials, it is important to continue to innovate the teaching of Vietnamese to ethnic minority primary students through approaches that are suitable for teaching Vietnamese as a second language. There has already been an extensive body of literature in foreign and second language education that future innovation can draw from. While basic literacy in Vietnamese, such as spelling, phonics, and reading, is important, meaning-based and communicative approaches, such as content-based instruction (CBI) and task-based language teaching (TBLT) may be applied to develop the learners' social and academic language to facilitate meaningful integration of ethnic minority groups into the larger society.

The innovation of the teaching materials also requires the modernization of teaching facilities and resources. Ethnic minority students have little exposure to Vietnamese. Therefore, apart from textbooks, students need to have access to supplemental materials, reference books, audiovisual materials, and technologies for more learning opportunities. They need to also be diverse, inclusive, and culturally relevant to the students. For example, these materials should be of different genres with topics that reflect the lands, people, and cultures of different ethnic groups. Works from authors that have written about ethnic groups (e.g., Tô Hoài, Học Phi, Ma Văn Kháng) as well as minority authors (e.g., Vương Trọng, Nông Quốc Chấn, Lò Ngân Sủn) should be made available to the students. By reading their works, they will see themselves and their cultures being reflected and appreciated, which can be a source of motivation to learn Vietnamese, master the language, and integrate into the wider society. Bilingual materials can also be a valuable source for the development of multilingual abilities.

Professional development for teachers is an important component in implementing any innovation. Teaching Vietnamese as a second language using contemporary approaches (e.g., CBI and TBLT) and culturally and linguistically responsive materials and pedagogies can be a topic of training workshops organized by the Ministry of Education. Through these workshops, teachers also have the opportunities to share experiences, ideas, and requests to relevant ministries and departments to effect meaningful and positive changes in the educational outcomes of their students.

Finally, primary schools in ethnic minority areas may implement programs to develop teachers' ability to use the mother tongue of ethnic minority students so that they can use it effectively in their teaching. Recruitment of teachers who are bilingual and engaging teachers in the materials development process itself can also be a fruitful endeavor. Since the majority of ethnic minority students have limited proficiency in Vietnamese, learning with teachers who can use their mother tongue will support the teaching and learning process. This can be a move toward bilingual and multilingual education options for ethnic minority students in the country.

Conclusion

This chapter reports an innovation in teaching Vietnamese to ethnic minority primary students in Vietnam. Specifically, the innovation involves the development and piloting of a Vietnamese practice book for Grade 5. Guided by the goals of developing pedagogically sound materials to facilitate students' acquisition of Vietnamese as an L2, we adopted a culturally and linguistically responsive approach to designing our materials. In developing the package, materials including texts and illustrations were adapted and selected to both represent the students' cultural values and practices and to facilitate their target language learning through their prior knowledge and mother tongue. The book includes examples of culturally and linguistically relevant visual illustrations, role models, texts and learning activities and received positive initial feedback from the teachers.

After piloting the materials, analyzing the teacher participants' feedback, and reflecting on the project, we suggest that further work be done in this area so that more and richer materials that cater to all ethnic minority groups are available to the teachers and students. The specific recommendations we put forward will start to fill the gaps in the instruction of Vietnamese to linguistically diverse learners in Vietnam and improve the learning outcomes of these learners.

References

Aide et Action. (2016). European Union-Vietnam: Cooperated to develop the first Viet-Mong bilingual supplementary learning materials for ethnic minority children in Lai Chau province, Vietnam. https://action-education.org/sea/en/launching-of-bilingual-materials/

Anderson, J. (2018). Reimagining English language learners from a translingual perspective. *ELT journal, 72*(1), 26–37. https://doi.org/10.1093/elt/ccx029

Baker, C. (2001). *Foundations of bilingual education and bilingualism* (3rd ed.). Multilingual Matters.

Clyne, M. (2005). *Australia's language potential.* UNSW Press.

Curtis, A. (2021). What do we mean by under-resourced context? In K. M. Bailey & D. Christian (Eds.), *Research on teaching and learning English in under-resourced contexts* (pp. 14–28). Routledge.

Do, P. T. (Project Coordinator). (2018). An experimental research on the methods of teaching Vietnamese as a second language for ethnic minorities primary students. *Project of Ministry of Education and Training,* Vietnam, code number: B. 2015-17-77.

Do, V. H., Nguyen, T. N. H., & Do, P. T. (2018). Integrating cultural and musical elements into teaching Vietnamese for ethnic minority students at primary level through song material sources. *Science Journal of Hanoi National University of Education, 63*(5), 120–129.

Ellis, R. (1994). *The study of second language acquisition.* Oxford University Press.

Gay, G. (2002). Preparing for culturally responsive teaching. *Journal of Teacher Education, 53*(2), 106–116.

Gay, G. (2010a). *Culturally responsive teaching: Theory, research, and practice.* Teachers College.

Hector-Alexander, A. (2019). Inclusive curriculum design. In R. Power (Ed.), *Technology and the curriculum* (pp. 193–204). Power Learning Solutions. https://pressbooks.pub/techandcurr2019/chapter/inclusive-curriculum-design/

Hollie, S. (2018). *Culturally and linguistically responsive teaching and learning classroom practices for student success* (2nd ed.). Shell Education.

Johnson, R. K., & Swain, M. (1997). *Immersion education. International perspectives.* Cambridge University Press

Kosonen, K. (2006). Multigrade teaching among ethnic minority children: The language issue. In L. Conish (Ed.), *Reaching EFA through multi-grade teaching: Issues, contexts and practices* (pp. 239–258). Kardoorair Press.

Krashen, S. (1985). *The input hypothesis: Issues and implications.* Longman.

Kumi-Yeboah, A., Onyewuenyi, A. C., & Smith, P. (2021). Teaching black immigrant students in urban schools: Teacher and peer relationships and academic performances. *Urban Reviro, 53,* 218–242. https://doi.org/10.1007/s11256-020-00570-2

Larsen-Freeman, D. E. (1976). An explanation for the morpheme acquisition order of second language learners. *Language Learning*, *26*(1), 125–135. https://doi.org/10.1111/j.1467-1770.1976.tb00264.x

Le, A., Nguyen, T. N. H., & Do, P. T. (2018). Teaching Vietnamese idioms to Tay—Thai elementary students in the direction of applying cultural knowledge and mother tongue (through the case of students Grade 5 Tay—Thai ethnic group learn some idioms with the words "animals"). *Journal of Educational by Ministry of Education and Training*, *428*(Second term), 24–29.

Lee, K. A., Cosby, B. C., & deBaca, C. D. (2007). *Cultural responsiveness*. Civil Rights Commission Education Steering Committee.

Long, M. (1996). The role of the linguistic environment in second language acquisition. In W. C. Ritchie & T. K. Bhatia (Eds.), *Handbook of second language acquisition* (pp. 413–468). Academic Press.

Lucas, T., & Villegas, A. M. (2013). Preparing linguistically responsive teachers: Laying the foundation in preservice teacher education. *Theory into Practice*, *52*(2), 98–109. https://doi.org/10.1080/00405841.2013.770327

Lyster, R. (2018). Roles for corrective feedback in second language instruction. In C.A. Chapelle (Ed.), *The encyclopedia of applied linguistics*. https://doi.org/10.1002/9781405198431.wbeal1028.pub2

Nation, I. S. P., & Macalister, J. (2009). *Language curriculum design* (J. Macalister & ProQuest, Eds.). Routledge.

Ngo, Q. Q. (2016). Full day schooling model: Sustainability and pervasion. (Mo hinh day hoc ca ngay: tinh ben vung va su lan toa). *Journal of Education-Special Edition*. https://tapchigiaoduc.moet.gov.vn/vi/magazine/so-dac-biet-thang-8/7-mo-hinh-day-hoc-ca-ngay-tinh-ben-vung-va-su-lan-toa-4430.html

Nguyen, X. N. M. C., & Nguyen, V. H. (2019). Language education policy in Vietnam. In A. Kirkpatrick & A. J. Liddicoat (Eds.), *The Routledge international handbook of language education policy in Asia* (pp. 185–201). Routledge.

Phan, L. H., Vu, H. H., & Bao, D. (2014). Language policies in modern-day Vietnam: Changes, challenges and complexities. In T. R. F. Tupas, P. G. Sercombe, T. R. F. Tupas, & A. Cincotta-Segi (Eds.), *Language, education and nation-building assimilation and shift in Southeast Asia* (pp. 232–245). Palgrave Macmillan.

Pienemann, M. (1995). *Second language acquisition: A first introduction*. National Languages and Literacy Institute of Australia.

Pienemann, M. (2007). Processability theory. In B. Van Patten & J. Williams (Eds.), *Theories in second language acquisition: An introduction* (pp. 137–154). Lawrence Erlbaum.

Siwatu, K. O. (2007). Preservice teachers' culturally responsive teaching self-efficacy and outcome expectancy beliefs. *Teaching and Teacher Education*, *23*(7), 1086–1101. https://doi.org/10.1016/j.tate.2006.07.011

Sobel, D. M. (2011). *Culturally responsive pedagogy teaching like our students' lives matter.* Emerald Group Publishing.

Socialist Republic of Vietnam. (2005). Education Law. http://www.moj.gov.vn/vbpq/lists/vn%20bn%20php%20lut/view:detail.aspx?itemid=18148

Swain, M. (1993). The Output Hypothesis: Just Speaking and Writing Aren't Enough. *The Canadian Modern Language Review, 50,* 158–164.

Thanh, H. (2010). Teacher quality: The key to teaching Vietnamese to ethnic minority students (Chat luong giao vien-Loi giai cho viec day tieng Viet cho hoc sinh dan toc thieu so). https://daibieunhandan.vn/van-hoa/Chat-luong-giao-vien%2D%2Dloi-giai-cho-viec-day-tieng-Viet-cho-hoc-sinh-dan-toc-thieu-so-i178593/

Tran, T. Y. (2016). Strengthening Vietnamese for ethnic minority primary school aged students: A proposed model (De xuat mo hinh tang cuong tieng Viet cho hoc sinh tieu hoc nguoi dan toc thieu so). *Journal of Education, 2*(394) https://tapchigiaoduc.moet.gov.vn/vi/magazine/so-394-ki-ii-thang-11/

Tran, T. Y. (2020). Researching on ethnic minority students at secondary school level dropping out of school: Current situation and solutions (Nghien cuu hoc sinh nguoi dan toc thieu so cap trung hoc co so bo hoc: Thuc trang va giai phap). *Vietnam National Institute of Educational Sciences, 2*(27). http://vjes.vnies.edu.vn/sites/default/files/bai_so_7_-_so_27_2020.pdf

Wallace, J., & Campbell, E. (2014). *Designing learning for culturally and linguistically diverse classrooms K-12.* Department of Education and Communities. https://www.arts.unsw.edu.au/sites/default/files/documents/Designing_learning_for_a_CALD_classroom_K12.pdf

CHAPTER 7

Pronunciation Teaching Innovation in the English as a Foreign Language Classroom

Loc Tan Nguyen ⓘ

BACKGROUND INFORMATION

Pronunciation plays a fundamental role in assuring mutual understanding between the speaker and the hearer in oral communication (Derwing, 2018; Foote & Trofimovich, 2018). In second/foreign language (L2) learning, learners who are incompetent in language use usually experience misunderstandings and/or breakdowns in both oral and written communication (Pennington & Rogerson-Revell, 2019). In the long run, such learners will be disheartened and lose their confidence and willingness to communicate in the target language. This is worrying because L2 learners need to be able to use the target language effectively for communication, both oral and written, in order to learn lesson contents and, for many

L. T. Nguyen (✉)
University of Economics Ho Chi Minh City (UEH),
Ho Chi Minh City, Vietnam
e-mail: loc.nguyen@ueh.edu.vn

© The Author(s), under exclusive license to Springer Nature
Switzerland AG 2024
L. Phung et al. (eds.), *Innovation in Language Learning and Teaching*, New Language Learning and Teaching Environments,
https://doi.org/10.1007/978-3-031-46080-7_7

others, to continue their education in English-speaking countries. Thomson and Derwing (2015) argue that learners with pronunciation problems are less likely to be properly understood in oral communication, no matter how excellent their lexical and grammatical knowledge is. In support of such an argument, Derwing and Munro (2015) and Pennington and Rogerson-Revell (2019) have presented research evidence showing that mispronunciation is one of the main causes of misunderstandings and/or breakdowns leading to potential discomfort that devalues the speaker's efforts in daily conversations. In this regard, a good command of pronunciation provides grounds for L2 learners' subsequent development of oral communication, specifically listening and speaking skills. As such, helping teachers and learners develop effective teaching and learning strategies to improve learners' pronunciation and oral communication generally is of paramount importance.

Communication as the primary focus of language learning posited in communicative language teaching has led many teachers to try to align their pronunciation teaching with a communicatively oriented methodology (Foote & Trofimovich, 2018). However, research has revealed that many L2 teachers generally receive little, if any, guidance on how to effectively implement communicative pronunciation teaching (CPT) in their language classes (Celce-Murcia et al., 2010; Derwing, 2018; Derwing & Munro, 2015) and have to rely mainly on controlled and semi-controlled techniques (Baker, 2014; Buss, 2017; Kochem, 2021). This line of inquiry has also shown pronunciation teaching to be unsystematic and ad hoc, usually in the form of recasts and/or prompts (Couper, 2017, 2019; Foote et al., 2016; Wahid & Sulong, 2013) despite growing research evidence on the efficacy of explicit pronunciation teaching on L2 learners' intelligibility and/or comprehensibility (Camus, 2020; Peltola et al., 2014; Zhang & Yuan, 2020). The underlying rationale for such instructional practices is that many teachers lack training and confidence to teach pronunciation (Bai & Yuan, 2019; Baker, 2014; Couper, 2017; Nguyen & Burri, 2022). Given this lack of pronunciation pedagogy training, teachers "may develop some teaching strategies that actually have little or no value or that may be counterproductive" (Derwing & Munro, 2005, p. 390). To accommodate this shortcoming, there have been continuous calls for more professional learning activities to promote L2 teachers' knowledge and pedagogical skills necessary to teach pronunciation effectively (Brinton, 2018; Derwing & Munro, 2015; Levis, 2018; Murphy, 2014; Nguyen & Newton, 2021).

Teacher professional learning (TPL) is conceptualized as a job-embedded learning activity for teachers to update knowledge, refine teaching skills, and subsequently transform these into actual teaching, which in turn improves student learning outcomes (Darling-Hammond et al., 2017; Diefes-Dux, 2014; Muijs et al., 2014; Timperley, 2011). In L2 pronunciation teaching, TPL enables teachers to advance their knowledge and pedagogical skills to teach pronunciation confidently and effectively (Derwing, 2018; Derwing & Munro, 2015; Levis, 2018). In a similar vein, Baker (2014) and Buss (2017) have argued that even a single course in pronunciation pedagogy can help teachers feel more confident and become more effective pronunciation instructors. However, there has been little research evidence on how teachers translate what they have learned from TPL activities into classroom practices. The research that is available dispersed across time and space. Burns' (2006) research was perhaps the first study to investigate how TPL enhanced ESL teachers' pronunciation pedagogy. Her research demonstrated that Australia-based teachers were not well-prepared to teach English pronunciation and needed more TPL activities. These findings laid the foundation for the implementation of a TPL package centering on pronunciation pedagogy at the national level. However, the findings relating to the effects of such a TPL program were not disseminated. Similarly, Hermans et al. (2017) investigated the impact of TPL on Dutch EFL teachers' pronunciation pedagogy and found that the TPL program enhanced the teachers' confidence and expertise in teaching English pronunciation.

These studies, though limited in their scopes, have pinpointed the value of TPL that is focused on pronunciation pedagogy to L2 teachers' knowledge gains and pronunciation teaching skills. These research findings have given me the impetus to conduct my doctoral study examining EFL teachers' pronunciation teaching practices and associating pedagogical beliefs and subsequently looking at the impact of TPL on the teachers' development of pronunciation pedagogy expertise at a public university in Vietnam, the context whereby the innovation was carried out.

THE CONTEXT OF INNOVATION

My doctoral research was a case study which was conducted in two phases across two consecutive semesters at a Vietnamese public university, one of the best 300+ universities in Asia, according to QS Asia Rankings 2023. At the time of the study, the university had 15 training faculties, and the

School of Foreign Languages (SFL) administered English teaching and learning. With a workforce of 40 full-time teachers, SFL had classes for English majors and nonmajors. The teachers all held an MA degree in TESOL, Applied Linguistics, or Education and had teaching experience ranging from 5 to 23 years. As statistics showed at the time of data collection, the university had a total of 16,000 full-time students, 80 of whom were studying French, 80 were English majors, and the others were English nonmajors. Most students had been learning English for at least seven years at secondary schools.

The curriculum for English nonmajors aimed to develop learners' listening, speaking, reading, and writing skills. As outlined in the program objectives, English was a mandatory subject designed with the ultimate goal of helping students build up their English competence and confidence in oral communication with both native and nonnative English speakers. The curriculum included 180 45-minute periods divided into four modules taught in four semesters. Each semester lasted for 11 weeks, with one class meeting held on a weekly basis. Four units from each of the two sources of instructional materials, namely *Market Leader* (a Business English textbook series) and *Practice Books* (supplementary materials compiled by SFL staff), were covered in each module. The teachers, in implementing the curriculum, reserved the right to decide on what to teach in class and what to assign as homework and/or self-study. As such, they were able to adapt materials from other resources for classroom instruction, providing that they completed all the prescribed tasks on schedule.

In terms of testing and assessment, students' final scores in each semester were earned from a mid-term test (30%) and a final exam (70%). Teachers might opt for an oral or a written test for the mid-term score, but the final exam was administered on the same day in the form of a written test for all students. The teachers who decided on an oral mid-term test typically asked their students to talk about a given topic for several minutes and then gave a score based on their own intuition of students' speaking ability without any conventional scoring criteria being specified. In the final written exam paper, students were tested on their knowledge of vocabulary, grammar, reading and listening comprehension, and business correspondence writing skills. This follows that pronunciation plays a very minor role in testing and assessment at the university.

In intact classes, the phase 1 study of my doctoral research showed that pronunciation teaching took place but was restricted to recasts and/or prompts in response to students' pronunciation errors and that the teacher participants (six volunteers, given the pseudonyms Quynh, Phuong, Diep, Nguyen, Khoa, Na) were insufficiently trained to teach English pronunciation (Nguyen & Newton, 2020). The phase 1 study further revealed that students held a negative view on the way the teachers addressed pronunciation in class and expressed a strong desire for CPT that can promote their pronunciation and oral communication in general (Nguyen, 2019). These findings provided grounds for the phase 2 study examining how TPL enhanced the teachers' knowledge gains and pronunciation teaching skills. The following section portrays the procedures in which the innovation on pronunciation teaching was implemented within a period of three months.

The Innovation

Given the teacher participants' lack of pronunciation pedagogy expertise and the students' consistent need for pronunciation instruction to include more communicative activities (Nguyen, 2019; Nguyen & Newton, 2020), an intervention was carried out in phase 2 of my doctoral research to innovate pronunciation teaching within the Vietnamese tertiary EFL classroom. The design of this intervention emerged from the phase 1 data and the principles for effective practice of pronunciation teaching in the current international literature. The pronunciation features targeted for the intervention were derived from the interview data with both the teacher and student participants in phase 1, triangulated with those documented in the current literature (Avery & Ehrlich, 2013; Lane & Brown, 2010; Smith & Swan, 2001). Overall, the phase 2 study commenced with a TPL workshop to help the teachers update on pronunciation pedagogy and refine their teaching skills, followed by individual lesson planning and sharing, experimental teaching, and finally tracking of classroom processes. These procedures will now be elaborated.

First, a three-hour TPL workshop focused on CPT was designed and delivered to the teacher participants. In this workshop, Celce-Murcia et al.'s (2010) framework for teaching pronunciation communicatively (Table 7.1) was introduced to the teachers through an illustration of a pronunciation lesson designed with a range of classroom tasks corresponding to the aims and objectives of the framework. During this lesson demonstration, I took the role of an English teacher and the teacher participants were EFL learners. After the lesson, I put the teachers in pairs to discuss two questions pertaining to (1) the number of stages through which the

Table 7.1 Celce-Murcia et al.'s (2010, p. 45) CPT framework

Stages	Descriptions
1. *Description and analysis*	Presents and explains how the target feature is produced and when it occurs within spoken discourse through oral and written illustrations
2. *Listening discrimination*	Provides focused listening practice accompanied by feedback on learners' ability to correctly discriminate the feature
3. *Controlled practice*	Raises learner consciousness via oral reading of minimal pair sentences, short dialogues, etc., with special attention to the highlighted feature
4. *Guided practice*	Enables learners to monitor for the specified feature through structured communication exercises, such as information gap activities and cued dialogues
5. *Communicative practice*	Gives learners an opportunity and requires them to attend to both form and meaning of their speech in less-structured, fluency-building activities such as role-play or problem-solving

lesson unfolded and (2) the aims and objectives of each stage. By engaging in the lesson demonstration and through discussions of the two questions, the teachers were able to independently explore and develop their understandings about the framework.

Second, to ensure the teachers' understanding about how the framework works in practice, I gave them two pronunciation textbooks and put them in pairs to plan a 45-minute pronunciation lesson they would like to teach by applying Celce-Murcia et al.'s communicative framework. After that, each pair of the teachers took turns to elaborate on their own lesson plans (LPs) and then discussed them as a whole group. The discussions centered on the extent to which the activities the teachers decided aligned with the aims and objectives in each stage of the framework. The data showed that the teachers demonstrated their understandings of Celce-Murcia et al.'s communicative framework and were all able to apply it in planning pronunciation lessons (Nguyen & Newton, 2021). Before the workshop ended, we discussed and finalized that each teacher would plan one CPT lesson covering one target pronunciation feature (e.g., long and short vowels or sentence stress), with one teacher voluntarily taking on two.

Third, the teacher participants started designing their communicative pronunciation LPs during the semester interval. To facilitate collaborative learning among the teachers, one of the most important qualities of effective TPL (Darling-Hammond et al., 2009; Diefes-Dux, 2014; Nguyen & Newton, 2021), they were asked to share their LPs within the group.

Specifically, one week before the second semester commenced, a meeting was set for the teachers to clarify their own LPs, followed by group discussions looking at how well the activities in each lesson plan fit into each stage of Celce-Murcia et al.'s communicative framework. In total, seven LPs were created (Table 7.2), including explicit phonetic explanation in stage 1 and two practice activities each for stages 2–5 (see Nguyen & Newton (2021) for details of the LPs).

These seven LPs were subsequently implemented in one of the teachers' scheduled classes in weeks 2, 4, 6, and 8 (two lessons per week, except for the last one) of the semester. For the teachers' autonomy and/or creativity in teaching, I confirmed with them, prior to the implementation of the CPT lessons, that it was their own decision to retain, adapt, or replace any of the activities in the LPs. To track classroom processes, I observed their classes, videotaped their lessons, and invited them to a review meeting after each lesson was completed. Review meetings were scheduled in weeks 3, 5, 7, and 9. The main aim of the review meetings was for the teachers to reflect on and discuss the lesson they had implemented to ensure they were all on the right track. The implementation of the seven lessons ended in week 8 of the semester, with the final review meeting being held in week 9.

Although the teachers reserved the right to adapt and/or replace the activities in the LPs, classroom observations showed that they retained them all and constructed the lessons as sequenced in the LPs. During the final review meeting, the teachers reported that they decided to keep the ready-made activities because of their appropriacy for classroom use. As

Table 7.2 The teachers' proportion of lesson planning

Teacher	Lesson and focus of instruction
Quynh	Lesson 1: *long and short vowels* (/iː/ vs. /ɪ/)
Phuong	Lesson 2: *long and short vowels* (/uː/ vs. /ʊ/)
Diep	Lesson 3: *sentence stress*; Lesson 4: *intonation*
Nguyen	Lesson 5: *troublesome consonants* (/ʃ/ vs. /ʒ/)
Khoa	Lesson 6: *troublesome consonants* (/tʃ/ vs. /dʒ/)
Na	Lesson 7: *final sounds and linking*

122   L. T. NGUYEN

they elaborated, the activities were aligned with the aims and objectives in each practice stage of the framework, feasible in their classes, and beneficial to student learning. For example, Na cited:

> I decided to use these activities because they're available, so no need to design new ones (…) It's a waste of time, not necessary (…) Moreover, the activities the teachers designed were suitable to carry out in each stage of the framework, so I just used them. And my students enjoyed them when they practiced (…).

Drawing on the observational data, I will now report on how the teachers innovated pronunciation teaching in their English classes by discussing selected instances of the teachers' pedagogical choices from the seven lessons. In the first stage of *Description and Analysis*, the teachers gave explicit phonetic instruction on how the target pronunciation feature(s) is produced through articulatory diagrams (for segmental instruction in lessons 1, 2, 5, and 6) and presentations and explanations of rules (for suprasegmental features in lessons 3, 4, and 7), followed by written and oral illustrations. They further explained some common errors Vietnamese EFL learners make regarding the pronunciation feature(s) in focus. To ensure students' comprehension of the articulation of the target feature, they then provided written examples, gave model pronunciation, and got the whole class to repeat. For instance, in lesson 2 focused on /uː/ and /ʊ/, after the teachers explained to students how these two vowels are articulated and what differences should be noted between the two, they provided common spellings for each vowel with illustrations of sample words and asked the whole class to listen and repeat after them. In lesson 3, teaching sentence stress, they presented the rules for sentence stress placement with sample sentences, explained the rules, and got students to repeat the sentences chorally.

Moving on to the second stage of *Listening Discrimination*, the teachers provided drills using minimal pairs to help students distinguish the target features or the feature in focus from other features (lessons 1–2 and 5–7). For instance, they got students to discriminate /tʃ/ from /dʒ/ or /tʃ/ from /ʃ/ in lesson 6 by listening to the recording of nine minimal pairs (e.g., *choice* vs. *Joyce*, *edge* vs. *etch*, and *mush* vs. *much*, etc.) and choosing the word they heard. For suprasegmental features, they had students listen to the recording and identify the stressed words (lesson 3) or draw lines that indicated the intonation contour in each individual utterance of a conversation (lesson 4). Specifically, the teachers had students look at a simple conversation with each line, including one or two words, listen to the recording and draw intonation lines illustrating either the rising or the falling tone at the end of each sentence. They then called for answers, let students listen again, and checked the answers together.

Each lesson then proceeded with two activities in the *Controlled Practice* stage that required students to focus mainly on the form of the target features rather than meaning. Overall, most of these mechanical tasks allowed students to replicate the production of the target features. For example, in lesson 7, teaching final sounds and linking, the teachers gave students 15 phrases in which consonant-vowel and consonant-consonant links are present, as in *correct answer*, *red door*, and *junk food*. They then explained the linking rules again and asked students to practice reading the phrases out loud to a partner. Finally, the teachers called some students to read the phrases to the whole class and gave feedback on their pronunciation.

However, some of the activities the teachers carried out at this stage of the lessons partly involved meaning-focused practice. Lesson 1 gave a clear example in which students were required to be slightly attentive to meaning in order to achieve classroom tasks. Specifically, controlled activity 1 in lesson 1 was for students to differentiate between long /i:/ and short /ɪ/ by listening to a partner reading a phrase or sentence that explained the meaning of a word and deciding which word best matched the definition. Although this activity required students to focus on the articulation of the two vowels, they would simultaneously need to understand the meaning of the words in each pair, for example, *live* and *leave*, *rich* and *reach*, or *ship* and *sheep*, and so on, to help them decide whether their partner's response was correct.

The *Guided Practice* stage of each lesson was conducted with structured communicative practice ranging from information gap activities to cued dialogues. In these tasks, students still stayed focused on the form of the target features but concurrently needed to shift attention to meaning slightly. As observed in lesson 6 focusing on /tʃ/ and /dʒ/, the teachers put students in pairs and gave them a table in two flashcards in which one student had some words their partner needed and vice versa. Students took turns asking such questions as what word is in 1a or what is the word in 1a and wrote the word their partner answered in their table. They kept asking and answering until all the words were filled in their table and finally crosschecked if the tables they had were identical. It was noted from the observational data that students engaged quite actively in these guided activities. Once they were given a task and their teacher finished explaining the task instruction, they quickly turned to each other and started talking.

For the final stage of *Communicative Practice*, the teachers engaged students in two meaningful, fluency-building activities in each lesson. Through these activities, students were given an opportunity to practice the target pronunciation feature(s) through debates, discussions, and free conversations, all of which involved both form and meaning focus. For example, the teachers had students discuss in pairs what two US students would miss about their hometown when they go to college in a different state far away from their home in lesson 1 or how they would spend their money if they become a billionaire in lesson 2. In other activities, students were put in pairs or groups to talk about how well they get along with their neighbors (lesson 3), how they plan a picnic at the weekend (lesson 4), what they did for their last vacation (lesson 5), which job is the best/ worst (lesson 6), or what can reduce or increase stress (lesson 7). Classroom observations showed that it was at this stage of the lessons when students were most enthusiastically involved in classroom learning. They started talking immediately after their teachers finished giving instruction on how to carry out the tasks. Since students were very interested in their discussions, the teachers had to stop them and invited some pairs/groups to speak up in front of the class. They then gave feedback on students' performance and finished the lesson.

Overall, the teachers successfully innovated their pronunciation teaching through a shift away from corrective feedback in response to students' individual pronunciation errors to a communicative methodology that involved a wide selection of classroom tasks ranging from mechanical to creative, meaningful activities. Although corrective feedback has been shown to be facilitative to L2 students' language development (Nassaji, 2017), not many learners are in favor of such an approach to pronunciation teaching (Couper, 2019) and thus express a strong need for more communication-oriented teaching practices (Nguyen, 2019). Most of the activities the teachers decided and implemented in their classes were found to be either strongly adherent or adherent to the aims and objectives stated in each stage of Celce-Murcia et al.'s communicative framework (Nguyen & Newton, 2021), leading to the teachers' and students' strong beliefs in the facilitative role of CPT to student learning (Nguyen & Hung, 2021). Such innovation has also responded to students' instructional need for more CPT that can facilitate their pronunciation and communication skills generally (Nguyen, 2019).

REFLECTIONS

Taken together, the data show that the teacher participants had successfully innovated their pronunciation teaching by applying Celce-Murcia et al.'s (2010) communicative framework in actual instructional practices. The five stages of the framework were sufficiently implemented in each of the seven lessons, with the aims and objectives of each stage being fully achieved through the teachers' conduct of different activities ranging from word to discourse level. From the viewpoint of an instructor, the teacher participants during their individual follow-up interviews reported that the implementation of CPT enabled them to (1) review pronunciation-related theories they learnt in EFL teacher education programs, (2) provide sufficient explicit phonetic instruction to learners, (3) raise students' awareness of their own pronunciation problems, and (4) make their pronunciation teaching more inspiring.

First, the teachers believed that CPT gave them the opportunity to revisit what they had learnt about English pronunciation as L2 learners. They reasoned that they did not teach pronunciation for so long that they almost forgot how to give precise explanations when addressing pronunciation in their English classes. For example, Phuong commented:

Frankly, I haven't taught pronunciation systematically for ages, so I've gradually forgot most of what I learnt at university, you know, things like place and manner of articulation or intonation patterns. But when I applied CPT in this semester, I had a chance to review stuff like how different sounds in English are produced, and how they're named and classified, etc. (…) This really helped because now I can explain these to my students in a clearer and more precise way.

Second, CPT enabled the teachers to provide an adequate amount of explicit phonetic explanations that helped students understand the mechanism of the pronunciation feature in focus. From the teachers' perspectives, sufficient explicit phonetic instruction provided grounds for students' subsequent practice and production, as illustrated in Khoa's response:

With CPT, I can provide students with basic knowledge about pronunciation like place and manner of articulation or how to apply linking in speaking English (…) Such basic knowledge can guide students' practice later either with friends or by themselves. For example, after I taught sentence stress, my students basically understood them and could apply them correctly in their speaking (...) With intonation, before students had no idea about how to use rising and falling intonation in their speaking (...) but after I gave explicit explanations on the use of different patterns, they understood and used them relatively appropriately in speaking practice.

Third, the teachers added that the CPT lessons helped students become more aware of their own pronunciation difficulties. They said that CPT allowed for awareness-raising activities through analysis of pronunciation errors that cause misunderstandings and/or breakdowns in oral communication. As the teachers saw it, such awareness-raising activities developed students' understanding of how important it is to overcome their pronunciation problems. For example, Diep explained:

CPT allows me to analyze students' pronunciation errors, explain these problems and then illustrate how these errors cause misunderstandings in oral communication. I think with this activity, I can raise students' awareness of the importance of pronunciation in listening and speaking. Maybe now they've realized how serious their pronunciation problems are in speaking English and will pay more attention to practicing pronunciation.

Finally, the teachers stated that CPT aroused students' interest in classroom learning, making pronunciation teaching and learning more welcoming and inspiring. The teachers noticed that most students in their classes were enthusiastic and actively involved in classroom activities, especially in communication tasks. Nguyen added:

I realized that students were very interested in learning. So, they engaged actively in classroom activities, especially communicative practice. Most students like listening and speaking activities. That's why they were very eager when I gave them communicative practice activities. I saw that they spoke enthusiastically with their classmates and it made the classroom atmosphere lively and more interesting.

Consistent with the teachers' beliefs, classroom observations revealed that students across the six classes whereby CPT was implemented actively engaged in classroom learning. When it came to speaking practice, especially with dialogs, discussions and debates, they quickly turned to each other to form pairs and/or groups and started talking. A possible explanation for this is that the students were excited in part at the communication tasks that immersed them in meaningful practice of the target feature in discourse. Together with explicit instruction on the target pronunciation feature, students were also given an opportunity to participate in some communicative activities, which they have perhaps not yet had in English learning. As EFL learners who had been learning English for at least seven years, the students who participated in focus group interviews also said that they found CPT interesting and were inspired to learn pronunciation through communicative activities. They said:

> Well, I enjoyed it a lot. CPT is more effective and more interesting than when teachers only ask us to listen and repeat after them. We've been learning English for nearly ten years... you know since we were in Grade 6 and even some started in Grade 3 or 4 but I wasn't taught pronunciation like this before. Usually, teachers corrected our pronunciation when we made it wrong (…). For me, I knew nothing about sentence stress or intonation before, so my speaking sounded flat and unlike other people. CPT method helps me know more about pronunciation like where to stress in a sentence and how to use rising and falling intonation, etc. I felt that the lessons are very interesting and enjoyable. (Student 1, focus group 3)
>
> Oh, I like it very much. I've never been taught pronunciation like this before. Frankly, I'm not very good at pronunciation, so my listening and speaking skills are below average (…) But the way the teacher taught pronunciation in this semester is very interesting. I felt that students in my class were very excited and they took part in activities very actively (…) Teaching pronunciation communicatively like in this semester is more helpful than teachers having us listen and repeat after them just like a parrot. (Student 4, focus group 6)

However, given the time constraints for the intervention, the students were not really satisfied with such a small number of seven 15-minute CPT lessons during a 12-week semester. From a learning perspective, the students thought such a limited time frame was insufficient for pronunciation improvement. They, therefore, expressed a wish for more instruction focused on CPT, as evident in the following responses:

> In this semester, my teacher taught us pronunciation but we also had the opportunity to practice listening and speaking (…) I found her teaching more interesting than teachers correcting our errors through listen-and-repeat activities. But I'm not very happy when such interesting teaching only took place for four days. Why didn't she teach us more? If she teaches pronunciation this way every day throughout the semester, we'll improve our pronunciation, I think. (Student 2, focus group 1)

> Well, I liked everything, but what disappointed me was that the time my teacher spent teaching pronunciation in this semester was too short. Why only four days? (…) It's a good way for us to practice speaking and listening skills too, so it'll be better if he teaches us more (…). I know it's not easy to improve our pronunciation and communication skills within a couple of days or weeks because it takes time. So, I hope we can learn pronunciation like this in the following semester. (Student 4, focus group 2)

These extracts reveal that the students perceived CPT as facilitative to not only their pronunciation but also their listening and speaking skills. Consequently, they expressed a strong need to engage in more CPT lessons. Previous research has also demonstrated EFL/ESL learners' desire for more opportunities to improve their pronunciation (Derwing & Rossiter, 2002; Nguyen, 2019; Pardede, 2018). The finding that students called for more CPT lessons suggests that instruction of this type is necessary to accommodate the students' wants, one of the three important needs analysis domains that needs to be addressed in designing a language curriculum (Macalister & Nation, 2020).

From a teaching perspective, the teachers reported that CPT was good, but it was not feasible for their tight schedule with many language inputs and skills that needed to be covered in class. They mentioned that they had to assign a considerable number of tasks for self-study so that they had time to enact the innovation. Nguyen commented:

> Difficulty? Uhm… I think maybe it's the time issue. As you can see, now the time allotted to English is too limited. Previously, English was taught in six 60-period semesters but now we only have four semesters, 45 periods each. This makes the curriculum overloaded, so it's hard for teachers when they don't have enough time to teach what they want (…) I had to ask students do more self-study so I could have time for these experimental teaching sessions (…). So, if we want to apply this CPT approach, then I think we'll need more credits for the English subject. Otherwise, we can only help correct students' pronunciation errors as we normally do.

As seen from the teachers' responses, time appeared to be a barrier that constrained their implementation of CPT in the classroom. According to the teachers, the credits for the English subject at the university had been abridged halfway from 360 to 180 periods, and they were already overloaded with the heavy mandated curriculum. Accordingly, they found it difficult to teach pronunciation the way they did during the intervention unless more time was allocated to English teaching at their university. To some extent, this finding aligns with Lee et al.'s (2016) research, which found that the limited time frame of the prescribed curriculum made it impossible for the teacher participants at a Hong Kong secondary school to successfully apply the feedback strategies they learnt from a TPL workshop in their EFL writing classes. Other studies have also found time constraints to be a factor that prevents teachers from putting their pedagogical beliefs into practice (Bai & Yuan, 2019; Wang, 2011).

In summary, triangulation of different data sources demonstrated that the teacher participants successfully transformed their pronunciation teaching from on-the-spot error correction to a more systematic approach that incorporates communicative activities. The teachers' and students' stated beliefs about the CPT lessons suggest that this approach to pronunciation teaching holds considerable promise within the context of the innovation. These findings lend support to a general claim that communicative activities promote L2 learners' comprehensibility and/or intelligibility (Gordon et al., 2013; Isaacs, 2009; Nguyen & Hung, 2021; Saito, 2012). According to Rogerson-Revell (2017), L2 learners, despite having been able to properly reproduce targeted pronunciation features in isolation, might still make pronunciation errors in discourse. Thus, such meaningful communication tasks as problem-solving or conversational activities are beneficial to learners' phonological development.

It is important to note that, apart from communication tasks, CPT methodology provides learners with detailed phonetic explanations during the stages of *Description and Analysis* and *Listening Discrimination*, followed by controlled and then semi-controlled activities in *Controlled* and *Guided Practice* stages. This suggests that the combination of all these three components is a key characteristic of this approach to pronunciation teaching. In addition, the role of teacher feedback is another highlighted feature of this teaching approach (Celce-Murcia et al., 2010). Research has shown that teachers' corrective feedback on learners' performance during communicative practice contributes to their pronunciation improvement (Saito & Lyster, 2012). Thus, it is necessary for teachers to scaffold instruction in order to create learning opportunities that enable learners to thoroughly understand the articulation of the target pronunciation features, followed by extensive practice that helps them proceduralize and then automatize declarative knowledge in more creative, fluency-building communication tasks.

Conclusion

In conclusion, the project has been a success in providing the kind of pronunciation pedagogy training the teachers needed to help them develop their expertise and refine their pronunciation teaching skills. Within a systematic pronunciation teaching methodology that started with explicit phonetic instruction and proceeded with controlled and semi-controlled and finally communicative activities, the teachers' pronunciation teaching innovation had met students' instructional needs regarding what and how they wanted to learn. These can all be considered key innovative aspects of the project.

Given such a success of the innovation project that was carried out for pronunciation instruction, it might also be meaningful for teachers to innovate their approach to teaching other skills or aspects of the English language such as grammar and vocabulary. In addition, studies on other instructional methods such as task-based pronunciation teaching would provide further insights into whether such an approach works in the same context. Finally, since the innovation was effective within the Vietnamese EFL context, it would be interesting to see if this innovation is applicable in similar settings in Asia or other L2 contexts.

Acknowledgments This work was funded by University of Economics Ho Chi Minh City (UEH), Vietnam.

References

Avery, P., & Ehrlich, S. (2013). *Teaching American English pronunciation*. Oxford University Press.

Bai, B., & Yuan, R. (2019). EFL teachers' beliefs and practices about pronunciation teaching. *ELT Journal, 73*(2), 134–143. https://doi.org/10.1093/elt/ccy040

Baker, A. A. (2014). Exploring teachers' knowledge of L2 pronunciation techniques: Teacher cognitions, observed classroom practices and student perceptions. *TESOL Quarterly, 48*(1), 136–163. https://doi.org/10.1002/tesq.99

Brinton, D. (2018). Innovations in pronunciation teaching. In O. Kang, R. I. Thomson, & J. Murphy (Eds.), *The Routledge handbook of contemporary English pronunciation* (pp. 449–461). Routledge.

Burns, A. (2006). Integrating research and professional development on pronunciation teaching in a national adult ESL program. *TESL Reporter, 39*(2), 34–41.

Buss, L. (2017). The role of training in shaping pre-service teacher cognition related to L2 pronunciation. *Ilha do Desterro, 70*, 201 226. https://doi.org/10.5007/2175-8026.2017v70n3p201

Camus, P. (2020). The effects of explicit pronunciation instruction on the production of second language Spanish voiceless stops: A classroom study. *Instructed Second Language Acquisition, 3*(1), 81–103. https://doi.org/10.1558/isla.37279

Celce-Murcia, M., Brinton, D. M., & Goodwin, J. M. (2010). *Teaching pronunciation: A course book and reference guide.* Cambridge University Press.

Couper, G. (2017). Teacher cognition of pronunciation teaching: Teachers' concerns and issues. *TESOL Quarterly, 51*(4), 820–843. https://doi.org/10.1002/tesq.354

Couper, G. (2019). Teachers' cognitions of corrective feedback on pronunciation: Their beliefs, perceptions and practices. *System, 84*, 41–52.

Darling-Hammond, L., Hyler, M., & Gardner, M. (2017). *Effective teacher professional development.* Learning Policy Institute. https://doi.org/10.54300/122.311

Darling-Hammond, L., Wei, R. C., Andree, A., Richardson, N., & Orphanos, S. (2009). *Professional learning in the learning profession.* National Staff Development Council.

Derwing, T. M. (2018). The efficacy of pronunciation instruction. In O. Kang, R. I. Thomson, & J. Murphy (Eds.), *The Routledge handbook of contemporary English pronunciation* (pp. 320–334). Routledge.

Derwing, T. M., & Munro, M. J. (2005). Second language accent and pronunciation teaching: A research-based approach. *TESOL Quarterly, 39*(3), 379–397.

Derwing, T. M., & Munro, M. J. (2015). *Pronunciation fundamentals: Evidence-based perspectives for L2 teaching and research* (Vol. 42). John Benjamins Publishing Company.

Derwing, T. M., & Rossiter, M. J. (2002). ESL learners' perceptions of their pronunciation needs and strategies. *System, 30*(2), 155 166

Diefes-Dux, H. A. (2014). In-service teacher professional development in engineering education. In S. Purzer, J. Strobel, & M. L. Cardella (Eds.), *Engineering in pre-college settings: Synthesizing research, policy, and practices* (pp. 233 257). Purdue University Press.

Foote, J. A., & Trofimovich, P. (2018). Second language pronunciation learning: An overview of theoretical perspectives. In O. Kang, R. I. Thomson, & J. Murphy (Eds.), *The Routledge handbook of contemporary English pronunciation* (pp. 75–90). Routledge.

Foote, J. A., Trofimovich, P., Collins, L., & Urzúa, F. S. (2016). Pronunciation teaching practices in communicative second language classes. *The Language Learning Journal, 44*(2), 181–196.

Gordon, J., Darcy, I., & Ewert, D. (2013). *Pronunciation teaching and learning: Effects of explicit phonetic instruction in the L2 classroom.* Proceedings of the 4th Pronunciation in Second Language Learning and Teaching Conference, : Iowa State University.

Hermans, F., Sloep, P., & Kreijns, K. (2017). Teacher professional development in the contexts of teaching English pronunciation. *International Journal of Educational Technology in Higher Education, 14*(1), 23–40.

Isaacs, T. (2009). Integrating form and meaning in L2 pronunciation instruction. *TESL Canada Journal, 27*(1), 1–12.

Kochem, T. (2021). Exploring the connection between teacher training and teacher cognitions related to L2 pronunciation instruction. *TESOL Quarterly.* https://doi.org/10.1002/tesq.3095

Lane, L., & Brown, H. D. (2010). *Tips for teaching pronunciation: A practical approach.* Pearson Longman.

Lee, I., Mak, P., & Burns, A. (2016). EFL teachers' attempts at feedback innovation in the writing classroom. *Language Teaching Research, 20*(2), 248–269.

Levis, J. M. (2018). *Intelligibility, oral communication, and the teaching of pronunciation.* Cambridge University Press.

Macalister, J., & Nation, I. S. P. (2020). *Language curriculum design* (2nd ed.). Routledge.

Muijs, D., Kyriakides, L., van der Werf, G., Creemers, B., Timperley, H., & Earl, L. (2014). State of the art–teacher effectiveness and professional learning. *School Effectiveness and School Improvement, 25*(2), 231–256.

Murphy, J. (2014). Teacher training programs provide adequate preparation in how to teach pronunciation. In L. Grant (Ed.), *Pronunciation myths: Applying second language research to classroom teaching* (pp. 188–224). University of Michigan Press.

Nassaji, H. (2017). The effectiveness of extensive versus intensive recasts for learning L2 grammar. *The Modern Language Journal, 101*(2), 353–368. https://doi.org/10.1111/modl.12387

Nguyen, L. T. (2019). Vietnamese EFL learners' pronunciation needs: A teaching and learning perspective. *The TESOLANZ Journal, 27*(2019), 16–31.

Nguyen, L. T., & Burri, M. (2022). Pronunciation pedagogy in English as a foreign language teacher education programs in Vietnam. *IRAL—International Review of Applied Linguistics in Language Teaching.* https://doi.org/10.1515/iral-2022-0126

Nguyen, L. T., & Hung, B. P. (2021). Communicative pronunciation teaching: Insights from the Vietnamese tertiary EFL classroom. *System, 101*(2021). https://doi.org/10.1016/j.system.2021.102573

Nguyen, L. T., & Newton, J. (2020). Pronunciation teaching in tertiary EFL classes: Vietnamese teachers' beliefs and practices. *The Electronic Journal for English as a Second Language (TESL-EJ), 24*(1), 1–20.

Nguyen, L. T., & Newton, J. (2021). Enhancing EFL teachers' pronunciation pedagogy through professional learning: A Vietnamese case study. *RELC Journal, 52*(1), 77–93. https://doi.org/10.1177/0033688220952476

Pardede, P. (2018). Improving EFL students' English pronunciation by using the explicit teaching approach. *JET (Journal of English Teaching), 4*(3), 143–155.

Peltola, M. S., Lintunen, P., & Tamminen, H. (2014). Advanced English learners benefit from explicit pronunciation teaching: An experiment with vowel duration and quality. *AFinLA-e: Soveltavan kielitieteen tutkimuksia, 2014*(6), 86–98.

Pennington, M. C., & Rogerson-Revell, P. (2019). *English pronunciation teaching and Research: Contemporary perspectives.* Palgrave Macmillan.

Rogerson-Revell, P. (2017). *English phonology and pronunciation teaching.* Continuum International Publishing Group.

Saito, K. (2012). Reexamining effects of form-focused instruction on L2 pronunciation development: The role of explicit phonetic information. *Studies in Second Language Acquisition, 35*(1), 1–29. https://doi.org/10.1017/S0272263112000666

Saito, K., & Lyster, R. (2012). Effects of form-focused instruction and corrective feedback on L2 pronunciation development of /ɹ/ by Japanese learners of English. *Language Learning, 62*(2), 595–633.

Smith, B., & Swan, M. (2001). *Learner English: A teacher's guide to interference and other problems.* Ernst Klett Sprachen.

Thomson, R. I., & Derwing, T. M. (2015). The effectiveness of L2 pronunciation instruction: A narrative review. *Applied Linguistics, 36*(3), 326–344.

Timperley, H. (2011). A background paper to inform the development of a national professional development framework for teachers and school leaders. *Australian Institute for Teaching and School Leadership (AITSL), 2011*(April), 1–26.

Wahid, R., & Sulong, S. (2013). The gap between research and practice in the teaching of English pronunciation: Insights from teachers' beliefs and practices. *World Applied Sciences Journal, 21*(Special Issue of Studies in Language Teaching and Learning), 133–142.

Wang, D. (2011). The dilemma of time: Student-centered teaching in the rural classroom in China. *Teaching and Teacher Education, 27*(1), 157–164.

Zhang, R., & Yuan, Z. (2020). Examining the effects of explicit pronunciation instruction on the development of L2 pronunciation. *Studies in Second Language Acquisition, 42*(4), 905–918. https://doi.org/10.1017/S0272263120000121

CHAPTER 8

Using a Mock Conference as an Innovative Internship Activity for Translation Education

Nguyen Thi Nhu Ngoc

INTRODUCTION

An internship course is usually a useful part of tertiary academic programs. Internships help students to acquire professional skills for a real working environment (Tobias, 1996). This hands-on course is a resource for students to apply theory to effective clinical practice (Levitov & Fall, 2009). Thus, more and more universities make it a compulsory course instead of an extracurricular activity so that they can provide students with real-life experiences and meet employers' demands.

In translation education, internships help students improve language skills, translation speed, confidence, independence, and teamwork; develop professional translation and management skills, apply classroom experience in the real world; gain knowledge of the industry, and attain real working exposure with career prospects (Astley & Hostench, 2017). In

N. T. N. Ngoc (✉)
University of Social Sciences & Humanities, Vietnam National University,
Ho Chi Minh City, Vietnam
e-mail: nhungoc@hcmussh.edu.vn

© The Author(s), under exclusive license to Springer Nature
Switzerland AG 2024
L. Phung et al. (eds.), *Innovation in Language Learning and Teaching*, New Language Learning and Teaching Environments,
https://doi.org/10.1007/978-3-031-46080-7_8

135

Vietnam, many language faculties provide internship courses for their senior translation majors. Students spend about two or three months working as interns in a company or organization to get familiar with the real working environment and get a sense of their future career prospects before graduation. However, a company internship does not always mean students can achieve all expected outcomes because they cannot apply both their written and spoken translation knowledge and skills through company work.

As Bezzaoucha (2021) suggests, "Simulations as a form of replicas make up for the lack of internship opportunities and bring the benefits of situated learning to traditional classrooms by providing access to authentic contexts" (p. 493). The Mock Conference (MC) in a translation program is a useful simulation, which is typically conducted as a cooperative activity inside the classroom where students take turns to be presenters and interpreters. The Faculty of English Linguistics and Literature (EF), the University of Social Sciences and Humanities, a member university of Vietnam National University Ho Chi Minh City (hereinafter called "VNUHCM-USSH") has embedded MCs as part of internship activities for senior translation majors to get hands-on experience since 2019.

The "mock conference" is a familiar concept in professional translation programs, especially at the master's level, in many other countries (Conde & Chouc, 2019; Bezzaoucha, 2021). Nonetheless, at the tertiary level in Vietnam, MCs are currently not as common as simulations in classrooms and video viewing for interpreting practice. The idea of organizing an MC as part of our internship course started in 2019 to ensure that translation students have experience in both written and spoken translations. After four years of implementation, we have identified a range of benefits and challenges, and have made adjustments to enhance its quality. This chapter provides a brief theoretical review and describes the use of MCs in translation education. Next, it describes the design and implementation of the MC as an internship activity for senior translation students and reports the results of an evaluation of the program from the students' perspective.

TRANSLATION EDUCATION AND MOCK CONFERENCE

The Situated Learning Approach to Translation Education

In the view of the situated learning approach, learning is an act of creation or co-construction of a new identity in partnership with others; it is situated in specific authentic contexts and embedded in specific social and physical environments and cultures that help learners find their performance more practical, meaningful, and transferable to similar contexts (McLellan, 1996; Wilson & Myers, 2000). Herrington and Oliver (2000, p. 26) offer a practical framework for designing a situated learning environment, which has nine features. These include: (1) provide authentic contexts reflecting the way the knowledge is used in real life; (2) provide authentic activities; (3) provide access to expert performance and the modeling of processes; (4) provide multiple roles and perspectives; (5) support collaborative construction of knowledge; (6) promote reflection to enable abstraction to be formed; (7) promote articulation to enable tacit knowledge to be made explicit; (8) provide coaching and scaffolding by the teacher at critical times; (9) provide for authentic assessment of learning within the tasks.

The situated learning approach has been employed as a theoretical foundation for tertiary translation education. Many scholars of situated learning, like Setton (2010) and Gillies (2013), affirm that translation trainers find that activities with real-life situations can help students connect their university learning with professional activities in a real working environment. Thus, the internship translation course should have some situated-learning activities. Mock conferences are one way of achieving this, and we will now describe what they involve.

THE MOCK CONFERENCE AS AN EFFECTIVE SITUATED LEARNING ENVIRONMENT FOR INTERPRETER EDUCATION

Kurz (1989) defines a mock conference as an exercise carried out at a later stage of a course involving a made-up conference involving role-play that mimics a real conference as closely as possible. Li (2015, p. 34) suggests an MC includes six components that can be summarized as follows: (1) Briefing: supervisors provide a brief of the event theme, background, speaker profiles, date, agenda, resources, tips for preparation, and so on; (2) Preparation: students perform background and documents research, analysis of parallel and comparable texts, glossary building, sharing of information and discussion, labor division, and so on; (3) Participant training: supervisors provide students with the last chance to make clarifications before the MC, checklists of rubrics generated through students and supervisor discussion to empower participants to evaluate their own weaknesses and strengths, and so on; (4) MC Day: students take turns to interpret; (5) Debriefing: students make self-assessment, and receive peer assessment, client and audience feedback, and supervisor or expert feedback and suggestions; and (6) Improvement: supervisors and students use assessment results to inform teaching and learning.

By its nature, the interpreting performance is done in live situations where the interpreter shares the same environment with the speaker and listeners and has access to the immediate and shared context, which keeps unfolding and changing as the communicative event proceeds; and the interpreter is expected to solve any translation problems as timely as possible by accessing to the immediate context to compensate for the temporal constraints (Setton, 2006). Therefore, using MCs can be quite effective for translation education. Also, to implement an MC as an internship activity, a group of relevant stakeholders has to go through a long procedure lasting at least two months for preparation and organization and make sure that the MC helps create an ideal situated learning environment with the nine features requirements aforementioned by Herrington and Oliver (2000).

The Use of the Mock Conference for Interpreting Practice

Research on the use of MCs for interpreting practice in a situated-learning environment has revealed that they can serve as a beneficial tool for students to practice interpreting skills. The employment of MCs for conference interpreter training shows some commendable benefits. First, MCs are used to develop relevant communication skills and promote interpreting skills such as professionalism, public speaking, and note-taking (Fomina, 2018; Conde & Chouc, 2019; Duyen & Huyen, 2019; Bezzaoucha, 2021; Duong & Nguyen, 2021). Second, MCs serve as a stimulating and beneficial experience to improve professional and psychological competence, a way to facilitate the internalization of learning motivation (Fomina, 2018; Gao, 2019; Duyen & Huyen, 2019). Third, MCs provide valuable authentic practice with a situated approach to interpreting teaching (Conde & Chouc, 2019; Gao, 2019; Duyen & Huyen, 2019; Bezzaoucha, 2021; Pérez, 2021). Fourth, MCs provide positive assessment of the learning outcomes and beneficial peer feedback thanks to the student-centered approach (Bezzaoucha, 2021; Pérez, 2021; Defrancq et al., 2022). Fifth, MCs improve students' strategic competence, good interpreting device management, and many other nonlinguistic dimensions more than in traditional interpreting classes under the teacher-centered teaching model (Fomina, 2018; Conde & Chouc, 2019).

Because of these benefits, MCs are often organized as an academic activity where students play the roles of speakers, interpreters, and participants. Students are free to choose different topics for their presentations related to the MC theme as requested by the teacher and spend at least two to four weeks preparing for their presentations and interpreting performance. In various education contexts, MCs are designed and implemented for simultaneous interpreting training (Conde & Chouc, 2019, Gao, 2019, Pérez, 2021, Defrancq et al., 2022) or consecutive interpreting training (Fomina, 2018; Duyen & Huyen, 2019; Bezzaoucha, 2021; Duong & Nguyen, 2021) in classrooms. Obviously, the use of MCs has been of great interest worldwide and focused more on simultaneous interpreting and graduate-level students. However, for large-sized undergraduate-level classes, it is difficult to do so. Thus, a mock conference focusing on consecutive interpreting is a better choice for all students to experience conference interpreting.

In the MC design and implementation of these studies, the students took turns to be speakers and interpreters in MCs; thus, the degree of authenticity was not as high as those of professional ones; the numbers of student participants varied from 3 to 35 students; the aims were to explore the MC benefits and challenges without focusing on factors/tactics that are effective for students' performance, and students' feedback and suggestions for the MC organization. Thus, this chapter aims to describe an innovative process of MC design and implementation in which the MC speakers were lecturers and administrators from different faculties and departments in the VNUHCM-USSH, which helped create a better professional and authentic environment and gave an opportunity for students to concentrate on the tasks and duties of professional interpreters. The data collected to evaluate this project came from a sample size of over 100 students; and the students' feedback involved all the components of the MC organization and performance.

The Mock Conference as an Innovative Internship Activity for Senior Translation Majors

The Impetus for the Use of The Mock Conference as an Innovative Internship

The EF's internship course started in 2013 to provide translation seniors with opportunities to become familiar with the working environment and meet the requirements of potential employers based on the students', lecturers', employers', and especially program-level assessors' feedback after the EF went under an external quality assessment for AUNQA accreditation (AUNQA refers to ASEAN University Network-Quality Assurance). We had a meeting with the EF's translation lecturers for some adjustments in the internship course syllabus and received the approval for revision from the EF's and the VNUHCM-USSH's academic councils.

From 2013 to 2017, the course consisted of three main activities: (1) working as an intern in a company within two or three months, (2) attending a field trip for further onsite translation practice and academic exchange with another university, and (3) writing an internship report to reflect on all the internship activities and lessons. In the academic year 2019–2020, the MC was first implemented as a compulsory internship activity after the syllabus revision to meet the students' needs for more professional expertise. Since then, the MC has been considered one distinctive internship activity of the EF and an exemplary activity for the other foreign language faculties at VNUHCM-USSH and other universities in South Vietnam. After four years of design and implementation (2019–2022), we have made some revisions. Then, in the academic year 2022–2023, the MC was upgraded into a university-level conference.

The Design and Implementation of the Mock Conference

The MCs were developed from the Annual Model of the United Nations conferences which simulate the United Nations General Assembly or Security Council conferences (Pérez, 2021; Defrancq et al., 2022). As for the design, we based it on the situated learning framework by McLellan (1996) and Wilson and Myers (2000) as well as the adjustments following previous MCs during four pilot years. In October 2022, a detailed MC plan was submitted for the university's approval. In terms of stakeholders, the EF translation lecturers, students, and academic staff, as well as relevant university support staff, all got involved in the MC organization procedure. In detail, the lecturers worked as internship supervisors and translation performance assessors, students as interpreters, and academic and support staff as MC organizers. This university-level mock conference took place in February 2023 and was funded by the USSH.

As for the implementation, in December 2022, the 110 students of Cohort 2019–2023 were divided into 14 groups of 7–10 students. One group, instructed by one teacher supervisor, worked with a specific translation topic and had a specific working scheme. Employing the six-procedure formulation by Li (2015), the students spent two months preparing their background and specific knowledge and skills before the MC Day under their supervisors' support. The schedule is explained below in detail:

Briefing (Week 1): A student-supervisor meeting was organized to provide all the information related to the presentations, speakers' profiles, speakers' journal papers, planned agenda, tips for preparation, conference interpreting skills, and assessment criteria.

Preparation (Weeks 2–3): The group leader worked with the supervisor on a working scheme and appropriate labor division in research of the background knowledge and relevant specialized documents related to the speaker's journal paper. The students worked together to analyze and understand their translation topic and the speaker's full paper, read some other comparable texts, share their research information, discuss building a bilingual word list, do a draft translation, and have peer evaluations before sending all their preparation products to their supervisor via email.

Participant training (Weeks 4–7): The students worked with their supervisor online and offline for further comments on their word list and draft translation and conducted at least two rehearsals under the supervisor's assessment. One week before the MC Day, they received and analyzed the speaker's PowerPoint slides in the way professionals receive from customers. The MC agenda was confirmed so that the students could check in on time and dress in the EF uniform.

MC Day (Week 8): The MC was organized with the procedure of a real conference. Two EF teachers hosted the MC as the masters of ceremony, coordinated the plenary section in the University Hall (with a capacity of 400 seats), introduced the conference agenda, organizers, and speakers, and invited the USSH and EF representatives to deliver the opening and welcome speeches. After that, one group would be assigned to be interpreters for the keynote speaker. Then students in the audience gave some feedback based on the given assessment criteria; and the supervisor gave detailed comments and assessments for each student interpreter, and the other supervisors might give some. After the plenary section, all the MC participants moved to the smaller parallel section rooms. There were two groups in one room, and the students took turns being interpreters. Besides, junior students were encouraged to attend.

Debriefing (30 minutes): After the speakers' finished their presentations and left, the students would listen to their peer and supervisor feedback and self-assess their performance.

Post-MC: A link to a Google form was sent to students to complete and evaluate the MC.

There are two innovative features in designing and implementing the MC as an internship activity:

Innovative Feature 1. It met all the nine requirements suggested by Herrington and Oliver (2000) to create a situated-learning environment with maximal authenticity. In detail, we worked with the relevant stakeholders to ensure:

(1) An authentic context: Creating a student-centered environment in which the students were the core of all the tasks of a conference interpreter;

(2) Authentic activities: Providing the students with authentic tasks and practice contexts to perform the consecutive interpreting as real conference interpreters, visualizing their future working scenarios;

(3), (4), (5) Access to expert performances and the modeling of processes, multiple roles and perspectives, collaborative construction of knowledge: Providing students chances to be in a translation practice community where they worked with each other from the first preparation stage to the final evaluation stage, spent time building the wordlists, searching for reference sources, doing translation drafts, giving feedback to each other and doing online and offline rehearsals in the role of interpreters and audiences to get familiar with the professional conference environment, and sharing of professional ethics and standards, and strategies to deal with arising interpreting problems;

(6) Reflection to enable abstraction to be formed: Encouraging the students to share feelings about their own and others' performances besides the supervisors' evaluation during the rehearsals and the MC Day so as to recognize strengths, weaknesses, and gaps between their levels and the professionals' for future improvement;

(7) Articulation to enable tacit knowledge to be made explicit: Developing interactive and collaborative relationships among the group members, teachers, and guest speakers during all the MC stages;

(8) Coaching and scaffolding by the teacher at critical times: Providing supportive assistance from the supervisors and the EF during the MC process in the form of task guides and resources to meet students' learning needs and help them achieve learning outcomes;

(9) Authentic assessment of learning within the tasks: Designing authentic assessment with specific criteria developed from translation quality assessment rubrics in a combination of the academic and professional environments, allowing students to be fully aware and effectively perform with acquired knowledge.

Innovative Feature 2. We developed our MCs based on the simulation of the United Nations conferences. However, the difference is that we invited real speakers from different faculties and offices of the USSH (including lecturers/experts from the Faculties of Sociology, Tourism, Urban Studies, Cultural Studies, Vietnamese Studies, Journalism; the University Library; the Administrative Affairs Office, etc.). The reasons for this choice are as follows:

(1) Time-saving: It would help the student interpreters save time and focus more on their preparation and training in the MC second and third procedures.

(2) Authentic professional experience: The students had to spend more time researching documents related to the translation topics in the way professional interpreters do.

(3) Authentic interpreting performance: Because the speakers were real, experienced ones with a lot of journal publications and real-life conference reports, the students would have a better experience of being professional interpreters and learn more strategies to deal with any translation problems arising, which also supported the ultimated learning approach.

(4) Exploration of the internal intellectual sources: Thanks to its members' number and quality of research publications, VNUHCM is currently one of Vietnam's top public universities with the high rankings in the QS and the World University Rankings (VNUHCM, 2023). Thus, the use of the publications by the academic and administrative staff at the USSH, a VNUHCM member, is quite encouraging. These papers examined different aspects of the fields of social sciences and humanities, and thus their English draft translations and interpreting performances at the MC did help students discover authentic data, real challenges, and possible

interpreting solutions. This indicates our creative utilization of the USSH's multidisciplinary education and helps establish good interdisciplinary relationships with the academic and administrative staff who are always ready to support us in implementing the MCs.

EVALUATION OF THE MC AS AN INNOVATIVE INTERNSHIP ACTIVITY

Collection of Students' Feedback

The MC model has been held for senior translation majors at the EF since 2019, and after an MC completion, we, including the teacher supervisors and MC organizers, had a meeting to discuss the MC strengths and shortcomings for improvement the next time. Thus, in the current MC, we only collected the feedback of students.

With a large number of participants, 110 students, we decided to employ a student questionnaire with five sections. As for the quantitative data, sections 1–4 consisted of some items using the Likert scale for their agreement or disagreement. As for the qualitative data, each section has one open item for students' further compliments, complaints, and/or suggestions for changes or improvements. All the questions were to explore how the students thought about *the quality of the MC organization, the quality of supervisors' support, and the benefits and challenges of the MC*. Section 5 had two open questions for the *student evaluation of factors and/or tactics effective for their interpreting performance at the MC*. The five sections are responding to all the steps in the six-procedure formulation of an MC suggested by Li (2015).

The MC Day took place in mid-February 2023, and the students were requested to submit their internship reports two weeks later. Then, an online questionnaire in Google form was sent to them in early March 2023, ensuring that the student interpreters really had careful thoughts after writing their internship reports and that their responses would be more accurate and reliable. In addition, to get reliable and valid data, the participants could complete the questionnaire within 14 days, a long time enough to recall experiences, make good decisions on answers, and provide in-depth recommendations or suggestions for the open questions. The data was then processed with SPSS version 2022.

Evaluation of the MC Design and Implementation

Students' Feedback on the Mock Conference Organization

The students highly appreciated the MC organization. Their positive feedback indicated that most of them completely supported the MC organization, which showed that the first procedure (*briefing*) and the fourth procedure (*MC Day*) were well-operated. In fact, to achieve such results, we provided all the supervisors and students with a detailed internship plan so that they all knew the timelines and completed their given tasks. This likely led to the students' feeling of being in a professional interpreting conference environment.

However, some students felt unsatisfied with the organization time and the arrangement of the MC operation. In fact, many students had internship/part-time jobs and prepared for the MC interpreting performance simultaneously; they had many deadlines and were under pressure. Some could manage the workload but others found it really tough. However, choosing a time that satisfied all the students was not easy. In addition, the schedule depended on external factors, such as the schedules of the speakers and the university's academic plan. Thus, it was a challenge and opportunity for the students to learn how to manage their time and a chance to deal with work pressure, which could be quite useful for their future careers.

We also had some unexpected problems in the facilities, such as seating and technical issues related to the sound quality of the microphones. In Pérez (2021), the students were aware that not everything would go as planned during the MC process, and unforeseen events could happen, such as sound and image problems. In our case, due to the high attendance of second and third-year students in the audience, some could not find seats in the parallel-section rooms. Besides, there was only one microphone in one of the seven parallel section rooms due to the sound system structure, so the interpreters had to speak up loudly. This was really inconvenient and out of our control, though we knew the sound quality affected the audience' ability to hear the speakers and interpreters.

Some students suggested organizing the MC outside the university and having more evaluators, which is worth considering. The MC can be held at a convention center, boosting the spirit of the would-be interpreters and creating a real-life environment. Besides, professional interpreters can be invited as MC assessors. However, it depends on the internship budget and the university's financial policy. The students' MC location preference is in line with Bezzaoucha (2021), in which students expected MCs to be held in venues different from their familiar environments.

Furthermore, some were concerned about the speakers' quality. It was indeed difficult for them because conference speakers had different styles of presentation, and they had to find appropriate tactics in specific contexts. In addition, many student groups expressed the desire to be on the stage and interpret the keynote speech. Ardito (1999) suggests that MCs are organized as authentically as possible to reflect the professional reality with the participation of international speakers to classrooms. However, this may work well with a small number of student interpreters. In our context, lengthening the MC agenda for some days is impossible, and a normal conference just has one or two keynote speeches. The student group to perform the keynote speech interpreting was chosen at random and announced right in the first student-supervisor meeting, which remains our best choice for the large sample size of our participants.

In short, the MC organization procedure worked well thanks to all the stakeholders' cooperation. Especially, the MC was innovatively conducted as a university-level conference funded by the university, though there existed some unavoidable problems. In addition, such problems turn out to be opportunities for students to learn how to prepare for their future careers.

Students' Feedback on the Teacher Supervisors' Support

The students valued their teacher supervisors, thinking that the supervisors had good professional support. This reflects our continuous efforts to find out our shortcomings and solutions for improvement in the next academic year and make a more detailed and carefully revised plan. Most of the students were satisfied with their supervisors' guidance. Specifically, they appreciated and respected the supervisors' dedication, constructive approach, and positive working attitude. This affirms the necessity and effectiveness of teacher supervisors.

Besides the good qualifications, useful advice, encouragement, tips, and experiences of their supervisors, some students expected to receive more detailed feedback for their translation work related to the wordlist, translation draft, and interpreting performance during the MC process; and felt unsatisfied with the supervisors' inappropriate time and place management for discussion and rehearsals due to their tight schedules. Some even expected more friendly behaviors and humor from their supervisors so that they could reduce stress and pressure in interpreting performance. These constructive suggestions should be seriously considered for supervisors' improvement and effectiveness. It is similar to the students' expectations in Bezzaoucha (2021) that supervisors would guide the students and enhance their confidence.

It can be concluded that the students are highly satisfied with the supervisors' quality, supportive behaviors, and useful experiences. However, some expected to receive more detailed feedback, more flexible schedules, and more friendly behaviors and humor from their supervisors.

STUDENTS' FEEDBACK ON THE BENEFITS OF THE MOCK CONFERENCE

The students affirmed that they learned professional interpreting and communication skills and broadened their views about interpreting tasks. In addition, they could familiarize themselves with the conference interpreting environment and felt interested in their future jobs. Their feedback is quite similar to those reported in Conde and Chouc (2019, pp. 9–11), where the students recognized the benefits of adequate preparation and agreed that participation in MCs as a situated learning activity, designed as a largely student-led exercise, could help consolidate their determination to become professional interpreters.

MCs are important activities in translation education because they provide notable career orientation and strong motivation for professional experiences for years (Lin, 2013). Our students' feedback confirmed these and other benefits. The students enjoyed a *natural exposure to different topics* because the speakers came from areas of social sciences and humanities, and the students were exposed to a lot of new vocabulary and subject knowledge, which was quite useful for widening their linguistic and background knowledge and preparing for their future jobs. Students also appreciated the opportunities to simulate real-life interpreting scenarios, including interpreting in real-time, dealing with technical equipment, and navigating the conference setting. Many particularly enjoyed the MC as an internship activity because all the MC tasks provided them *authentic practice* in the form of hands-on experience to gain the skills essential for real-life interpreting situations. In addition, the MC allowed students to receive *constructive assessment* in the form of feedback and evaluation from their peers and supervisors, which were seen as really essential for them to refine their professional skills. Finally, the MC offered students *a supportive network* with other student interpreters and professionals. Students all had a chance to build connections and learn about career opportunities.

STUDENTS' FEEDBACK ON THE CHALLENGES OF THE MOCK CONFERENCE

Although the students put great effort into their interpreting performance, many felt worried due to the challenging MC atmosphere and problems with difficult vocabulary and specific text contents in translation. Obviously, the MC atmosphere was more real life than that of a traditional interpreting class, and some students might have felt nervous or stressed. However, this turned out to be a positive backwash effect because it exposed students to different degrees of anxiety, which could be helpful for them to learn to psychologically manage their anxiety, overcome translation barriers, and prepare them for the market better than practice in traditional classrooms (Lin et al., 2004). This implication is also affirmed by Alexeeva and Shutova (2010), who suggest that pressure is one of the aspects relevant to real-life practice, given that it is an experience as near to a real-life environment as feasible, and hence favorable to the so-called stress of working in front of a real audience (p. 14), which is quite essential for students to learn to manage. Besides, some students expected to feel the most challenging moments of interpreting the keynote speech under the witness of the biggest audience, but it was impossible for 110 student interpreters in this MC. However, in Pérez (2021), students got similar fear when a speaker did not provide any documents beforehand. In short, their challenges came from their levels of experience with the professional working environment and their translation competency.

Other challenges reported by the students include the *limited scope* of the translation topics in the MC, which did not cover natural sciences and other fields and other possible topics or scenarios students may encounter in their future work. Although simulating real-life situations, the MC might have *limited authenticity* in that many students might not experience the same level of pressure and stress as in a real conference. In addition, the one-day MC format and scale might affect the amount of individual exploration, feedback, and evaluation for all the 110 student interpreters, while some of the supervisors might have *limited feedback and limited time* for fully detailed individual assessment, which may not have allowed the students to fully explore all the nuances of the translation topics or receive as much feedback as expected. Finally, the MC in this academic environment offered the students *limited language variety* to interpret, while in a real conference there may be multiple languages involved. The students were requested to interpret from Vietnamese to English, and each performed for about seven to ten minutes. We could not extend the MC Day and invite English-speaking presenters for more practice due to time and budget constraints, so there might be some limitations on the students' exposure to and practice with interpreting in multiple languages.

Students' Feedback on the Influential Factors and Effective Tactics

The students thought that eight factors might be influential for their performance at the MC, including: *aptitude, listening, memory, psychology, note-taking, speaker's quality, teamwork,* and *translation topic.* Noticeably, *memory* was mentioned as the top factor. Besides, many students provided the most important aspects or tactics that they believed in and/or applied to help better their performance. In detail, they felt more confident with *good preparation* through building and learning the word list, reading the translation documents and reference documents, and doing rehearsals. Students found it essential to *understand the translation topics carefully* so that they could prepare and use relevant terminologies. They noted that their good *mental control* helped them to deal with challenges in their performance because they felt calm, comfortable, confident and able to maintain composure to boost credibility and deal with any rising problems/troubles. Their *teamwork skills* helped them to engage in working with the other members of the interpreter group, listening to their translation and supporting those in need, being ethical and professional. Their appropriate use of *translation skills* such as note-taking skills and memory tactics really helped them to remember the ideas and details, and employ translation techniques to transfer the ideas and messages appropriately with accuracy and fluency, and deliver the speaker's ideas and nuances at a suitable pace.

150 N. T. N. NGOC

Their suggested tactics quite match the eight influential factors that they mentioned in their responses to our survey. This means during the MC's six-procedure formulation, the students were fully aware of what to do, such as having good preparation, using teamwork skills, knowing how to control their mental states, having a good understanding of the translation topics, applying interpreting skills to deliver ideas with accuracy and fluency in the conference, and interpreting performance.

PEDAGOGICAL IMPLICATIONS

MCs can be used as "a bridge between classroom realism and professional realism" to give students the way to enter the industry, and students perceive MCs as "good, beneficial, and stimulating learning experiences", though MCs are challenging tasks (Li, 2015, pp. 328, 338). Based on our evaluation of the MC as an internship activity, some pedagogical implications for the use of MCs are as follows:

To maximize the benefits of a situated learning activity, teachers can use MCs for undergraduate translation-majored seniors to have hands-on consecutive interpreting practice as compensation for the lack of translation opportunities in their company internship. As part of the internship course, it can be officially and advantageously funded for the organization. To be a good internship supervisor in an MC, teachers are supposed to play many roles, such as a good listener, a good assessor, and even a good partner with friendly and humorous manners.

To deal with the major MC challenges, some solutions may be applied. First, to expand the MC scope, it is encouraging to invite guest speakers from different fields to provide more diverse content. A course or module of conference interpreting may be supplemented for students' additional practice opportunities. To increase authenticity, teachers should encourage students to spend more time and effort to practice their skills to meet professional assessment criteria, and familiarize themselves with more background materials, glossaries, translation topics, and terminologies. In addition, to increase feedback and practice time for a large number of student interpreters while the time is limited, supervisors should be patient and give them more guidance and support through rehearsal, provide constructive feedback on interpreting skills, encourage peer feedback, and even record students' interpretation practice for students' self-review. Finally, because MCs may not reflect the full diversity of language varieties and accents like real ones, supervisors should encourage students to practice interpreting more in various contexts outside the classroom to enrich their language and dialect exposure.

Thus, to help students improve their MC interpreting tactics is a long-term learning process. Some applicable suggestions for classroom practice include using role-play scenarios to simulate real conferences because role-plays can be done easily in class for interpreting speeches, giving questions and answers, and working on their memory tactics, note-taking skills, teamwork skills, and aptitude, which will really help students to be more confident and perform better in the big mock conference like the one in this study. Furthermore, teachers can use technology like online platforms to simulate conference settings and allow students to practice remote interpreting, a popular form of interpreting especially after Covid-19, which helps save classroom time. Another suggestion is that teachers can focus on developing students' time management skills with more exercises to improve their speed and accuracy. Another idea is giving students various forms of cooperative learning in their translation courses to foster their sense of community and mutual support. Finally, teachers may encourage and even require students to attend university conferences to obtain valuable real-life experience.

The MC evaluation in this chapter serves as confirmation of its usefulness as an internship activity that deserves teachers' and students' time and effort. The insights gained from the project will help to improve the quality of the EF's internship course in not only our program but also similar translation education programs at the tertiary level worldwide.

References

Alexeeva, I., & Shutova, E. (2010). Elements of the intensive post-graduate translator/interpreter training programme at SPbS. In I. Shpiniov & A. Antonova (Eds.), *Training the next generation of professionals: The St Petersburg School of conference interpreting and translation* (pp. 11–18). St Petersburg Herzen University Press. https://scit.herzen.spb.ru/wp-content/uploads/2016/04/training_generation_x.pdf

Ardito, G. (1999). The systematic use of impromptu speech in training interpreting students. *Interpreters' Newsletter, 9*, 177–189.

Astley, H., & Hostench, O. T. (2017). The European graduate placement scheme: An integrated approach to preparing master's in translation graduates for employment. *The Interpreter and Translator Trainer, 11*(2), 204–222. https://doi.org/10.1080/1750399X.2017.1344813

Bezzaoucha, I. (2021). Mock conference as a situated learning activity in Algeria: Consecutive interpreter training as a case study, its design and effect as perceived by trainee interpreters. *Cahiers de Traduction, 24*(1), 490–503. https://www.asjp.cerist.dz/en/downArticle/224/24/1/154826

Conde, J. M., & Chouc, F. (2019). Multilingual Mock Conferences: A Valuable Tool in the Training of Conference Interpreters. In *The Interpreters' Newsletter 2019 (24), Trieste, EUT Edizioni Università di Trieste*, 1–17. https://doi.org/10.13137/2421-714X/29521

Defrancq, B., Delputte, S., & Baudewijn, T. (2022). Interprofessional training for student conference interpreters and students of political science through joint mock conferences: An assessment. *The Interpreter and Translator Trainer, 16*(1), 39–57. https://doi.org/10.1080/1750399x.2021.1919975

Duong, D. A., & Nguyen, T. L. P. (2021). Using mock conference to teach consecutive interpreting—A case study at Vinh University. *International Journal of Education and Social Science Research (IJESSR), 4*(6), 361–384. https://doi.org/10.37500/IJESSR.2021.4627

Duyen, T. L., & Huyen, L. T. (2019). The effects of using mock conferences to teach interpretation skills to the 4th year cadets of the English Department at Military Science Academy. *Science Journal of Military Foreign Language, 19*(5), 14–36. https://eng.vn/tai-lieu/the-effects-of-using-mock-conferences-to-teach-interpretation-skills-to-the-4th-year-cadets-of-the-english-department-at-5463/

Fomina, M. (2018). The mock conference as a teaching tool to promote communication and interpreting skills. In *ICERI2018 Proceedings*, IATED, 4312–4318. https://doi.org/10.21125/iceri.2018.1959

Gao, M. J. (2019). Mock conferences' impact on internalizing translating and interpreting learners' motivation. *Journal of Contemporary Educational Research, 3*(3), 55–71. https://doi.org/10.26689/jcer.v3i3.616

Gillies, A. (2013). *Conference interpreting. A student's practice book*. Routledge.

Herrington, J., & Oliver, R. (2000). An instructional design framework for authentic learning environments. *Educational Technology Research and Development, 48*, 23–48. https://doi.org/10.1007/BF02319856

Kurz, I. (1989). The use of video-tapes in consecutive and simultaneous interpretation training. In L. Gran & J. Dodds (Eds.), *The theoretical and practical aspects of teaching conference interpretation* (pp. 213–215). Campanotto.

Levitov, J. E., & Fall, K. A. (2009). *Translating theory into practice: A student guide to practicum and internship*. Waveland.

Li, X. (2015). Mock conference as a situated learning activity in interpreter training: A case study of its design and effect as perceived by trainee interpreters. *The Interpreter and Translator Trainer, 9*(3), 323–341. https://doi.org/10.1080/1750399X.2015.1100399

Lin, W. (2013). Why Do Students Learn Interpreting at the Graduate Level? A Survey on the Interpreting Learning Motives of Chinese Graduate Students in BFSU. *T&I Review, 3*, 145–168.

Lin, J., Davis, C., & Liao, P. (2004). The effectiveness of using international mock conference in interpreting courses. *Studies of Translation and Interpretation, 9*, 81–107.

McLellan, H. (1996). Situated learning: Multiple perspectives. In H. McLellan (Ed.), *Situated learning perspectives* (pp. 5–17). Educational Technology Publications.

Pérez, P. S. P. (2021). Mock conferences in simultaneous interpreting training. *Transletters—International Journal of Translation and Interpreting, 5*, 163–182. https://journals.uco.es/tl/article/view/12937

Setton, R. (2006). Context in simultaneous interpretation. *Journal of Pragmatics, 38*(3), 374–389. https://doi.org/10.1016/j.pragma.2005.07.003

Setton, R. (2010). From practice to theory and back in interpreting. *The Interpreters' Newsletter, 15*, 1–18. https://core.ac.uk/download/pdf/41173596.pdf

Tobias, A. J. (1996). Internships, coop experience provide an edge. *Electronic Engineering Times, 921*, c4–c6.

VNUHCM.(2023).https://vnuhcm.edu.vn/su-kien-sap-dien-ra/bao-cao-thuong-nien-2022/343835326864.html

Wilson, B. G., & Myers, K. M. (2000). Situated cognition in theoretical and practical context. In D. Jonassen & S. Land (Eds.), *Theoretical foundations of learning environments* (pp. 57–88). Erlbaum.

PART III

Technology Integration

CHAPTER 9

Enhancing Student Participation in Online Collaborative Learning Groups, Using a Design Framework and Accessible Technologies

Vu Thi Thanh Nha

INTRODUCTION

Collaborative learning has been documented to provide multiple educational benefits for students in both face-to-face and online learning environments (Harsch et al., 2021; Ingram & Hathorn, 2004; Lapitan et al., 2023; Le et al., 2018; Ng, 2012; Nokes-Malach et al., 2015; Roberts, 2004; Zhang et al., 2021). It is an active learning strategy to enhance achievement, personal development, and psychological health (Khalil & Ebner, 2017; Ng, 2012; Razzouk & Johnson, 2012; Slavin, 2010; Stephens & Roberts, 2017). Covid-19 breakout forced many ELT teachers in Vietnam to adopt full online classes with inadequate preparation for

V. T. T. Nha (✉)
VNU University of Languages and International Studies,
Vietnam National University-Hanoi, Hanoi, Vietnam
e-mail: nhavtt@vnu.edu.vn

© The Author(s), under exclusive license to Springer Nature Switzerland AG 2024
L. Phung et al. (eds.), *Innovation in Language Learning and Teaching*, New Language Learning and Teaching Environments, https://doi.org/10.1007/978-3-031-46080-7_9

157

the switch (Le et al., 2022). One common complaint about online classes is the challenge to implement group work and increase student participation (Harsch et al., 2021; Tao & Gao, 2022). Previous studies have identified some solutions, including group size (Luo et al., 2023), role assignment (Luo et al., 2023), flipped classrooms (Lapitan et al., 2023), and instructional planning strategy to facilitate collaboration in online groups (Stephens & Roberts, 2017). However, as Ng (2012) points out, online learners' perception is crucial for effective learning. She explains:

> we cannot assume that students will automatically tune in to this new approach to learning. They need to perceive online collaborative learning as useful and motivating. (Ng, 2012, p. 2497)

This chapter, therefore, reports findings from an action research project that adopted a design framework to facilitate collaboration in online groups to enhance student participation in a postgraduate course at a Vietnam public university. It aims to address the following questions:

1. How can the facilitator support online group work effectively?
2. What are learners' attitudes toward online group work?

To address the questions, this chapter, therefore, first reviews the online collaborative learning principles and strategies to increase student participation in online environments. It then analyzes an action research study conducted to apply these principles in the context of Vietnam, followed by detailed discussions of the findings and implications for future research and instruction.

LITERATURE REVIEW

Online Collaborative Learning Pedagogy

Collaborative learning refers to learning that occurs when a group of learners work together toward a common goal (Ingram & Hathorn, 2004; Ng, 2012; Roberts, 2004). Collaborative learning is sometimes contrasted with cooperative learning in terms of philosophy and organizational techniques. While collaborative learning focuses on constructing knowledge together, cooperative learning puts more emphasis on the completed work assembled from the share of individual group members. The former requires learners to closely work in a team toward the final goal, whereas the latter does not require the company of group members to complete the task. Ingram and Hathorn (2004, p. 216) highlight the differences between the two strategies regarding the merging point and the complexity of the interactions. While cooperation is labeled as 'divide-and-conquer' in which students can complete their share in isolation and then 'stitched together' to finish the assignment, collaboration requires students to continuously work together for joint products.

It is, however, noted that the two concepts (cooperative and collaborative learning) are also interchangeably used in some situations (Arends & Kilcher, 2010; Slavin, 2010). This study adopted collaborative learning principles to organize group work and focused on learning processes in an online environment with three important elements of collaboration, namely participation, interactions, and synthesis (Ingram & Hathorn, 2004). Group members must participate in group work through interactions to achieve a synthesized product from individual inputs.

Collaborative learning is intellectually supported by three educational perspectives: (1) social interdependence, (2) constructivism, and (3) behavioral learning theories (Razzouk & Johnson, 2012). First, social interdependence theory views that positive interdependence (cooperation) results from promotive interaction as individuals encourage and facilitate each other's efforts to learn. If group members work separately, the group lacks functional interdependence and interactions. Second, constructivism largely drawing from the work of Vygotsky and Cole (1978) reveals the social nature of knowledge-building processes. Learners are engaged in joint activities to learn, understand, and solve problems. Third, behavioral learning theory provides theoretical background for the academic and social impacts of interactions and group rewards on learning (Slavin, 1987).

When learning is structured in online environments, collaborative learning still has its original educational values (Davis et al., 2022; Hernández-Sellés et al., 2019; Lehtinen et al., 1999; Miller & Young, 2023; Ng, 2012; Roberts, 2004). In addition, it offers flexibility in joining the conversations from differing locations and points of time due to technology-based tools (Bennett, 2004; Lehtinen et al., 1999). Lehtinen et al. (1999) have reviewed numerous advantages of online collaborative learning in several aspects:

1. Communication: Enabling students with diverse backgrounds and from differing locations to communicate so that multiple perspectives and solutions to problems could be obtained.
2. Student-centered learning: Facilitating student-centered learning in authentic and collaborative learning settings.
3. Active learning: Fostering active and independent learning.
4. Academic gain: Enabling learners to discuss their subject matter in greater depth and thus considerably enhance their critical thinking skills.
5. Motivation: Increasing learner involvement and incentives to learn, leading to a wider and more complete understanding of the subject knowledge.

Challenges of Online Collaborative Learning

In addition to reported benefits, there are some observed challenges of group work in the literature. Roberts (2004) summarizes some challenges such as the existence of free rider members who do not work but get credit for group work, the negative attitudes toward slow students, and the divide among group members. Le et al. (2018) find four obstacles Vietnamese students perceived of collaborative learning, including lack of collaborative skills, free-riding effects, competence status leading to the dominating roles of more competent students in group discussions, and friendship that distracts students from meaningful and focused collaboration. Later works report more disadvantages, specifically for online group work, namely time management, lack of personal interaction, reduced accountability, and technical challenges:

1. Time management difficulties: It can be challenging to coordinate schedules and ensure that all team members are available for online group work. (Bakir et al., 2020; Graham & Misanchuk, 2004; Koh & Hill, 2009).
2. Insufficient personal interaction: Online group work lacks personal interactions and nonverbal cues that are present in face-to-face meetings, leading to difficulty in building trust, establishing rapport, and resolving conflicts, especially in heterogeneous groups (Bakir et al., 2020; Graham & Misanchuk, 2004; Harsch et al., 2021).
3. Reduced accountability: Online group work might be challenging to monitor progress, hold team members accountable for their

actions, and ensure that everyone is committed to contributing (Bakir et al., 2020; Bennett, 2004; Graham & Misanchuk, 2004; Koh & Hill, 2009).

4. Technical difficulties: Technical issues, namely slow Internet connectivity or software or hardware problems, can disrupt online group work and reduce its effectiveness and equal participation among members (Bennett, 2004; Koh & Hill, 2009).

It is important to be aware of these drawbacks to mitigate them to enhance online group work and achieve the best outcomes.

Strategies for Effective Online Group Work

There have been numerous strategies applied to ensure effective collaborative learning, in both online and face-to-face environments. Educators looked at group structures (Stephens & Roberts, 2017), member roles (Luo et al., 2023), and reward mechanisms (Arends & Kilcher, 2010). In this study, I adopted a design framework for facilitating collaboration in online groups (FCOG) proposed by Stephens and Roberts (2017) with four steps:

1. Creating groups: Small group sizes allow interactions and flexibility in arranging group meetings. Giving students options to choose groups also facilitates group scheduling and consensus in the group. Themes that reflect the interest areas are created to name groups.

2. Establishing expectations: All group members are aware of group expectations and activities and resources (e.g. reading or quiz) they have to go through in the course.

3. Communication tools: Communications tools, which can include rather-than-LMS (Learning Management System) options for group members, are critical for online groups. Learners may have guided sessions to use the tools.

4. Assignments and activities: Online assignments and activities should integrate the use of technology tools. Assignment questions allow open and multiple answers with authentic products.

Tools for Online Group Work

There are a range of tools for online group work, which can be classified based on the nature of communication, asynchronous or synchronous. Asynchronous communication takes place outside of real time. For example, a learner sends an e-mail message to other group members, who later read and respond to the message. There is a time lag, though short, between the time the learner sends the message and other members reply. Asynchronous communication takes place whenever learners have the time to complete them. Viewing videos linked to the course site, reading a textbook, and writing a paper are all asynchronous activities. Some tools for asynchronous group communication include emails, blogs, Padlet, LMS, Google Docs, and websites. These tools allow group members to communicate over one topic at a time and place of their own choice. However, several limitations of asynchronous communication have been reported: delayed feedback, missed turns, inadequate time, and feelings of social disconnection (Khalil & Ebner, 2017).

In contrast, synchronous, or real-time, communication takes place like a conversation. For example, in a chat session of a writing class, learners get online in the same chat room and type questions, comments, and responses in real time. Synchronous activities may include chat sessions, whiteboard drawings, and other group interactive work. Some tools for synchronous communication are Zoom, Facebook Messenger, Teams Meeting, and Google Meet, which allow real-time communication and collaboration in a "same time-different place" mode (Khalil & Ebner, 2017, p.531). Synchronous tools are best to facilitate brainstorming and quick sharing activities among group members (Ingram & Hathorn, 2004). Their disadvantages, however, have been reported to include hardware requirements (microphone or video camera), Internet connection, discussion moderation, and equal member participation (Khalil & Ebner, 2017).

In selecting tools for this online class, I considered three aspects: nature of communication, access, and text type support, as summarized in Table 9.1.

Detailed use of these applications will be provided in the following section.

9 ENHANCING STUDENT PARTICIPATION IN ONLINE COLLABORATIVE... 163

Table 9.1 Descriptions of communication tools for online group work

Tools	Description	Features		
		Nature of communication	Access	Text type support
Google Docs	An application that allows students to write or insert texts online.	Both synchronous and asynchronous	Fairly easy with user accounts and Internet access	Texts, images
Padlet	An online bulletin board that allows students to share and collaborate on ideas, notes, and documents.	Both synchronous and asynchronous	Fairly easy with Internet access	Texts, images, videos, audio, files
Zoom	A videoconferencing platform that allows for virtual meetings, webinars, and screen sharing, making it a useful tool for group discussions and presentations.	Synchronous and asynchronous for selected functions	Fairly easy with Internet access and video and audio equipment	Texts, images, videos, audio, files
Google Classroom	An LMS that allows facilitators to give assignments, create a forum discussion, provide materials, and send messages	Both synchronous and asynchronous	Medium easy with account login and Internet access	Texts, images, videos, audio, files
Zalo	A communication app that allows users to send instant messages, make video or audio calls.	Both synchronous and asynchronous	Medium easy with account login using a mobile phone number and Internet access	Texts, images, videos, audio, files
Email	An application that allows users to exchange messages	Asynchronous	Fairly easy with an account log in and Internet access	Texts, images, videos, audio, files

IMPLEMENTING ONLINE COLLABORATIVE LEARNING

The Research Context

The study was developed in the context of a three-credit training course on material and curriculum development offered in 2022. This is an English-medium course toward a 27-credit postgraduate diploma in teaching English as a foreign language with 11 subjects for six months. The course was 100% online via Zoom Meeting for synchronous sessions with the support of Google Classroom for classroom management. Padlet was used for during-class interactions and note-taking.

This six-week course lasted 45 hours. It aimed to provide students with knowledge and skills in curriculum development so that they can write or evaluate a curriculum. It also develops some academic skills to read academic texts and work in groups, and develop some personal attributes such as honesty, collaboration, and proactive attitudes. Assessments for the course include online quizzes, group work, and a final assignment.

The facilitator was also the researcher of the study with 25 postgraduate students aged 23 to 33, 1 Chinese and 24 Vietnamese. However, the Chinese student rarely interacted with others due to Internet restrictions. Their English proficiency was at least B2 (CEFR levels). They had varied work experience, the majority being English teachers (75%) and 12.5% being school or center managers or administrative staff. These teachers worked in various teaching contexts. Fourteen participants mainly worked at primary schools (years 1–5), 11 worked at lower secondary schools (years 6–9), high schools (years 10–12), and universities, and 9 worked at kindergartens.

Data Collection

Data were collected along with teaching activities (Burns, 2010) to explore students' opinions and performance. The researcher used questionnaires, students' work and reflections as well as course materials and observation notes by the facilitator for data collection in four action research stages: plan, action, observe, and reflect (Burns, 2010).

There were two questionnaires: a needs analysis questionnaire delivered at the first session with 23 respondents, coded NQ1-NQ23, and an evaluation questionnaire at the final session with 24 respondents, coded EQR1-EQR24. The first questionnaire was delivered to collect the participants' needs and expectations for the course. It included personal information about their jobs, workplaces, and teaching experience. Meanwhile, the second one evaluated their experience with the course. It consisted of standard course evaluation items of objectives, design, delivery, learning, administration, and open-ended questions to elicit their opinions about group work.

Another type of data was students' guided reflections collected after the course, which aimed to help the students be more mindful of group work experiences and future applications (Bulman, 2008). The students wrote to respond to six prompt questions about their role, how they arranged group work, the problem they encountered and solutions, their gain from group work, the most enjoyable aspects, and suggestions for future group work. Twenty students submitted their reflections which were coded from R1 to R20.

Other data, including the facilitator's during-the-course feedback and students' works, was also examined to reflect on the project implementation.

Data Analysis

Data analysis in this exploratory research was an iterative process (Creswell & Clark, 2011), which involved both data analysis and collection. Data was analyzed to inform subsequent data collection activities, providing inputs for new data analysis. Close-ended questions were described in tables and charts. Open-ended questions and students' reflection notes were analyzed, using a constant comparative analysis method (Creswell, 2007), to identify key themes. The participants were anonymized and numbered consecutively.

Procedures

Group work was organized corresponding to four-phase action research: plan, action, observe, and reflect. Activities were adjusted based on information collected from each phase. Students worked in two types of groups. fixed groups to complete an assignment making up 30% of the total course scores and random group discussions during synchronous facilitator-led sessions.

Planning

The planning stage was conducted before and during the first session. Its purpose is to identify the what, who, and how issues in action research (Burns, 2010). The "what" issues refer to the focus of the research, which was meant to examine online group work and students' experience when they switched to a new mode of learning. People involved in this study were the course facilitator (also the researcher), and 25 postgraduate students enrolled in this course. To better understand the students, a needs analysis questionnaire was delivered at the first session to collect background information about the learners, including demographic, gender, work, experience in curriculum development, and expectations for the course (see the context of the study). Only 23 out of the total 25 students responded to the questionnaire as one Chinese student could not access the Google form, and another missed the first session.

This stage adopted a four-step planning form for facilitating collaboration in online groups (Stephens & Roberts, 2017).

Creating Groups

The lecturer provided eight discussion topics under the course outline and selected eight team leaders who could choose a topic of interest before they recruited another two members for their team. One problem was that the students seemed to favor certain topics, which were more aligned with their interests or scheduled later in the course so that they could have more preparation time. The group leaders then had to negotiate and select one topic per group and decided on the contact information in the table for group communication (Table 9.2).

Establishing Expectations

To help the students be aware of course expectations, the facilitator briefed them about the assessment policy and responded to any questions from the students at the first session. Accordingly, students had to work in groups to complete a lecture guide, a group presentation, a quiz, and a writing reflection. Assessment criteria included content, collaboration, visual aids, delivery, time limit (for oral presentation), and references (Table 9.3). These criteria evaluated both collaboration (reflected in the process and final product) and individual efforts (oral presentation).

9 ENHANCING STUDENT PARTICIPATION IN ONLINE COLLABORATIVE... 167

Table 9.2 Examples of group setup by theme

Date of presentation	Topics	Group leader and contact	Group members
2022-04-22	Group 1: Approaches to curriculum design	Email and phone number	
2022-04-22	Group 2: Needs and environment analysis	Email and phone number	
2022-04-29	Group 3: Principles and method	Email and phone number	
2022-04-29	Group 4: Goals, content (language), and sequence; format and presentation	Email and phone number	
2022-05-06	Group 5: Monitoring and assessment	Email and phone number	
2022-05-06	Group 6: Curriculum evaluation	Email and phone number	
2022-05-20	Group 7: Evaluating materials	Email and phone number	
2022-05-20	Group 8: Adapting textbooks	Email and phone number	

Table 9.3 Assessment criteria for group assignment

Assessment criteria	Description
Content	Related to the topic and include examples and explanations that reflect the student's understanding of the topics
Visual aids (oral presentation)	Well designed and supportive to understand the presentation
Delivery (oral presentation)	Personal presentation of the content (voice and clarity)
Time limit (oral presentation)	The presentation is within 40 minutes
References	Updated and relevant to the content
Collaboration	Allows group members to work independently and collaboratively to complete the task. A reflection note that reflects their authentic experience in group work is included.

Communication Tools

The online course applied multiple technology tools for both asynchronous and synchronous communication. First, Google Classroom was officially mandated as an LMS to manage group learning where the enrolled students could receive course materials and announcements and submit their homework assignments. All students could access Google Classroom except one Chinese student residing in China who did not have Gmail access during the course. Second, Zoom and Padlet were used for synchronous communications to communicate with the whole class. The students, however, could opt for their preferred modes of communication when they work in small groups, for example Quizizz, Kahoot, Google Form or Google Docs, Canva, and Zalo (an app similar to WhatsApp for messaging) (Table 9.1).

Assignments and Activities

The course combined various activity formats. Each session is usually comprised of six main activities, in which presentation and quiz are the activities facilitated by one student group for 40 minutes out of the total 120 minutes (see Fig. 9.1).

A warm-up activity started with brainstorming questions about the session topic. Students could provide their responses on Padlet about their related experiences and concern. This could make use of wait time and lead the students in the session topic. After that, the facilitator summarized previous content in the review activity to anchor their understanding of the topic before introducing a group presentation with a follow-up quiz for 40 minutes. Group work activity during the Zoom sessions required students to work in random groups, using the Zoom Meeting breakout function, to complete a task related to the presentation to further analyze the content and applications in authentic contexts. For example, after a presentation about material evaluation, the students were asked to work in groups to plan an evaluation. This synchronous group work provided a model and facilitator support for the students. It could also avoid a free-rider phenomenon when only members of the presentation group worked.

Fig. 9.1 A typical lesson structure for a Zoom session

The last activity wrap-up was a whole class activity by the facilitator to comment or conclude on issues discussed in break-out sessions.

Action and Observation
During the action phase, from Session 3 to Session 11, the facilitator provided support to groups via email. Some common questions were about access to materials, difficulty in understanding the materials, or group work assessment. The facilitator, and also researcher, observed student activities during the Zoom sessions and took note of emerging issues to address directly during or after the session. For example, when Group 2 encountered some design issues in their presentation, the facilitator gave guidelines about how to make effective PowerPoint slides.

Reflection
This phase reflects the effectiveness of the activities and processes implemented in earlier phases and suggests modification for the following cycle (Burns, 2010). Reflection was based on data from the evaluation survey at the final session with 2 responses and 20 students' guided reflections, which will be analyzed in the finding section.

FINDINGS

This section discusses findings from two main data types to explore learners' attitudes toward group work: an evaluation survey at the final session with 24 responses and 20 students' guided reflections. Generally, the students expressed positive attitudes toward group work, which seemed to be useful in understanding the course content and developing social and personal attributes as described in the course objectives.

Findings from Evaluation Survey

An anonymous survey aimed to evaluate the entire course and both asynchronous and synchronous group work. It included some close-ended standard items examining the course objectives, delivery, and student satisfaction, as summarized in Table 9.4. Item 10 was added to elicit information about group work. Meanwhile, open-ended answers were coded to identify categories and patterns. Overall, the students had positive attitudes toward the course and group work activities. As can be seen in the

170 V. T. T. NHA

Table 9.4 A summary of students' responses to the evaluation questionnaire

	Strongly agree (4)	Agree (3)	Disagree (2)	Strongly disagree (1)	NA	Mean
1. This course met my expectations.	9	14	1	0	0	3.3
2. The course was challenging.	12	11	1	0	0	3.5
3. The course provided effective online opportunities for active participation.	12	12	0	0	0	3.5
4. My contributions to the course were responded to.	8	16	0	0	0	3.3
5. The online course design was excellent.	8	15	1	0	0	3.3
6. The learning activities were clearly explained and covered the ideas and concepts in the subject area.	10	13	1	0	0	3.4
7. The information/course materials provided were useful.	11	13	0	0	0	3.5
8. The administration and enrollment procedures of the course were efficient.	6	17	0	0	1	3.1
9. Overall, I was satisfied with the quality of this course.	13	11	0	0	0	3.5
10. Group work is effective.	10	13	1	0	0	3.4

table, 100% of the students were satisfied with the course to some extent. Some aspects that were evaluated higher were course materials (mean = 3.5), online opportunities for active participation (mean = 3.5), challenging courses (mean = 3.5), learning activities (mean = 3.4), and group work (mean = 3.4). Feedback to students' contribution and course design seemed to be less favored while administration and enrollment procedures gained the lowest score (mean = 3.1).

One respondent was not happy with the course and gave negative scoring on several aspects of the course (design, learning opportunities, and interest in the course). However, he/she still benefited from the course and liked the group discussions, as described below:

I am sorry but I am not really interested in the course although I find it useful. It is not easy at all but if I am motivated, I think I can do better. But I respect and appreciate the different activities that you integrate into the course. They are challenging and difficult and force me to read and study more. (EQR13)

Some questions in the evaluation survey specifically examined students' attitudes toward group work. Out of 2 respondents (95.8%) 23 participated in both synchronous and asynchronous group work activities. Three aspects they gained the most from these collaborative activities were course content understanding (23 selections), discussion skills (23 selections), and collaboration (22 selections); time management skills and teaching knowledge were less often observed benefits, making up 58.3% and 66.7%, respectively. Unfortunately, English skills were the least reported gain in this English-medium course with only five selections (see Fig. 9.2).

When the respondents were asked to report their favorite aspects of group work, they listed six areas as summarized in Table 9.5. It seems that communication was the most popular aspect with 9 mentions, followed by motivation (6), understanding (5), and critical thinking (4). Collaborative skills (2) and peer support (2) were two areas with the fewest observed cases.

The respondents also revealed they disliked some aspects of group work. Although 5 participants out of total 24 respondents deliberately stated that they could not find any unfavorable aspects of group work, other respondents reported six areas they disliked about working collaboratively. The top-cited feature was time management (6 mentions),

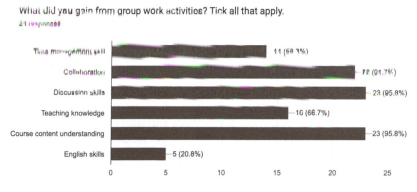

Fig. 9.2 Reported benefits of group work

172   V. T. T. NHA

Table 9.5 Favorite aspects of group work

Aspects	Mention frequency	Examples from questionnaire respondents' comments
Communication	9	We can share our opinions without the limitation of shame, gender, culture, and also gaps of knowledge (EQR19)
Motivation	6	My classmates are fantastic; they have a wealth of expertise from which I may benefit by conversing with them. This course's group work activities clearly demonstrated the value of peer learning (EQR17)
Understanding	5	I like to collaborate with other people, which makes me understand more about the content of the course. In addition, I think I benefit from listening to others' perspectives (EQR15)
Critical thinking	4	We can discuss and see different aspects/ views on 1 issue (EQR2)
Collaborative skills	2	I can work with many people with different tasks (EQR22)
Peer support	2	I can exchange ideas and explore areas I am a bit weak at. (EQR8)

followed by difficult tasks (4 mentions), and participation (3 mentions). Work allocation, Internet connectivity, and arguments were some unfavorable features of group work with one mention each (see Table 9.6).

Findings from the Guided Personal Reflections

After the joint presentations, the students were asked to reflect on their experience, using guided questions about what they did, how they felt, what problems they faced, and what benefits they gained from the task. In all, 20 out of 25 students submitted their reflections, which were qualitatively coded and presented under recurring themes: collaboration mechanism, attitudes, and lesson withdrawal.

Most students described collaborative principles in their group work experience. They could work independently and then meet for feedback or update. The final product (slides and oral presentations) resulted from enhanced individual works. One student described how they collaborated to complete the task:

> After receiving the topic, we agreed on a time to plan for the presentation and did several online meetings before the official presentation before class.

9 ENHANCING STUDENT PARTICIPATION IN ONLINE COLLABORATIVE... 173

Table 9.6 Unfavorable aspects of group work

Dislike aspects	Mention frequency	Examples from questionnaire respondents' comments
Time management	6	I think our time management skills still need to improve, so the given time is too short for us (EQR19)
Difficult task	4	It's not that I detest it; it's just that we don't always have enough time to brainstorm and debate things thoroughly, especially because the activities are often extremely challenging for me (EQR17)
		I think I need more detailed guidance (sample, template, ideas) for each task on [Google] Classroom because some of them are difficult for me to understand and get the right point. And maybe some feedback from teachers after I submit the assignment so that I can know whether I meet the requirements or not (EQR14)
Participation	3	At first, there are some moments when we are shy and not active in sharing. And also some people tend to talk less even though they have great ideas (EQR24)
Internet connectivity	1	Sometimes Internet disconnection (EQR23)
Arguments	1	Sometimes group work activities were not effective as we had some arguments. And the time was also limited, so we could not finish the tasks (EQR15)
Work allocation	1	The division of work is not really clear (EQR6)

I dealt with "content and sequencing", which was the first part of the chapter. I scrutinized my chapter to understand it at a deep level, before moving on to the other 2 parts of my teammates. (R2)

They recognized the importance of individual members in the joint project:

We acknowledged that the strength of the team was the strength of each individual, so each of us had an equal role in the group work. (R12)

One respondent really appreciated the online mode where collaboration was effectively supported:

What I enjoyed most in our group work was that I could contact each other regularly and effectively on Zalo and we could submit all the result tasks together on Google Drive. I had never experienced this comfortable working environment before. (R20)

Regarding attitudes, data revealed that the students generally had positive attitudes, mainly related to two-way communication among members. Some students commented:

> I enjoyed writing the lecture note and having my work commented on by my teammates the most. They gave me lots of questions, which prompted me to reflect on the concepts and read more. (R3)

> [What I like most about the group work was] the discussion time. We discussed a lot and worked out many things to make our presentation better. (R9)

The discussions helped them to solve problems and be engaged in the materials at greater depth as described by two other students:

> We not only learn how to cooperate and collaborate but how to solve problems together. For example, when I found supplementary reading materials, I was confused by different sources on the internet. TC supported me to find suitable materials for that. (R18)

> When we saw each other's work and then gave feedback. Each of us learned from those comments (and other parts of the presentation) and tried to make them better. (R5)

Another plus of group work that the students reported was social support from their peers:

> Having my friends talking to me and commenting on my notes makes the work much more bearable and I think the feeling is shared among our group members. (R3)

This helped them develop personally and academically:

> Through the discussion process, I have been amazed by others' critical thinking and innovative ideas. Instead of accepting everything even though it was not really a good one as I was afraid of offending people, my group

mates have taught me to question, not to spot others' errors but to come up with an improved version with the whole group. (R6)

However, some negative experiences were also reported regarding time management, group conflict, and online interactions:

[One problem was] scheduling a group meeting. Since we were all working on the weekdays and attending classes on the weekends, it was not easy to arrange a group meeting. And even when we did find an available time slot, something came up, and we had to move the meeting to another day. (R12)

It was unavoidable that members would have opposing viewpoints during the presentation process. We had some disagreements about the sub-titles or some points in the content. (R11)

Online teamwork was also a hindrance because we don't have face-to-face meetings, so we're still a bit apprehensive and lack motivation. (R15)

Luckily, they managed to overcome these problems and withdrew practical lessons about collaboration, time management, and presentation:

First, I think that I learned how to cooperate and collaborate with my team members, even at first, we were all strangers. Second, I learn how to improve my critical thinking by giving and sending feedback from my team members. Last but not least, we learn how to solve some problems which happened such as time management or different opinions. (R13)

We still missed the deadline for individual work that we set before. As a result, we just had a little bit of time to improve the final version and rehearse our scripts before presentation day. We also run out of time in our presentation, then we had to go through quickly the last part of it. We did learn from this case that we need to use our time wisely and commit to the deadline and the time frame. (R10)

Some expressed that they would not hesitate to be engaged in future group work activities when they gained these practical lessons:

If I have a group work assignment again, I would like to take more time discussing with my teammates and encouraging them to share their difficulties so that I can support them on time and have no rush for deadlines. (R4)

If I have a group work assignment again, I really love to meet face-to-face because I believe that offline discussions can evoke more ideas. (R12)

In short, findings from both the evaluation survey and guided reflections consistently revealed mostly positive group work experiences. The participants benefited from personal development (communication and collaborative skills), academic gains (critical thinking, understanding), and social support (peer support, motivation). They, however, reported some challenges in time management, technical glitches, participation, group harmony, work allocation, and task difficulty.

DISCUSSION

Tools to Support Online Collaborative Learning

The study revealed that students enrolled in the course could operate multiple collaborative tools for different communication purposes. They could use Zoom meetings for real-time communication, Zalo and Padlet for near-synchronous communication, and Google educational tools (Classroom, Google Docs, Google Sheets) for asynchronous information exchange. The participants did not report any challenges in using technical tools to complete the online collaborative tasks, involving strategic planning, task execution, reflection, and adaptation of a group. This enabled social-emotional interactions, leading to better learning outcomes (Huang & Lajoie, 2023). Occasionally, the students experienced unstable Internet connectivity and Google access as in the case of a Chinese student, but it did not hinder intragroup communication and their joy of two-way communication via technology tools. This was an advantage for organizing online collaboration for this group of Vietnamese learners. The finding confirms the relationships between online tools, emotional support, and effective collaborative work as highlighted in Hernández-Sellés et al. (2019).

Student Participation in Online Group Work

In this project, the students demonstrated active participation in the course collaborative activities with three types of interactions: teacher–student interaction, content–student interaction, and student–student interaction. The joint presentation provided ample opportunities for peer communication. They discussed how to complete the task, work allocation, and feedback to other members' work, and even life stories. The reflective notes show abundant evidence of this collaborative process and students' enhanced learning, which have been described as "socially shared regulation of learning (SSRL)" (Huang & Lajoie, 2023, p. 1). This type of interaction is critical for effective collaboration with proven beneficial effects on both cognitive knowledge gain and emotional interactions (Huang & Lajoie, 2023).

However, it seemed that when the students worked on collaborative tasks that required open answers as recommended by Stephens and Roberts (2017) to facilitate joint efforts, they felt less confident in their peer authority in course content. They found the tasks challenging and failed to find the answers only with peer support. They preferred to receive sample answers or feedback from the facilitator about their discussion results.

Students Perceived Benefits of Online Collaborative Learning

The students generally held positive attitudes toward group work. Their course satisfaction was rated relatively high and expressed their enjoyment in collaborating with their classmates. It was evident in the study that group work led to personal development, academic achievement, and mental health support. The findings again support findings from previous studies (Bennett, 2004; Davis et al., 2022; Graham & Misanchuk, 2004; Huang & Lajoie, 2023; Koh & Hill, 2009). It was noted that the students' experiences illustrated the relationships among these factors. When they were emotionally supported by group members, they were open to sharing and accepting alternative perspectives and individual differences. In that way, they developed collaborative skills and critical thinking, which helped them to achieve better understanding and task completion.

Students' Perceived Challenges of Online Collaborative Learning

In this project, students reported several hindrances of online collaborative tasks. The most concern was time management to complete the task. There could be several explanations for this response. First, most of them had full-time jobs and spent only the weekends on the course. Second, on the timetable, the students had two three-hour sessions per day, which left little preparation time for group work. Another challenge observed was task difficulty. The participants were overwhelmed with the information about the course. This was partly explained by the needs analysis at the first session. Most of the participants were in their first five years of teaching and had never been involved in designing or developing a syllabus.

Interestingly, participation was reported as a challenge in the evaluation survey, but not present in the reflection note about fixed group arrangement. It could be explained that participation was probably a perceived problem of a random group setup which did not allow them to select members they knew or obtained the emotional support they needed (Koh & Hill, 2009). An alternative explanation was that random groups involved more members, which limited interaction time as reported in Harsch et al. (2021). To take advantage of collaborative learning, the students are expected to adjust their roles and enhance their self-directed learning skills.

Conclusion and Implications

This action research project has examined a group work innovation in an online English-medium class with 25 postgraduate students at a public university. It aimed to enhance student participation in online collaborative learning activities, using a four-step design framework for facilitating collaboration in online groups (Stephens & Roberts, 2017). The students were asked to complete two types of group work, asynchronous and synchronous. The asynchronous activity involved students in fixed groups to make a joint presentation while the synchronous group work arranged them in random discussion groups. Data were collected from students' work, reflection notes, and an evaluation survey during the course. Findings revealed that the planning framework was helpful to create positive learning experiences via these collaborative activities. Some benefits reported were personal development (communication and collaborative skills), academic gains (critical thinking and understanding), and social support (peer support and motivation). They, however, reported some challenges in time management, technical glitches, participation, group harmony, work allocation, and task difficulty.

As the study was conducted in a natural setting of an online postgraduate course in a public university in Vietnam, it had some research limitations. First, it had to follow the official guidance for online learning of the institution such as time allocation and assessment. The students had to take two 3-hour sessions per day, which might have affected the time available for group work and the effectiveness of the learning activities. Second, as the course was entirely implemented online in the emergency of the Covid-19 outbreak, little technical support was available to monitor all group work interactions and analyzed other aspects of group work. Third, this group of adult learners had good English proficiency and did not experience technical or linguistic barriers in group communication. Caution, however, should be noted to other learner populations.

The study offers some implications for online educators to effectively facilitate collaborative learning. First, the course facilitators should create ample interaction opportunities, which are critical to achieving collaborative learning benefits. This can be done through the application of multiple online communication technologies that encourage both asynchronous and synchronous communication and the adoption of a four-step framework for facilitating collaboration in online groups (Stephens & Roberts, 2017). Second, students should be scaffolded for completing open-ended tasks which are beneficial for group discussions but might increase the task difficulty when the facilitator cannot provide timely and extensive support. For example, some sample products or detailed instruction worksheets (Cortázar et al., 2022) can be provided for performance tasks or the facilitator gives feedback on discussion questions. Third, for effective group work, time is a critical factor. Learners should be given adequate time for outside-classroom group work as well as in-class discussions. Unfortunately, the evidence in this study was insufficient to recommend measurable amounts for specific collaborative task types. In future studies, it might be practical to examine the effects of different group dynamics including time and English usage on students' learning and the effects of group work in a blended mode. This could be a new tendency in future classrooms where more language teachers will be working with accessible online technologies (Güzer & Caner, 2014).

References

Arends, R., & Kilcher, A. (2010). Cooperative learning. In D. Arends & A. Kilcher (Eds.), *Teaching for student learning: Becoming an accomplished teacher* (pp. 305–323). Routledge.

Bakir, N., Humpherys, S., & Dana, K. (2020). Students' perceptions of challenges and solutions to face-to-face and online group work. *Information Systems Education Journal, 18*(5), 75–88.

Bennett, S. (2004). Supporting collaborative project teams using computer-based technologies. In T. S. Roberts (Ed.), *Online collaborative learning: Theory and practice* (pp. 1–27). Idea Group Publishing.

Bulman, C. (2008). An introduction to reflection. *Reflective Practice in Nursing*, 1–24.

Burns, A. (2010). *Doing action research in English language teaching: A guide for practitioners*. Routledge.

Cortázar, C., Nussbaum, M., Alario-Hoyos, C., Goñi, J., & Alvares, D. (2022). The impacts of scaffolding socially shared regulation on teamwork in an online project-based course. *The Internet and Higher Education, 55*, 100877. https://doi.org/10.1016/j.iheduc.2022.100877

Creswell, J. W. (2007). *Qualitative inquiry & research design* (2nd ed.). Sage.

Creswell, J. W., & Clark, V. L. P. (2011). *Designing and conducting mixed methods research* (2nd ed.). Sage.

Davis, L. L., Bhatarasakoon, P., Chaiard, J., Walters, E. M., Nance, J., & Mittal, M. (2022). Use of collaborative online international learning to teach evidence-based practice. *The Journal for Nurse Practitioners, 104498*. https://doi.org/10.1016/j.nurpra.2022.11.008

Graham, C. R., & Misanchuk, M. (2004). Computer-mediated learning groups: Benefits and challenges to using group work in online learning environments. In T. S. Roberts (Ed.), *Online collaborative learning: Theory and practice* (pp. 181–202). Idea Group Publishing.

Güzer, B., & Caner, H. (2014). The past, present and future of blended learning: An in-depth analysis of literature. *Procedia—Social and Behavioral Sciences, 116*, 4596–4603. https://doi.org/10.1016/j.sbspro.2014.01.992

Harsch, C., Müller-Karabil, A., & Buchminskaia, E. (2021). Addressing the challenges of interaction in online language courses. *System, 103*, 102673. https://doi.org/10.1016/j.system.2021.102673

Hernández-Sellés, N., Pablo-César, M.-C., & González-Sanmamed, M. (2019). Computer-supported collaborative learning: An analysis of the relationship between interaction, emotional support, and online collaborative tools. *Computers & Education, 138*, 1–12. https://doi.org/10.1016/j.compedu.2019.04.012

Huang, X., & Lajoie, S. P. (2023). Social emotional interaction in collaborative learning: Why it matters and how can we measure it? *Social Sciences & Humanities Open, 7*(1), 100447. https://doi.org/10.1016/j.ssaho.2023.100447

Ingram, A., & Hathorn, L. (2004). Methods for analyzing collaboration in online communications. In T. Roberts (Ed.), *Online collaborative learning: Theory and practice* (pp. 215–241). Information Science Publishing.

Khalil, H., & Ebner, M. (2017). Using electronic communication tools in online group activities to develop collaborative learning skills. *Universal Journal of*

Educational Research, 5(4), 529–536. https://doi.org/10.13189/ujer.2017.050401

Koh, M. H., & Hill, J. R. (2009). Student perceptions of group work in an online course: Benefits and challenges. *International Journal of E-Learning & Distance Education/Revue Internationale du e-learning et la formation à distance, 23*(2), 69–92.

Lapitan, L. D. S., Chan, A. L. A., Sabarillo, N. S., Sumalinog, D. A. G., & Diaz, J. M. S. (2023). Design, implementation, and evaluation of an online flipped classroom with a collaborative learning model in an undergraduate chemical engineering course. *Education for Chemical Engineers, 43*, 58–72. https://doi.org/10.1016/j.ece.2023.01.007

Le, H., Janssen, J., & Wubbels, T. (2018). Collaborative learning practices: Teacher and student perceived obstacles to effective student collaboration. *Cambridge Journal of Education, 48*(1), 103–122.

Le, V. T., Nguyen, N. H., Tran, T. L. N., Nguyen, L. T., Nguyen, T. A., & Nguyen, M. T. (2022). The interaction patterns of pandemic-initiated online teaching: How teachers adapted. *System, 105*, 102755. https://doi.org/10.1016/j.system.2022.102755

Lehtinen, E., Hakkarainen, K., Lipponen, L., Rahikainen, M., & Muukkonen, H. (1999). Computer-supported collaborative learning: A review. *The JHGI Giesbers Reports on Education, 10*, 1999.

Luo, H., Chen, Y., Chen, T., Koszalka, T. A., & Feng, Q. (2023). Impact of role assignment and group size on asynchronous online discussion: An experimental study. *Computers & Education, 192*, 104658.

Miller, J. A., & Young, C. A. (2023). Cooperative learning in virtual high school English language arts: An action research study. In J. Keengwe (Ed.), *Handbook of research on facilitating collaborative learning through digital content and learning technologies* (pp. 106–131). IGI Global.

Ng, E. M. W. (2012). Online collaborative learning. In N. M. Seel (Ed.), *Encyclopedia of the sciences of learning* (pp. 2497–2499). Springer.

Nokes Malach, T. J., Richey, J. E., & Gadgil, S. (2015). When is it better to learn together? Insights from research on collaborative learning. *Educational Psychology Review, 27*(4), 645–656. https://doi.org/10.1007/s10648-015-9312-8

Razzouk, R., & Johnson, T. E. (2012). Cooperative learning. In N. M. Seel (Ed.), *Encyclopedia of the sciences of learning* (pp. 812–815). Springer.

Roberts, T. S. (2004). *Online collaborative learning: Theory and practice.* Idea Group Publishing.

Slavin, R. E. (1987). Cooperative learning: Where behavioral and humanistic approaches to classroom motivation meet. *The Elementary School Journal, 88*(1), 29–37. https://doi.org/10.1086/461521

Slavin, R. E. (2010). Cooperative learning. In P. Peterson, E. Baker, & B. McGaw (Eds.), *International encyclopedia of education* (3rd ed., pp. 177–183). Elsevier.

Stephens, G. E., & Roberts, K. L. (2017). Facilitating collaboration in online groups. *Journal of Educators Online, 14*(1), n1.

Tao, J., & Gao, X. (2022). Teaching and learning languages online: Challenges and responses. *System, 107*, 102819. https://doi.org/10.1016/j.system.2022.102819

Vygotsky, L. S., & Cole, M. (1978). *Mind in society: Development of higher psychological processes.* Harvard University Press.

Zhang, Z., Liu, T., & Lee, C. B. (2021). Language learners' enjoyment and emotion regulation in online collaborative learning. *System, 98*, 102478. https://doi.org/10.1016/j.system.2021.102478

CHAPTER 10

Revitalizing Language Education: An Exploratory Study on the Innovative Use of Mobile Applications in English Language Teaching at a State University in Vietnam

Nghi Tin Tran, Phuc Huu Tran, and Vu Phi Ho Pham

INTRODUCTION

Language education has undergone significant transformations due to technological innovations and constantly evolving educational approaches and methodologies in recent decades. The outdated teacher-focused mode

N. T. Tran (✉)
Faculty of Foreign Languages, Ho Chi Minh City University of Industry and Trade, Ho Chi Minh City, Vietnam
e-mail: nghitt@huit.edu.vn

P. H. Tran
Faculty of English, University of Foreign Language Studies,
The University of Da Nang, Da Nang City, Vietnam
e-mail: thphuc@ufl.udn.vn

© The Author(s), under exclusive license to Springer Nature
Switzerland AG 2024
L. Phung et al. (eds.), *Innovation in Language Learning and Teaching*, New Language Learning and Teaching Environments,
https://doi.org/10.1007/978-3-031-46080-7_10

of language instruction has been supplanted by learner-focused techniques that prioritize autonomy, involvement, and communication (Mayer, 2017).

Facilitating successful language acquisition remains a significant challenge for language educators. Insufficient student motivation, inadequate opportunities for interaction, and outdated teaching methods are some of the difficulties they encounter (Kukulska-Hulme & Shield, 2008). Nevertheless, the emergence of mobile language learning applications introduces a potential solution to these hurdles. These apps provide new prospects for both language learners and educators as they have been recognized as effective tools in improving language acquisition outcomes (Klimova et al., 2023). Unlike traditional instructional models, mobile apps offer unique advantages such as personalized interaction and flexible learning experiences. Additionally, these apps can facilitate autonomous learning and self-directed practice, which play an integral role in successful language acquisition (Metruk, 2021).

The incorporation of mobile applications in English language teaching (ELT) is a relatively new research area, particularly in the Vietnamese context. To bridge this gap, this study investigated the potential of mobile apps to enhance language learning and teaching. The study used a questionnaire and focus group interviews with language teachers and students to gain insights into their experiences and perception of the use of mobile apps in language learning. This chapter presents the study findings, highlighting the advantages of mobile apps in improving students' English language proficiency, motivation, and involvement.

Literature Review

Traditional Language Education and its Challenges

Traditional language education has been criticized for having limited interaction, low student motivation, and outdated pedagogical approaches (Bax, 2011; Kacetl & Klímová, 2019; Warschauer & Matuchniak, 2010). One of the main limitations of traditional language education is the focus

---

V. P. H. Pham
Faculty of Foreign Languages, Van Lang University,
Ho Chi Minh City, Vietnam
e-mail: ho.pvp@vlu.edu.vn

on the rote memorization of grammar rules and vocabulary rather than the development of communicative competence (Nunan, 1991). This approach often results in students lacking confidence in their ability to use the language in real-life situations (Larsen-Freeman & Anderson, 2011).

Regarding the lack of student motivation, the traditional classroom setting can leave students feeling passive, causing them to disengage, as they have little opportunity for interaction or collaboration (Bax, 2011; Van et al., 2021). Additionally, the lack of relevance to students' interests and daily lives may further contribute to their lack of motivation (Dörnyei, 1998).

It is clear that the traditional approach to teaching languages has several drawbacks, and it will need to be updated to better engage learners and improve instructional effectiveness. Language education is currently characterized by a shift toward student-centered approaches, which prioritize learner autonomy, engagement, and interaction (Mohammadi et al., 2023). As a result of technological advancements, language learners can now access authentic target language materials and communicate with native speakers of that language more easily. Modern learners, who are increasingly tech savvy and expect personalized, interactive learning experiences, may not appreciate outdated teaching methods. Therefore, it is important for educators to innovate their teaching methods and incorporate new technologies into their instruction.

Mobile Applications in Language Education

The use of mobile applications is a burgeoning innovation in language teaching and learning, as evidenced by its successes (Huertas-Abril et al., 2023; Zheng & Warschauer, 2015). With such apps, students can experience language learning in more engaging and interactive ways, which ultimately boosts their motivation and confidence in speaking (Akçayır & Akçayır, 2017; Castañeda & Cho, 2016; Haleem et al., 2022). Intelligent tutoring systems and adaptive algorithms found in language learning apps cater to individual needs and preferences (Kukulska-Hulme, 2009), while gamification features like points, badges, and leaderboards boost learner engagement and motivation (Burston, 2014; Chinnery, 2006; Luo, 2023). With increased interaction, customization, and adaptability, these apps provide a unique learning experience. The independent study and self-guided practice that they offer present students with an opportunity to improve their skills.

Common learning activities in mobile apps are vocabulary development, linguistic games, and pronunciation exercises (Boroughani et al., 2023), which allow students to study at their preferred pace and in accordance with their unique learning preferences (Zheng & Warschauer, 2015). Research conducted by Chen and Hsu (2020) highlights the effectiveness of mobile apps in building vocabulary and improving listening skills, emphasizing their positive impact on language education. Kholis (2021) investigates the role of mobile apps in providing pronunciation guidance, demonstrating that apps with pronunciation features significantly improve learners' pronunciation skills and boost their confidence in speaking. Furthermore, studies by Liu et al. (2016) and Li et al. (2022) focusing on the impact of mobile apps on specific language learning settings, such as Chinese, Japanese, and English language instruction, respectively report the effectiveness and potential of mobile apps in language learning in these contexts.

Collectively, these studies provide evidence supporting the effectiveness of mobile apps as tools for language acquisition. However, despite the advantages, there are limitations to consider, particularly in terms of quality of the materials and instruction provided to students (Kukulska-Hulme & Shield, 2008). In addition, while mobile apps are valuable tools, they cannot fully replace the benefits of face-to-face communication and immersion in the target language (Warschauer & Matuchniak, 2010). Another challenge is finding apps that align with educational goals (Akçayır & Akçayır, 2017). Additionally, the effectiveness of mobile apps in improving learning outcomes may be dependent on external factors such as quality educational resources and teacher support (Pechenkina et al., 2017).

Looking to the future, personalized AI/ML-based language learning apps offer promising opportunities (Baars et al., 2022). Integrating virtual and augmented realities into language learning apps could further enhance motivation and involvement (Punar et al., 2022; Santos et al., 2013). However, concerns related to the quality and effectiveness of these applications call for further research into the incorporation of mobile apps in language learning and teaching. This study presents findings regarding teacher and students' experience with mobile apps in English language teaching at a public university in Vietnam.

The Present Study

The Objectives of The Study

Our study aimed to explore teachers and students' experience of using mobile apps in ELT at a Vietnamese university. The following research questions guided our investigation:

RQ1: What are the perceptions of students and teachers regarding the benefits and challenges of using mobile apps for language learning?

RQ2: Considering the benefits and challenges identified, how can the utilization of mobile apps in ELT be optimized to enhance English proficiency, student motivation, and engagement both in Vietnam and other contexts?

Methodology

This study employs mixed methods to investigate the utilization of mobile applications in English Language Teaching at a public university in Vietnam. It gathers both quantitative and qualitative data to evaluate the experience of integrating apps in language instruction, with a specific emphasis on their benefits for student engagement, learning outcomes, and teacher satisfaction.

Participants

The study included three English language instructors and a group of 166 students who actively utilized mobile apps in their language learning. The students were selected through a selective sampling method from English language courses at a Vietnamese public university. This means that instead of selecting participants randomly, the researchers specifically recruited students who showed a particular interest in using mobile apps for language learning.

Similarly, the instructors were chosen based on their enthusiasm and expertise in integrating mobile apps into language education. Rather than randomly selecting any English language instructors, the researchers deliberately asked those who demonstrated a keen interest in incorporating mobile apps as a teaching tool. Table 10.1 shows the specific information of the two groups of participants.

Table 10.1 Demographic characteristics of participants

	Teachers (n = 3)	Students (n = 166)
Gender	2 male, 1 female	40 males, 126 females
Age	35–48 years	18–25 years
Major	English language	English language
Experience	5–10 years	N/A

Survey

Exploring language student experiences, attitudes, and perceptions of mobile app usage, the study used a survey consisting of online closed- and open-ended questions. The inquiry spanned multiple topic areas, including mobile app frequency and duration of use, benefits and challenges experienced with mobile app language learning, and the convergence of emerging technologies with language learning apps (see Appendix 1).

Focus Group Interviews

Two focus groups were formed: one consisted of three teachers, and the second included six students. The focus group discussions comprised semi-structured questions delving into the participants' experiences, viewpoints, and impressions of the use of mobile apps for language learning (see Appendix 2). The focus group interviews also enabled participants to give their perspectives, insights, and recommendations for better utilization of mobile apps in language education.

Data Analysis

The collected data from the survey and focus group discussions were subjected to both quantitative and qualitative analyses. Descriptive statistics were employed to summarize and present the data. Subsequently, content examination was conducted to identify and categorize patterns that emerged from the qualitative data. Finally, a theme-based analysis was utilized to uncover underlying patterns and connections within the data. This comprehensive approach allowed for a robust exploration of the participants' perspectives and experiences.

Ethical Considerations

The study adhered to ethical principles and obtained informed consent from all involved individuals. Participants' confidentiality and privacy were safeguarded, and their personal details remain undisclosed. Furthermore, participants were made aware of their ability to opt out of the study whenever they chose.

RESULTS

Overview of Participants and Data Collected

A total of 3 language teachers and 166 students participated in the study. The majority of the students were females (76%) aged between 18 and 25 years (cf. Table 10.1). The teachers had an average of seven years of experience teaching English. The data collected from the participants included information on the frequency of mobile app usage, the most useful mobile apps for language learning, the advantages and disadvantages of mobile app usage, and the extent to which mobile apps improve language learning outcomes.

Results from the Survey

Frequency of Mobile App Usage

Table 10.2 revealed that 72% of the students reported using mobile apps either sometimes, often, or always as part of their courses or on their own. Among the teachers, all of them reported using mobile apps for teaching, *with 67% reporting using them often or always.* The most frequently mentioned mobile apps were Duolingo (67%), Quizlet (49%), and Memrise (41%) (see Table 10.3).

The participants' responses on the frequency and average duration of mobile app utilization are portrayed in Table 10.4.

Table 10.4 shows that mobile apps are regular feature practice of most language learners and their instructors, with both groups spending around 2 hours each week utilizing these applications.

Table 10.2 Frequency of mobile app usage

	Never	Rarely	Sometimes	Often	Always
Students	28%	12%	25%	22%	13%
Teachers	0%	33%	0%	33%	33%

Table 10.3 Most useful mobile apps for language learning

	Frequency
Duolingo	67%
Quizlet	49%
Memrise	41%
Other apps	24%

Table 10.4 Frequency and duration of mobile app usage in language learning

	Weekly basis	Average duration (hours/week)
Language teachers	Majority	2
Language students	Majority	2

Extent to Which Mobile Apps Can Improve Language Learning Outcomes

The participants' perceptions of the extent to which mobile apps can enhance language learning outcomes were assessed. Table 10.5 presents the findings of the students' and teachers' responses to each of these questions.

The findings from Table 10.5 reveal a predominantly positive perception of mobile apps for language learning among both students and teachers. A significant portion of students (48%) and all the three teachers (100%) find mobile apps to be very useful for language learning. Additionally, 37% of students consider the apps somewhat useful, further highlighting their utility in supporting language learning.

The study also indicates that mobile apps are perceived as effective tools for improving language skills. A notable 35% of students and 67% of teachers believe the apps to be very effective, while 50% of students and 33% of teachers rate them as somewhat effective. These findings underscore the recognition of the positive impact of mobile apps on language learning outcomes by both students and teachers.

Furthermore, the results demonstrate that mobile apps are highly engaging for learners. A significant 43% of students and all teachers (100%) find the apps to be very engaging, and an additional 37% of students perceive them as somewhat engaging. This indicates that mobile apps successfully capture learners' attention and interest, potentially contributing to an engaging language learning experience.

10 REVITALIZING LANGUAGE EDUCATION: AN EXPLORATORY STUDY... 191

Table 10.5 Perceived improvement of language learning outcomes through mobile app usage

Question	Response	Students (%) (n = 166)	Teachers (%) (n = 3)
11. Usefulness	Very useful	48	100
	Somewhat useful	37	0
	Not very useful	9	0
	Not at all useful	6	0
12. Effectiveness	Very effective	35	67
	Somewhat effective	50	33
	Not very effective	8	0
	Not at all effective	7	0
13. Engagement	Very engaging	43	100
	Somewhat engaging	37	0
	Not very engaging	15	0
	Not at all engaging	5	0
14. Adaptability	Very well	34	100
	Somewhat well	46	0
	Not very well	12	0
	Not at all well	8	0
15. Integration	Very well	25	100
	Somewhat well	60	0
	Not very well	9	0
	Not at all well	6	0

Additionally, the study highlights the adaptability of mobile apps to cater to individual learning paces and styles. Notably, 34% of students and all teachers (100%) rate the adaptability as very well, while 46% of students perceive it as somewhat well. These findings emphasize the apps' ability to accommodate diverse learning preferences and individual needs.

Moreover, the findings indicate that mobile apps effectively integrate emerging technologies, such as AI and gamification, into the language learning experience. Specifically, 25% of students and all teachers (100%) rate the integration as very well, and 60% of students perceive it as somewhat well. This suggests that mobile apps successfully leverage modern technologies to potentially enhance the language learning process.

Both students and teachers acknowledge the usefulness, effectiveness, engagement, adaptability, and integration of mobile apps as valuable assets in enhancing language learning outcomes. These predominantly positive perceptions underscore the potential of mobile apps to play a significant

192 N. T. TRAN ET AL.

role in facilitating effective and engaging language learning experiences for learners and educators alike.

Table 10.6 presents the advantages and disadvantages of mobile app usage as reported by the study participants.

The advantages highlighted by the participants include increased motivation (81%), flexibility in learning (72%), and improved access to learning resources (65%). On the other hand, the participants also identified several disadvantages, such as limited interaction with teachers (49%), limited interaction with other students (47%), and potential distractions (41%). These findings showed that proper balance between independent learning and interaction with teachers and other students must be achieved to optimize the effectiveness of mobile app usage.

When asked about more specific benefits that language learning apps provide, the majority of students reported the following benefits: increased motivation (81%), convenience (76%), and flexibility in learning (72%), personalization (68%), adaptive learning (60%), and self-directed learning (57%). These findings suggest that mobile apps can enhance the language learning experience significantly by addressing individual needs and preferences while offering more autonomy in the learning process.

However, participants also identified further challenges that may hinder learning outcomes. The most commonly reported challenges include lack of engagement (55%), difficulty in retaining information (48%), mobile apps not being challenging enough (37%), and insufficient feedback on progress (31%). These concerns highlight areas for improvement in the design of language learning apps and how they should be used in language instruction.

Table 10.6 Advantages and disadvantages of mobile app usage

	Advantages	*Disadvantages*
Increased motivation	81%	N/A
Flexibility in learning	72%	N/A
Improved access to learning resources	65%	N/A
Limited interaction with teachers	N/A	49%
Limited interaction with other students	N/A	47%
Potential distractions	N/A	41%

Integration of Emerging Technologies

Regarding the integration of emerging technologies, the majority of participants expressed a desire for the integration of emerging technologies, such as AI (74%) and AR (62%), into mobile apps for language learning. The participants believed that these technologies would enhance the learning experience and offer innovative ways of learning. The findings suggest that developers and educators should explore the potential of incorporating emerging technologies to improve the effectiveness of mobile apps in language education.

Results from the Focus Group Interviews

In addition to the survey, focus group interviews were conducted with three teachers and six students to better understand their experiences with mobile applications in English language teaching. The focus group interviews with the teachers were conducted separately from those with the students.

Teacher Focus Group Interviews

The following themes emerged from the teachers' focus group interviews.

Benefits of mobile apps in ELT: According to the teachers interviewed, using mobile apps in English language teaching has various advantages. These benefits consist of enriching the learning experience, boosting student engagement, and accommodating personalization and individualization. Using Duolingo and Quizlet mobile apps has been found to boost student engagement, according to Teacher 1. These apps come with gamification features that make learning enjoyable and therefore increase participation rates. Individualization through mobile apps has been witnessed by Teacher 2. Teacher 2 has noticed that through apps like Memrise, customization is allowed, leading to a more personalized learning journey for students. This individualization eventually leads to better engagement and improved effectiveness of learning experiences.

Challenges in implementing mobile app usage: The integration of mobile app usage has faced numerous challenges for teachers. Access to technology was oftentimes limited, and integrating apps into lesson plans has been difficult. Additionally, due to the absence of necessary training and support, the implementation process has proven arduous. Teacher 2 voiced his agreement, "Proper training and support are lacking, and integrating apps into lesson plans and limited technology access pose some of the challenges at hand."

App selection and creation: The successful implementation of mobile app usage in ELT was reportedly contingent on proper app selection and instructional material creation, as teacher feedback indicated. Teacher 3 emphasizes the significance of choosing suitable apps and crafting effective instructional materials to guarantee the triumphant use of mobile apps in ELT.

Student Focus Group Interviews

The following themes emerged from the student focus group interviews:

Benefits of mobile apps in language learning: Mobile apps, as per student feedback, boosted motivation, allowed for self-directed learning, and created an immersive and engaging learning environment. "I find my motivation to learn languages really boosted when using interactive and engaging mobile apps." Student 1 expressed their enjoyment in using apps to learn languages.

Challenges in using mobile apps: In their feedback, the students brought up various obstacles they encountered when utilizing mobile apps: from glitches with the technology, to insufficient guidance and help, to being sidetracked by other diversions. "Offering opportunities for self-directed learning, which is great," Student 2 commented. "But there are some challenges that come with it, such as the lack of guidance and support, as well as technical issues."

App features: Providing multimedia content, customization options, and interactive exercises were the favored features of mobile apps among the students. "Apps that offer multimedia content, interactive exercises, and customization options are my favored ones, although they can be distracting," said Student 3.

Integration of mobile apps into ELT: In a systematic and purposeful manner, with clear learning objectives and assessment criteria, the students were of the opinion that incorporation of mobile apps in ELT was essential. Mobile apps in ELT can be maximized by integrating them systematically and purposefully. Assessment criteria and clear learning objectives are integral in this process according to Student 4.

In summary, support and training are crucial when considering the implementation of mobile apps in language education, as noted by both teachers and students. While acknowledging its potential, the integration of mobile apps in ELT demands a well-planned selection process, systematic incorporation into lesson plans, and support for educators and learners alike. Overall, the study underscores the importance of careful consideration when integrating mobile apps into language education.

DISCUSSION

In recent years, the emergence of mobile language learning apps has gained popularity. These technologies have been widely embraced by language educators and learners (Kukulska-Hulme, 2009; Punar et al., 2022). Focusing on both the teaching and learning experiences, this study sought to gain insights into teachers' and students' attitudes, perceptions, and experiences regarding the use of language learning apps. The study investigated the current app usage and integration of up-and-coming technologies, allowing for a comprehensive understanding of both teacher and student perspectives.

Throughout this study, we collected a variety of perspectives on the use of mobile apps in language learning through focus group interviews. These findings further support previous research by Burston (2014) and Stockwell and Hubbard (2013) in that teachers acknowledged the benefits of mobile apps, such as increased student motivation and engagement, but also expressed the challenges of evaluating progress and ensuring effective app usage. Meanwhile, students praised mobile apps for their fun and engaging approach to language learning, leading to increased motivation to learn.

Consistent with previous studies (Chen et al., 2018; Chen & John, 2016; Chen & Hsu, 2020), focus group participants generally expressed optimism toward emerging technologies in mobile language learning apps. They believed that these advancements could optimize learning, offering novel approaches that could greatly enhance the learning experience. However, the importance of striking a balance between face-to-face interaction and technology was also emphasized, as technology alone could not supersede the value of human interaction and personal connections.

Within the survey, a substantial portion of students and instructors utilizing mobile apps in their language programs on a frequent basis were reported. Feedback indicated that these devices contribute to learning by increasing interest and making it more accommodating, which reinforces prior research (Burston, 2014; Chen et al., 2018; Stockwell & Hubbard, 2013).

RECOMMENDATIONS

Current Problems in English Language Teaching in Vietnam and the Call for Using Mobile Applications in Teaching

In Vietnam, the traditional approach to language teaching predominantly relies on grammar and vocabulary drills, which have their limitations. To enhance English language learning in this context, the incorporation of mobile applications presents a logical solution. These apps offer interactive and stimulating content, making the learning process simpler and more engaging. By providing learners the freedom to access these resources beyond the confines of the classroom, mobile apps can serve as a valuable tool for supplementary education and self-directed learning. The adaptability of these apps allows for personalized learning experiences tailored to individual needs, ensuring a more effective learning process. Moreover, the immediate feedback feature of mobile apps enables learners to quickly identify and rectify their mistakes, facilitating their language development. The study emphasizes several benefits of mobile apps in language learning.

Procedures to Use Mobile Apps to Teach a Foreign Language in a Classroom Setting

The use of mobile apps in language learning has the potential to revolutionize the way we teach and learn. These platforms offer greater interactivity and flexibility, which can lead to more effective and engaging learning experiences. We will discuss the steps involved in using mobile apps to teach foreign languages in a classroom setting based on the findings of this study, our experience as educators, and existing literature. We will begin by discussing the importance of aligning mobile apps with the specific goals and objectives of the language course. We will then explain how to research and select suitable mobile apps as well as how to introduce these apps to students. Finally, we will discuss how to incorporate mobile apps into classroom activities and monitor and evaluate students' progress.

Step 1: Identify the Goals and Objectives of the Course
The first step in using mobile apps to teach a foreign language is to identify the specific goals and objectives of the course. What are the specific skills and knowledge that students are expected to acquire by the end of the course? Once the goals and objectives have been identified, it is then

possible to select mobile apps that align with these goals. For example, if the goal of the course is to improve students' speaking skills, then mobile apps that focus on speaking exercises and conversation practice would be suitable. Similarly, if the goal of the course is to improve students' vocabulary knowledge, then mobile apps that focus on vocabulary games and flashcards would be suitable.

Step 2: Research and Select Suitable Mobile Apps
There are a wide variety of mobile apps available for language learning. Some apps focus on specific aspects of language learning, such as listening, speaking, grammar, vocabulary, and reading. Other apps offer a more comprehensive approach to language learning.

When researching and selecting mobile apps, it is important to consider the following factors:

- The specific goals and objectives of the course
- The age and level of the students
- The learning style of the students
- The technical capabilities of the students
- The cost of the apps

Step 3: Introduce Mobile Apps to Students
To effectively introduce students to chosen mobile apps, it's key to provide the right instruction. Demonstrations or tutorial sessions can both work well, as long as students can access the apps. It's worth noting that different schools have different policies on this, with some asking students to bring their own devices and others offering them on site. Regardless, app introduction is a valuable part of the process to minimize technical difficulties and distractions.

Step 4: Incorporate Mobile Apps into Classroom Activities
Students' learning experience can be elevated with mobile app utilization in classroom activities. In-class activities or homework can be supplemented with mobile app-assigned exercises and quizzes by teachers. Language skill enhancement can also be achieved through group activities where students collaboratively use mobile apps. For example, the ESLA app helps students improve English pronunciation through immediate feedback. The teacher may introduce vocabulary related to a theme and provide meanings and example sentences, and students use the app to

access phonetic transcriptions and audio pronunciations. They practice individually, record themselves, and get peer feedback. Classroom discussions encourage sharing experiences and challenges. A fun pronunciation game with an app rewards accuracy. Follow-up homework includes pronunciation exercises with reminders and progress tracking. This integrated approach enriches students' pronunciation skills interactively and effectively.

Step 5: Monitor and Evaluate Students' Progress

When utilizing mobile apps within the classroom, keeping tabs on and assessing students' progress is critical. The data extracted from the mobile apps allows instructors to observe their students' success rates, enabling them to single out deficiencies within the students' academic performance and edify accordingly. With the information at their disposal, they can cater to each student's individual learning needs and offer constructive feedback.

Tips for Encouraging Students and Teachers to Use Mobile Apps

The use of mobile apps in foreign language teaching has gained significant attention as a promising approach to enhance language learning outcomes. However, successful implementation of this pedagogical tool requires concerted efforts from both teachers and students. In this regard, this chapter presents practical tips and recommendations for guiding teachers and students in maximizing the benefits of mobile app integration in language education.

Tip 1: Encouraging Student Engagement through Gamification Incentives

One crucial aspect of fostering successful app integration lies in motivating students to actively engage with language learning applications. Leveraging the principles of gamification, as proposed by Hamari et al. (2014), teachers can create fun and interactive activities in language learning apps to spark students' interest. Gamified features can be used to encourage regular app usage, increasing student enthusiasm. Additional rewards can also be provided to motivate students further and keep them engaged over time.

Tip 2: Empowering Teachers through App-focused Training

To optimize the quality of language instruction, it is imperative that educators receive comprehensive training on utilizing mobile apps effectively. Workshops and online courses tailored to the integration of language learning apps can play a pivotal role in equipping teachers with the necessary skills and knowledge. As noted in a report by Samson and Collins (2012), such training has been identified as a critical component in fostering effective language education. Ensuring that teachers are well versed in leveraging app features to complement their teaching methodologies enables a more seamless incorporation of technology in the classroom.

Tip 3: Synergizing Mobile Apps with Traditional Teaching Methods

A successful integration of mobile apps within language education involves leveraging the strengths of both technology and traditional teaching approaches. Li et al. (2022) highlighted the significance of gamification incentives in motivating regular app usage among language learners. By integrating fun and interactive tools, teachers can inspire a deeper sense of enthusiasm among students. By thoughtfully aligning app-based activities with the overall curriculum, teachers can further enhance the learning experience and encourage learners to actively participate in language learning.

Tip 4: Selecting Appropriate Language Learning Apps

The efficacy of mobile app integration significantly depends on the selection of appropriate applications specifically designed for language learning. As emphasized in a study conducted by Li et al. (2022), language learning apps that encompass grammar lessons, vocabulary exercises, and pronunciation practice have demonstrated remarkable potential in improving language learning outcomes. Teachers and students should prioritize apps that cater explicitly to language education to maximize the benefits of technology in the learning process.

Tip 5: Encouraging Students to Monitor Language Learning Progress with App Tracking Features

To improve language proficiency, it's essential to regularly assess strengths and weaknesses. Language-learning apps often come with tracking features that can be incredibly helpful in achieving this goal. Teachers can encourage students to make it a habit to use these tools and monitor their progress over time. By keeping track of their performance, they can identify areas that need more practice and focus, leading to more effective language learning.

The current problems in English language teaching in Vietnam call for the use of mobile applications to enhance language learning. The traditional approach in Vietnam primarily relies on grammar and vocabulary drills, but the incorporation of mobile apps can provide interactive and stimulating content, making learning more engaging and flexible. Mobile apps offer the freedom for learners to access resources beyond the classroom, fostering self-directed learning and supplementary education. Additionally, mobile apps' immediate feedback feature allows learners to quickly identify and correct mistakes, further facilitating language learning progress. By addressing these challenges and using mobile apps strategically, language education in Vietnam can experience significant improvements.

Conclusion

By conducting both survey and focus group interviews, the study sought to get a holistic view of how teachers and students viewed the use of mobile apps for language learning. Language educators, app developers, and educational policy makers gained insights from the findings of the study. First, mobile apps can offer language learners a learning experience that is individualized and satisfying. The learners reported finding the mobile apps interactive and engaging, and they appreciated the customizable pace of instruction. Second, mobile app-based language learning comes with its own share of challenges. The availability of technology, compatibility, and the necessity for continuous support and training for both teachers and students were all cited as problematic areas. Third, the need to provide language learners with effective and engaging mobile technology experiences is highlighted by the results of this study, which can inform future language education research. Last, with a focus on applying mobile apps in language teaching, the chapter provides guidance in the form of concrete procedures and practical tips. Future research may continue with the development and analysis of mobile app-based language learning programs, considering the needs and points of view of both teachers and students.

Appendix 1: Online Survey

Part 1: Demographic Information

1. Age: _____
2. Gender:

   - Male
   - Female
   - Other

3. Occupation: _____
4. Current Language Learning Status:

   - Beginner
   - Intermediate
   - Advanced

5. How long have you been learning this language? _____

6. What is your primary reason for learning this language? _____

Part 2: Mobile App Usage

7. Have you used a mobile app for language learning before?

   - Yes
   - No

8. If yes, how often do you use the mobile app for language learning?

   - Daily
   - Weekly
   - Monthly
   - Rarely

9. What type of language learning activities do you engage in using the mobile app?

- Listening and speaking exercises
- Reading and writing exercises
- Grammar and vocabulary exercises
- Cultural activities
- Games and simulations

10. Have you used a mobile app that integrates emerging technologies, such as AI and gamification, for language learning?

- Yes
- No

Part 3: Perceptions of Mobile Apps for Language Learning

11. How useful do you find the mobile app for language learning?

- Very useful
- Somewhat useful
- Not very useful
- Not at all useful

12. How effective do you think the mobile app is in improving your language skills?

- Very effective
- Somewhat effective
- Not very effective
- Not at all effective

13. How engaging do you find the mobile app for language learning?

- Very engaging
- Somewhat engaging
- Not very engaging
- Not at all engaging

14. How well does the mobile app adapt to your learning pace and style?

- Very well
- Somewhat well
- Not very well
- Not at all well

15. How well does the mobile app integrate emerging technologies, such as AI and gamification, into the language learning experience?

- Very well
- Somewhat well
- Not very well
- Not at all well

Part 4: Open-Ended Questions

16. What do you like about using the mobile app for language learning?
17. What do you dislike about using the mobile app for language learning?
18. What improvements would you suggest for the mobile app to enhance the language learning experience?

Appendix 2: Focus Group Interview

Part 1: Introduction and Background Information

1. Can you tell us a little about your background and experience with language learning and teaching?
2. How familiar are you with the use of mobile apps for language learning?

Part 2: Mobile App Usage

3. Can you describe your experience using mobile apps for language learning?
4. How often do you use mobile apps for language learning?

5. What features do you look for in a mobile app for language learning?

Part 3: Integration of Emerging Technologies

6. How do you believe the integration of emerging technologies, such as AI and gamification, enhances language learning in mobile apps?
7. Can you provide an example of a mobile app that effectively integrates emerging technologies for language learning?

Part 4: Perceptions of Mobile Apps for Language Learning.

8. How do you believe mobile apps compare to traditional language learning methods (e.g. textbooks, language classes, etc.) in terms of effectiveness?
9. What do you see as the strengths of using mobile apps for language learning?
10. What do you see as the weaknesses of using mobile apps for language learning?

Part 5: Future Use of Mobile Apps for Language Learning

11. Do you plan to continue using mobile apps for language learning in the future?
12. If yes, what features or technologies would you like to see integrated into mobile apps for language learning in the future?

References

Akçayır, M., & Akçayır, G. (2017). Advantages and challenges associated with augmented reality for education: A systematic review of the literature. *Educational Research Review, 20,* 1–11. https://doi.org/10.1016/J.EDUREV.2016.11.002

Baars, M., Khare, S., & Ridderstap, L. (2022). Exploring students' use of a mobile application to support their self-regulated learning processes. *Frontiers in Psychology, 13,* 585. https://doi.org/10.3389/FPSYG.2022.793002/BIBTEX

Bax, S. (2011). Normalisation revisited. *International Journal of Computer-Assisted Language Learning and Teaching, 1*(2), 1–15. https://doi.org/10.4018/IJCALLT.2011040101

Boroughani, T., Xodabande, I., & Karimpour, S. (2023). Self-regulated learning with mobile devices for university students: Exploring the impacts on academic vocabulary development. *Discover Education*, *2*(1), 1–10. https://doi.org/10.1007/S44217-023-00028-Z

Burston, J. (2014). MALL: The pedagogical challenges. *Computer Assisted Language Learning*, *27*(4), 344–357. https://doi.org/10.1080/0958822 1.2014.914539

Castañeda, D. A., & Cho, M. H. (2016). Use of a game-like application on a mobile device to improve accuracy in conjugating Spanish verbs. *Computer Assisted Language Learning*, *29*(7), 1195–1204. https://doi.org/10.1080/09588221.2016.1197950

Chen, C. M., Chen, L. C., & Yang, S. M. (2018). An English vocabulary learning app with self-regulated learning mechanism to improve learning performance and motivation. *Computer Assisted Language Learning*, *32*(3), 237–260. https://doi.org/10.1080/09588221.2018.1485708

Chen, X., & John, S. (2016). Evaluating language-learning mobile apps for second-language learners. *Journal of Educational Technology Development and Exchange*, *9*(2), 39–51.

Chen, Y. L., & Hsu, C. C. (2020). Self-regulated mobile game-based English learning in a virtual reality environment. *Computers & Education*, *154*, 103910. https://doi.org/10.1016/J.COMPEDU.2020.103910

Chinnery, G. M. (2006). Emerging technologies going to the MALL: Mobile assisted language learning. *Language Learning & Technology*, *10*(1), 9–16. http://llt.msu.edu/vol10num1/emerging/

Dörnyei, Z. (1998). Motivation in second and foreign language learning. *Language Teaching*, *31*(3), 117–135. https://doi.org/10.1017/S026144480001315X

Haleem, A., Javaid, M., Qadri, M. A., & Suman, R. (2022). Understanding the role of digital technologies in education: A review. *Sustainable Operations and Computers*, *3*, 275–285. https://doi.org/10.1016/J.SUSOC.2022.05.004

Hamari, J., Koivisto, J., & Sarsa, H. (2014). Does gamification work?—A literature review of empirical studies on gamification. *Proceedings of the Annual Hawaii International Conference on System Sciences.* https://doi.org/10.1109/HICSS.2014.377

Huertas-Abril, A., Palacios-Hidalgo, F. J., Chung, S.-J., & Choi, L. J. (2023). The use of mobile instant messaging in English language teaching: The case of South Korea. *Education Sciences*, *13*(2), 110. https://doi.org/10.3390/EDUCSCI13020110

Kacetl, J., & Klímová, B. (2019). Use of smartphone applications in English language learning—A challenge for foreign language education. *Education Sciences*, *9*(3), 179. https://doi.org/10.3390/EDUCSCI9030179

Kholis, A. (2021). Elsa Speak app: Automatic Speech Recognition (ASR) for supplementing English pronunciation skills. *Pedagogy: Journal of English Language Teaching, 9*(1), 1–14. https://doi.org/10.32332/JOELT.V9I1.2723

Klimova, B., Pikhart, M., Polakova, P., Cerna, M., Yayilgan, S. Y., & Shaikh, S. (2023). A systematic review on the use of emerging technologies in teaching English as an applied language at the university level. *Systems, 11*(1), 42. https://doi.org/10.3390/SYSTEMS11010042

Kukulska-Hulme, A. (2009). Will mobile learning change language learning? *ReCALL, 21*(2), 157–165. https://doi.org/10.1017/S0958344009000202

Kukulska-Hulme, A., & Shield, L. (2008). An overview of mobile assisted language learning: From content delivery to supported collaboration and interaction. *ReCALL, 20*(3), 271–289. https://doi.org/10.1017/S0958344008000335

Larsen-Freeman, D., & Anderson, M. (2011). *Techniques and principles in language teaching* (3rd ed.). Oxford University Press.

Li, F., Fan, S., & Wang, Y. (2022). Mobile-assisted language learning in Chinese higher education context: A systematic review from the perspective of the situated learning theory. *Education and Information Technologies, 27*(7), 9665–9688. https://doi.org/10.1007/S10639-022-11025-4/FIGURES/4

Liu, Y., Holden, D., & Zheng, D. (2016). Analyzing students' language learning experience in an augmented reality mobile game: An exploration of an emergent learning environment. *Procedia—Social and Behavioral Sciences, 228*, 369–374. https://doi.org/10.1016/J.SBSPRO.2016.07.055

Luo, Z. (2023). The effectiveness of gamified tools for Foreign Language Learning (FLL): A systematic review. *Behavioral Science, 13*(4), 331. https://doi.org/10.3390/BS13040331

Mayer, R. E. (2017). Using multimedia for e-learning. *Journal of Computer Assisted Learning, 33*(5), 403–423. https://doi.org/10.1111/JCAL.12197

Metruk, R. (2021). The use of smartphone English language learning apps in the process of learning English: Slovak EFL students' perspectives. *Sustainability.* https://doi.org/10.3390/su13158205

Mohammadi, Z. Z., Admiraal, W., & Saab, N. (2023). Learner autonomy, learner engagement and learner satisfaction in text-based and multimodal computer-mediated writing environments. *Education and Information Technologies.* https://doi.org/10.1007/S10639-023-11615-W/TABLES/10

Nunan, D. (1991). *Language teaching methodology: A textbook for teachers.* Prentice Hall.

Pechenkina, E., Laurence, D., Oates, G., Eldridge, D. S., & Hunter, D. (2017). Using a gamified mobile app to increase student engagement, retention and academic achievement. *International Journal of Educational Technology in Higher Education.* https://doi.org/10.1186/s41239-017-0069-7

Punar, O. N., Yangin, E. G., & Baturay, M. H (2022). Augmented Reality (AR) in language learning: A principled review of 2017–2021. *Participatory Educational Research, 9*(4), 131–152. https://doi.org/10.1727/5/per.22.83.9.4

Samson, J. F., & Collins, B. A. (2012). *Preparing all teachers to meet the needs of English language learners applying research to policy and practice for teacher effectiveness.* Center for American Progress. www.americanprogress.org

Santos, S. N., Belén, M., Mesa, S., Area, A., & Manuel, M. (2013). Students' ICT practices at La Laguna University and their influence on learning processes. *Procedia—Social and Behavioral Sciences, 93,* 1451–1455. https://doi.org/10.1016/j.sbspro.2013.10.062

Stockwell, G., & Hubbard, P. (2013). Some emerging principles for mobile-assisted language learning. *TIRF Report, 29*(3), 201–218.

Van, L. K., Dang, T. A., Pham, D. B. T., Vo, T. T. N., & Pham, V. P. H. (2021). The effectiveness of using technology in learning English. *AsiaCALL Online Journal, 12*(2), 24–40. https://asiacall.info/acoj/index.php/journal/article/view/26

Warschauer, M., & Matuchniak, T. (2010). Chapter 6: New technology and digital worlds: Analyzing evidence of equity in access, use, and outcomes. *Review of Research in Education, 34*(1), 179–225. https://doi.org/10.3102/0091732X09349791/ASSET/IMAGES/LARGE/10.3102_0091732X09349791-FIG4.JPEG

Zheng, B., & Warschauer, M. (2015). Participation, interaction, and academic achievement in an online discussion environment. *Computers & Education, 84,* 78–89. https://doi.org/10.1016/J.COMPEDU.2015.01.008

CHAPTER 11

Factors Affecting EFL Lecturers' Implementation of Blended Learning in Vietnamese Universities

Thi Nguyet Le

INTRODUCTION

In light of the digital era, traditional face-to-face teaching has revealed many limitations of an outdated and ineffective method (Musdalifah et al., 2021; Nuri & Bostanci, 2021). The rapid growth of Web 2.0 and digital technologies has resulted in innovations and reforms in English language teaching and learning in higher education worldwide (Ivanova et al., 2020). This has led to the emergence of "blended learning" (BL), which refers to the combination of online teaching/learning and face-to-face teaching/learning with the aim of motivating students and enhancing their learning (Alblladi & Alahareef, 2019; Nuri & Bostanci, 2021; Sheerah, 2020). BL is believed to be an optimal approach as it maximizes the advantages of both face to-face and online learning (Mulyono et al.,

---

T. N. Le (✉)
People's Security University, Ho Chi Minh City, Vietnam

© The Author(s), under exclusive license to Springer Nature
Switzerland AG 2024
L. Phung et al. (eds.), *Innovation in Language Learning and
Teaching*, New Language Learning and Teaching Environments,
https://doi.org/10.1007/978-3-031-46080-7_11

209

2021) and minimizes limitations of those delivery modes (Musdalifah et al., 2021).

In response to the increasing trend of global economic integration, the Vietnamese government has enforced many higher education reforms to improve the quality of teaching and learning in the country (Le, 2017). The government has identified English as the most important foreign language to help the country achieve the goals of higher education reforms as well as promoting successful global integration (Hoang, 2015). The government has emphasized the importance of English education reforms by having implemented Vietnam's National Foreign Language 2020 Project along with the enforcement of many documents such as Decision No. 1400/QD-TTg, Decision No. 2080/ QD-TTg, and Decision No.1659/QD-TTg to enhance the quality of EFL education at different levels (Ngo, 2016; Nguyen, 2019; Tran, 2020). Moreover, having realized the benefits of digital technologies, the Vietnamese government has issued many policies to promote the use of ICTs, focusing on integrating online learning with traditional learning to achieve the goal of EFL education reforms (Hoang, 2015; Tran, 2020). A clear understanding of the combination of these two traditional and online components, also known as blended learning, will lead to an effective application of this delivery mode. However, the term "blended learning" itself has not been explicitly described in the policy documents of the Vietnamese government (Nguyen, 2017), which resulted in a confusion in lecturers' understanding and implementation of this delivery mode. BL has been considered an optimal solution to Vietnamese government's EFL education transformation (Hoang, 2015); and the quality of implementing it in reality depends on various factors (Tran, 2020). For example, Vietnamese EFL lecturers are still unfamiliar with integrating online learning into face-to-face classrooms (Bouilheres et al., 2020; Hoang, 2015; Tran, 2020). In practice, their teaching methods are still heavily influenced by the Confucian traditions which prioritize face-to-face, teacher-centered teaching methods (Nguyen, 2019; Tran, 2020). Moreover, Vietnamese universities' provision of technologies is limited (Hoang, 2015). However, very few studies have been done to investigate factors affecting the success or failure of implementing BL in the Vietnamese tertiary context. This research project was, therefore, conducted to investigate the underlying factors affecting EFL lecturers' implementation of BL in their teaching practice, which was expected to make some contributions to the increased quality of EFL education at Vietnamese universities.

An Overview of the Literature on Blended Learning: Issues and Contexts

Definitions and Understandings of Blended Learning in EFL Education

The term "blended learning" appeared in the early twenty-first century (Wright, 2017), and has been used interchangeably with other terms such as "hybrid learning," "flipped classrooms," "distributed learning," "flexible learning," and "blended learning pedagogies" (Riel et al., 2016; Vymetalkova & Milkova, 2019). Furthermore, there has been no real consensus on how BL has been defined (Eshreteh & Siaj, 2017; Radia, 2019). First, BL has been viewed as "a combination between face-to-face learning and online" (Zaim & Mudra, 2019, p. 209). Other researchers have used various expressions to define BL such as "the mixing of language learning content with online activities" (Alsowayegh et al., 2019, p. 268), "a combination of traditional and technology-enhanced learning" (Hosseinpour et al., 2019, p. 99), and "the attributes of both online synchronous-asynchronous learning and offline face-to-face language learning" (Wang et al., 2019, p. 4). These definitions are all viewed from the perspectives of researchers toward the process of language learning. A second set of perspectives on BL concentrates on the teaching dimension only. Wright (2017, p. 64) viewed BL as "a combination of traditional face-to-face teaching and online teaching." Elsewhere, BL is expressed as "an integration of online education with traditional methods" (Rahim, 2019, p. 1168) and "a combination of face-to-face and online instruction" (Zhang & Zou, 2020, p. 41).

One distinctive form of BL which has been recently adopted in EFL in Vietnamese universities is the "flipped classroom" (Bui, 2022). In this pedagogical design, students are required to read texts and watch videos to develop foundational knowledge before class. Once in the classroom, they will apply that learned knowledge in higher-order activities and join thoughtful discussions in classrooms (Sulaiman, 2018).

Overall, there is no consensus on how to define the term "blended learning" in previous studies as researchers see it from different perspectives. The context of this study covers ten different universities in Vietnam, and BL has been defined in these universities differently due to many factors that will be covered in the following sections. In this study, BL must include two components: face-to-face and online; it should be used for language teaching and learning; and it also refers to the ultimate goal of improving learning outcomes. Therefore, BL is defined as an appropriate blend of face-to-face and online dimensions in EFL education to achieve effective English learning.

Types of Blended Learning in Educational Contexts

An analysis of previous studies on the types or models of BL reveals how this delivery mode has been implemented in EFL education so far. This forms a theoretical basis to compare the types of BL used in English language teaching in Vietnamese higher education and those in the literature.

The six most traditional models of BL in the literature include: Face-to-Face Driver, Flex, Rotation, Online Lab, Self-Blend, and Online Driver (Horn & Staker, 2011). The Face-to-Face Driver model involves the delivery of curricula face-to-face in class, while technology is used outside classrooms to support or supplement traditional teaching. In the Rotation model, students rotate their learning between face-to-face learning in physical classrooms and online learning in computer laboratories or from home. The Flex model refers to the delivery of courses mostly through online materials, and small group sessions or in-person tutoring sessions are provided when necessary. The Online Lab model refers to the delivery of entire content on an online platform in computer laboratories and this online learning is supervised by a lab assistant. The Self-Blend model refers to a type of BL in which learners can select some supplemental online courses to support face-to-face learning. Finally, the Online Driver model refers to the delivery of content mostly on an online platform, while face-to-face check-ins are sometimes optional and sometimes required. From another perspective, Norberg et al. (2011) proposed a time-based BL model, which refers to a blend of two technology-enabled elements: synchronous meetings and asynchronous activities. Synchronous elements include face-to-face meetings, chats, videoconference meetings, and webinars, all of which take place in real time. On the other hand, asynchronous elements comprise recorded lectures, assignments, asynchronous research, book readings, collaboration, and discussions. Generally, BL has been categorized into various models that differ in the components they blend, and the roles of each component in the blend.

Factors Affecting the implementation of BL in EFL Education

Across several research studies, three groups of factors appear to affect the implementation of BL in EFL education: individual, institutional, and sociocultural. First, individual factors are mentioned the most in previous research, and they consist of the following: teachers' perceptions of BL; their pedagogical knowledge (PK); their English language proficiency; their technological competence; their understanding of students' backgrounds and characteristics; their motivation, beliefs, and attitudes; and their experience in integrating BL into EFL teaching.

Perceptions of Blended Learning

How teachers perceive the value of BL contributes to the outcomes of implementing it. Sheerah (2020, p. 205) explains that positive perceptions help teachers "embrace this concept to improve their classroom practice and enhance their delivery of the curriculum." Conversely, Hoang (2015) argues that when teachers are doubtful about the benefits of BL, they tend to refuse it in their teaching.

Pedagogical Knowledge

In his study on Vietnamese teachers' crucial knowledge in BL environments, Hoang (2015) argues that an understanding of pedagogies leads to better teaching practices, and as a result, improvements in students' learning. Mishra and Koehler (2006) emphasize the importance of pedagogical knowledge of blended teachers in their technological pedagogical content knowledge (TPACK) model. PK refers to teachers' understandings of teaching methods/approaches and classroom management strategies as well as learner characteristics, and strategies for assessing students' performance (Koehler & Mishra, 2009).

English Language Proficiency

Mishra and Koehler (2006) also emphasize the role of content knowledge (CK) that EFL teachers need to teach the subject content effectively. CK refers to teachers' sufficient English proficiency or their mastery of linguistic components such as phonetics, syntax, pragmatics, morphology and semantics, communication strategies, language skills, and sociocultural knowledge (Hoang, 2015). On the contrary, Hoang indicates EFL teachers' lack of English competence leads to the low quality of English teaching and learning at Vietnamese universities.

Technological Competence

BL requires teachers to have necessary technological skills and knowledge to deliver English courses successfully because it is basically a technology-enhanced approach (Mozelius & Hettiarachchi, 2017). Hoang (2015) emphasizes that the use of BL required EFL lecturers to "have some advanced knowledge and skills related to computers and online tools" (p. 79).

Understanding of Students' Backgrounds and Characteristics

Successful teachers using BL need to have a good understanding of students' needs, backgrounds, preferences, and their information technology (IT) competence so that the teachers can integrate web-based technologies into English classrooms successfully (Okaz, 2015). Such awareness assisted teachers in designing, organizing, and balancing appropriate teaching activities in classrooms and online (Wu & Liu, 2013).

Motivation, Beliefs, and Attitudes

Personal motivation encourages teachers to use BL and assists them to maintain effort and persistence in improving EFL education using BL (Copriady, 2015; Ibrahim & Nat, 2019; Rahim, 2019). Moreover, when teachers have positive attitudes toward BL, they are encouraged to use these delivery modes to increase students' learning outcomes (Tawil, 2018). When they believe in the benefits of using BL, they will put more commitment and devotion in implementing it (Hoang, 2015). Thus, teachers' motivation, beliefs, and attitudes have a positive impact on the use of BL in EFL education (Ibrahim & Nat, 2019).

Experience in Integrating Blended Learning into EFL Teaching

Previous research has shown that teachers seem to be quite comfortable in a traditional, face-to-face environment, whereas many feel unfamiliar with online elements of a virtual learning environment (Garner & Rouse, 2016; Mozelius & Hettiarachchi, 2017). Thus, blended teachers must be experienced in blending face-to-face and online learning environments. Hayati et al. (2021) argue that teachers can benefit from the experience of "engaging the students in a blended learning class by getting attention and students' interest with fully applying technology" (p. 775).

Second, various institutional factors also play an important role in enhancing the quality of implementing BL in EFL education. These include the following: infrastructure, resources and technology; support and incentives; training and professional development; policies; budget; course design and evaluation; and ethical issues.

Infrastructure, Resources, and Technology

Successful implementation of BL at an institution lies in the availability and accessibility of infrastructure, resources, and technology (Bowyer & Chambers, 2017; Hamzah et al., 2020; Tran, 2020). Thus, technological infrastructure has been highly emphasized in previous studies because it contributes to a successful BL environment (Chen & Yao, 2016; Futch et al., 2016; Mozelius & Hettiarachchi, 2017).

Support and Incentives

Several studies provide evidence for both teachers and students needing to access technical support, affective support, and/or academic support to be comfortable in BL environments (Al-Saleh, 2018; Bojović, 2017). The challenges students and teachers have when working with web-based technologies and resources are alleviated by technical support, which in turn facilitates technology-mediated teaching and learning. Hoang (2015) argues that when teachers lack technical support, they cannot design and deliver BL courses effectively. Moreover, Graham et al. (2013) agree that institutional incentives can increase opportunities for implementing BL successfully.

Training and Professional Development

It behooves universities to provide teachers with the necessary training so that they can deal with the multiplicity of problems that emerge in BL environments (Ivanova et al., 2020; Okaz, 2015). Moreover, training enables teachers to appreciate and make use of the benefits of both face-to-face learning and online learning (King, 2016). Teachers can overcome difficulties or challenges of BL environments with sufficient training in how to implement BL approaches in teaching (Koşar, 2016). Moreover, EFL teachers often lack the capacity to deal with digital technology problems, so they need professional development programs on pedagogical and technological skills and effective strategies of using BL (Ibrahim & Nat, 2019). Not surprisingly, Tran (2020) confirms that a lack of professional development opportunities led to EFL teachers displaying insufficient competence and low confidence when using BL.

Policies

In light of the institutional factors explained above, university policies are an umbrella factor that can contribute to successful implementation of BL. Graham et al. (2013) assert that a clear institutional policy direction contributes to the successful adoption of BL. Effective institutional policies around the implementation of BL motivate teachers to use this delivery mode (Ibrahim & Nat, 2019). Additionally, institutional advocacy among leaders and staff contributes to an effective implementation of BL (Tran, 2020). By contrast, the lack of clear institutional policies to support the implementation of BL has a negative impact on learning outcomes (Hoang, 2015).

Budget

Costs are a vital factor in adopting BL because institutions need to make investments to establish and maintain technological infrastructure (King, 2016). Additional costs lie in technology servicing, administration, class content, faculty, and student services. Thus, consideration of cost effectiveness plays a vital role in making the implementation of BL effective because technological infrastructure is the core of an BL environment (Mozelius & Hettiarachchi, 2017).

Course design and Evaluation

Appropriate blended course design involves finding the ideal "combination of online and classroom activities" (McGee, 2014, p. 33), which can increase learner engagement, reduce teaching time in classrooms, and promote the use of information technology. In addition, ongoing evaluation of BL courses are essential to inform thorough and multifaceted reflection on the results of the courses and propose solutions to improve the courses' quality (Bowyer & Chambers, 2017).

Ethical Issues

BL environments require educational institutions to follow ethical practices which guarantee the effective implementation of BL (Partridge et al., 2011). Those ethical issues are mainly around online learning, such as data quality, plagiarism, intellectual property rights, and privacy (Alebaikan, 2010).

Finally, the success of the implementation of BL may be impacted by sociocultural factors (Okaz, 2015). For example, how to develop policies connected with the use of BL and how to design technology-enhanced learning systems depend on cultural elements of specific regions (Pillay & James, 2014).

The three groups of factors, including: individual, institutional, and sociocultural ones play an important role in guiding the data collection for the current study. Thus, four main questions were addressed to achieve the research objectives:

1. How is BL being implemented in EFL education across ten Vietnamese universities?
2. How do Vietnamese EFL lecturers perceive their implementation of BL in English teaching?
3. What factors positively affect those lecturers' implementation of BL?
4. What factors negatively affect their implementation of BL?

The chapter now continues with a description of the research design and methodology, and then the major findings.

Research Design and Methodology

This chapter employed a qualitative research design which aims to explore a problem, develop an in-depth understanding of a central phenomenon, and build theories from data patterns (Creswell, 2012; Taylor et al., 2016). Moreover, using interpretivism, the study seeks an in-depth understanding of people's views, thoughts, beliefs, or perspectives to explore a phenomenon (O'Donoghue, 2007, 2018). The chapter focused on investigating the perspectives that the 20 Vietnamese lecturers held about the various factors affecting the implementation of BL in their EFL education, the outcomes of their implementing BL, and factors affecting the lecturers' success or failure.

Data for this research was collected through semi-structured interviews with 20 EFL lecturers across ten universities in Vietnam. These universities are located in two metropolitan cities, Hanoi and Ho Chi Minh city, where BL has been increasingly enacted to improve English language education. The Deans of the faculties/departments of English at these universities gave consent to support the research and allow the lecturers to participate. The interviews were conducted between February and April 2019. Each interview lasted between 30 and 45 minutes and consisted of open questions around four main issues related to the four research questions: (i) how BL was being implemented at their institutions; (ii) how the

EFL lecturers perceived the outcomes of implementing BL in their English teaching; (iii) what factors they identified as having a positive impact on the implementation of BL; and (iv) what factors they identified as having a negative impact on that implementation.

The participants were EFL lecturers aged 25 to 55 years old, and had experience in applying BL in English teaching. Fourteen out of the 20 participants had a master's degree; four had a doctorate; and two had bachelor's degrees in TESOL methodology, Education, and Applied Linguistics. Not only did they consent to the research, but they also expressed their strong willingness to participate in it, clearly very appreciative of the opportunity to provide their opinions on the matter.

Each of the interviews was electronically recorded, saved in audio files, and subsequently transcribed in the Vietnamese language. The interview transcripts were translated into English and saved in NVivo™ 12 files. The transcripts were coded using NVivo™ 12 for storage and categorizing. Two or three levels of codes emerged from the analysis, depending on specific data. NVivo™ 12 also allowed the data to be displayed in detail, as seen in the findings section. The data analysis was conducted in line with Miles et al. (2014)'s framework consisting of three stages: "data condensation, data display, and conclusion drawing and verification" (p.12).

The coding process was conducted at two or three levels to obtain the data for answering the four research questions. At two levels, selected excerpts from the 20 interviews were grouped into level-two child nodes of similar themes. Then, those level-two child nodes were grouped into two parent nodes, namely: (i) "stated types of BL," which revealed evidence of various categories of BL used in EFL education across ten Vietnamese universities; and (ii) "stated results of implementing BL," which provided information on how the EFL lecturers viewed the outcomes of their implementation of BL in their English teaching.

In addition, other selected excerpts from the 20 interviews were grouped into level-three child nodes of similar themes. Then, those level-three child nodes were grouped into level-two child nodes, namely: (i) "positive personal factors"; (ii) "positive institutional factors"; (iii) "negative personal factors"; and (iv) "negative institutional factors." Finally, those level-two child nodes were grouped into two level-one parent nodes, namely: (i) "stated positive factors"; and (ii) "stated negative factors." These parent nodes were predetermined codes which revealed the evidence of positive and negative factors affecting the lecturers' implementation of BL.

FINDINGS

The findings that emerged from the data analysis are presented below in terms of addressing the four main research questions regarding categories of BL implemented by the participant lecturers; outcomes of their implementation of BL; factors contributing to their success; and factors causing their failure in implementing BL.

How is BL Being Implemented in EFL Education Across Vietnamese Universities?

The first group of findings emerged from the analysis of the qualitative data extracted from the 20 EFL lecturers' responses when the lecturers were asked about how they were using a mix of face-to-face learning and online learning in their English teaching.

The results from the data analysis indicated that five types of BL were employed in EFL education across the ten universities. The most dominant type of BL, stated by 16 out of the 20, was a blend of face-to-face learning in classrooms as the main component and online learning as a supportive component. The second type of BL, stated by six of the participants, referred to the rotation between face-to-face learning in classrooms and online learning in computer laboratories. The third type of BL, stated by two participants, was a mixture of a face-to-face English course and a supportive online course. The last two types, each mentioned by only one participant, comprised the following: (i) a blend of online self-study before class, face-to-face practice of English skills in classrooms, and online exercises after class—a sort of flipped classroom; and (ii) a synchronous delivery of face-to-face learning and online learning in a computer laboratory.

How do Vietnamese EFL Lecturers Perceive their Implementation of BL in English Teaching?

The second group of findings emerged from the analysis of the qualitative data extracted from the 20 EFL lecturers' responses when the lecturers were asked about how they perceived the outcomes of their implementation of BL in English teaching.

Across the 20 participants, the most startling result was that three-quarters of the participants could find few positive things to say about their use of BL. Those 16 participants all said that they were failing to manage the use of BL in their teaching. They struggled to exploit web-based technologies and learning platforms to enhance students' learning outcomes. For example, Lecturer 2 confirmed that "learning English writing skills with the LMS system is not very effective." Moreover, Lecturer 6 was doubtful about this delivery mode when stating:

> As far as I can tell, that students can have better academic results is not due to blended learning... Students are more and more aware of their English learning ... Their parents have equipped them with the English language since high school... I don't dare to assert whether students' better academic results are due to blended learning or not because it depends on many other factors.

The participants also found it hard to check and monitor students' learning progress in BL environments. For example, some stated:

> Most of them [lecturers] worry that when teaching in such an LMS, they cannot control student learning as well as in a traditional environment. (Lecturer 3)

> I still have difficulty controlling whether students have done homework by themselves or have copied answers from friends. (Lecturer 18)

Most importantly, those participants complained of ever-increasing workload demands and more technical problems to deal with in their BL environments. When expressing their views about this drawback, they used similar expressions such as "have to work harder" (Lecturers 2 and 6); "workload increases" (Lecturer 3), and "a burden for me" (Lecturer 10).

By contrast, only four stated that they were managing their use of BL successfully. Two of those were a deputy dean and a senior EFL lecturer who were working at the same university where the introduction and implementation of BL were well planned and well prepared in advance. The deputy dean oversaw planning, designing, evaluating, and making changes to the implementation of BL in EFL teaching at her university as well as being an active EFL lecturer. She proudly stated, "I think our success is that our students can produce more work and speak more English in classrooms with teachers' guidance, control and support." Of the other two who were positive about their use of BL, one managed her university's combined center for foreign languages and technology. She proudly stated that she was provided with appropriate policies, sufficient technologies, training and support to ensure a successful implementation of BL in EFL education. She was also an EFL lecturer with practical experience of using BL in English classrooms. When asked about how she viewed the use of BL, she said, "It [the use of BL] is of course better. Students are more active and they are always looking for ways to access technology, so they will have more initiatives in their learning." The fourth satisfied lecturer was another dean of an English Department, who also had some authority and empowerment on how BL was implemented. He took advantage of expertise and experience of using educational technology to increase the quality of English learning in higher education. In brief, all four explained that their use of BL in English teaching was effective because it had helped to improve their students' learning results; they were also convinced that BL brought benefits for students, lecturers, and their institutions.

What Factors Positively Affect those Lecturers' Implementation of BL?

The third group of findings emerged from the analysis of the qualitative data extracted from the 20 EFL lecturers' responses when the lecturers were asked about what factors positively affected those lecturers' implementation of BL.

The four lecturers who were managing their use of BL successfully spoke to a range of personal factors and institutional factors that contributed to their success. The set of personal factors they referred to consisted of the following: (i) a well-developed understanding and experience of using BL in EFL education; (ii) effective teaching methods in BL environments; and (iii) a positive sense of professional agency. They agreed on a group of institutional factors as well: (i) clear and unified policies and procedures for implementing BL in EFL education; (ii) appropriate syllabi and textbooks; (iii) adequate infrastructure, technology, and resources; and (iv) sufficient support, incentives, and professional development. From the lecturers' perspectives, they could effectively manage their implementation of BL in EFL teaching when these personal and institutional factors were positive. As an evident example of positive personal factors, Lecturer 3 showed his understanding and experience of using BL in EFL education when stating:

with some English courses, I followed the PALM model (Plan, Activate, Learning activities, Management). For some other courses, I consulted the framework of University of Oregon, USA, which also includes warm-up activities, then receptive activities such as reading, listening, then the stage of production. It is a bit like the sequence of teaching an English lecture including pre-teaching, while-teaching, and post-teaching.

I have used many different tools on the LMS to interact and communicate with students. I can use a forum, video-conferencing, chat tools, even tools for collecting questionnaire feedback … lots of different tools.

Lecturer 3 also indicated that his university facilitated the use of BL. He said:

The university supports facilities and training sessions, encourages research such as writing newspapers, implementing scientific projects … The university encourages lecturers to apply blended learning. If anyone wants to use the LMS, they are free and comfortable to use it, so they don't have to fulfill their compensatory teaching hours.

Another participant, Lecturer 18, explained how her institution supported the implementation of BL in English teaching and learning. He stated:

IT staff are available and ready to assist us. Wi-Fi works well everywhere. We can have support and assistance in the cooperation with the Faculty of Informatics and other departments during the implementation of blended learning. This blended program has helped us increase our commitment, passion and enthusiasm in teaching because we can work together and share much with each other.

What Factors Negatively Affect their Implementation of BL?

The last group of findings emerged from the analysis of the qualitative data extracted from the 20 EFL lecturers' responses when the lecturers were asked about what factors negatively affected those lecturers' implementation of BL

This subsection addresses one of the more significant outcomes of the research, which also explains why the 16 lecturers' use of BL was ineffective. The participants identified a range of factors that contributed to their failure to manage the implementation, including a number of personal and

11 FACTORS AFFECTING EFL LECTURERS' IMPLEMENTATION OF BLENDED... 223

institutional factors as detailed in Table 11.1. Evaluating the table, one can see that the same factors are repeated across most of the participants

The three major personal factors reflected a sense of personal inadequacy. First, they had an insufficient understanding of what BL meant in practice. This was clearly expressed in what Lecturer 19 said, "I used to hear about the term blended learning, but I don't clearly understand this concept. I cannot explain what it exactly refers to." Second, they lacked any effective pedagogies for successfully implementing BL. For example, Lecturer 11 explained, "there are no documents regarding how to use blended learning, how to define it or specific steps to apply it in English lessons." Consequently, they assumed a low-level professional agency to enact any positive change in their practice. Some participants expressed their similar views when they made statements such as "online learning in the computer laboratory is a burden for me" (Lecturer 10); and "online lectures have been sketchily designed to meet the minimum requirements of our university's policies of implementing BL" (Lecturer 11). In addition, they also indicated four institutional factors, one of which was that they found policies for implementing BL in English teaching at their universities confusing and unhelpful. The institutions failed to provide them with necessary resources, adequate technological infrastructure and digital resources, and supportive syllabi and textbooks. They also received inadequate support and incentives from their institutions, and insufficient and irrelevant training to implement BL effectively. For example, Lecturer 4 complained that "the university has no policy to encourage lecturers...

Table 11.1 Underlying factors negatively affecting the EFL lecturers' implementation of BL

Underlying factors	Stated supportive findings	NVivo™ References
Personal factors	Insufficient understanding of BL	16
	Ineffective pedagogies of implementing BL	16
	Low professional agency	14
Institutional factors	Unclear policies for implementing BL	16
	Insufficient provision of technological infrastructure and resources	16
	Inappropriate course syllabi and textbooks	16
	Inadequate support and incentives from institutions	14
	Insufficient and irrelevant training	13

This university has problems with policies." In a similar vein with many participants who were dissatisfied with the lack of BL-related training, Lecturer 19 confessed that "my university does not have any training sessions on pedagogies with blended learning, so lecturers are flexible in using it, each will apply it in a different way." These obstacles led to the lecturers' dissatisfaction and demotivation in using BL, which in turn contributed to their failure in implementing BL effectively in their EFL teaching. Moreover, the payment for online teaching was considered a demotivating factor. Lecturer 4 explained, "whether lecturers don't use technology to save time or they try hard to invest their efforts in using technology in their teaching, their salary is still the same... the same price policy is not acceptable."

The findings of this study also revealed a group of contributory factors that were indirectly referred to, the sociocultural and economic factors, which mostly hindered the lecturers' implementation of BL. One of the most pervasive factors was the traditional Confucian teaching culture. For centuries, teachers and students in Vietnam have valued traditional, face-to-face teaching methods, where each had distinctive roles to uphold and play. Brought up in this tradition, many participants in this study spoke about the conflict between these classroom-based pedagogies and the implementation of BL. Lecturer 17 blamed her failure on Confucian teaching traditions when stating that "traditional teaching methods are deeply rooted in our minds, making us prefer teaching English to students in the outdated ways we were taught before." Even Lecturer 9 wondered, "So what is the difference?" when she tried to distinguish BL and traditional teaching methods. Most of the lecturers confessed that they tended to ignore and disregard BL, and gradually they could not maintain their interest, commitment, and time investment to implement this delivery mode in their teaching. The economic factors centered on Vietnam as a middle-income country with limited resources to feed its educational demands. Consequently, they said openly that their universities did not have sufficient financial and capital resources to provide them with the necessary technological infrastructure to support and maintain the implementation of BL. Lecturer 7 blamed this on Vietnam's economic context:

> because our country is still poor, it can't be compared to Australia where universities are well equipped with technological infrastructure ... the use of technology must be very smooth ... but if technical problems occur frequently, they will make us uncomfortable.

The sum of all the factors outlined in the subsection represent the barriers and drawbacks which hindered the implementation of BL among the majority of the participants.

DISCUSSION

The implementation of BL was considered an innovation to many Vietnamese EFL lecturers, although BL is not a novice concept worldwide. The findings revealed that the EFL lecturers implemented five various types of BL in their teaching, depending on many personal and institutional factors. The first four categories have been mentioned in detail in previous research (Horn & Staker, 2011), except the last type in which the lecturer conducted a blend of synchronous face-to-face learning and online learning in a computer laboratory. The most widely used category in EFL education was still a combination of face-to-face learning as a main component and online learning as a supportive one. This confirms that EFL teaching and learning in the Vietnamese universities were strongly influenced by traditional teaching methods and Confucian traditions. This finding supports what has been found in previous research (Hoang, 2015; Tran, 2020). Generally, there was not a fixed category of BL applied at ten universities, and there were no clear regulations on this issue.

Although BL was recognized to provide many educational benefits in EFL education, not all EFL lecturers implemented BL as successfully as expected. In revealing the lecturers' views on how they managed the implementation of BL in their English teaching, only a quarter of them openly said that they were successful in doing so. Three-quarters frankly admitted that they were not managing BL well. The success or failure of those lecturers depended largely on the impact of personal and institutional factors and also on whether these two factors were positively or negatively aligned. In addition, in the context of these universities, the sociocultural and economic factors hindered the effectiveness of the implementation of BL.

On the other hand, the success of a small number of the EFL lecturers was related to their leadership roles and empowerment with their adoption of BL, their decision-making roles with BL courses, and the institutional support of technologies and policies. Significant among the four successful participants was that they had a decision-making position in the workplace, and they were empowered to control policies and practices in their teaching environment. Such influence ensures that the relevant personal and institutional factors were positive. The three-fourths of the participants were unable to manage their implementation of BL effectively due to the negative impact of personal and institutional factors. Those who admitted to being unsuccessful in their practices of BL revealed a sense of helplessness. They lacked personal resources to implement BL effectively, and as they sensed failure, their sense of agency declined, and that helplessness multiplied in a vicious, downward spiral. In addition, those lecturers blamed their failure on the obstructive impact from institutional factors, including institutional policies; syllabi and textbooks; technological infrastructure; professional development, support, and incentives, which did not facilitate the lecturers' implementation of BL in their teaching. These findings implied that successful implementation of BL in Vietnamese EFL higher education required improvements in both personal and institutional factors. Moreover, consistent with the existing literature (Hoang, 2015; Tran, 2020), the sociocultural factors were viewed as obstacles which hindered the quality of implementing BL. Although these factors may not be as prominent as the first two, the implementation of BL in Vietnamese EFL education would be better if the negative impact of those sociocultural and economic factors was reduced.

From the findings emerging from the current study, a conceptual framework has been refined for Vietnamese EFL lecturers to manage their implementation of BL effectively in English teaching (see Fig. 11.1 below). This framework consisted of two groups of overt, predominant factors and a group of contextual, contributory factors. The first group were personal ones, with three sub-components: Vietnamese EFL lecturers' perspectives of BL; their BL-based pedagogies; and their sense of professional agency in implementing BL. The second group of major factors were institutional ones. Here, there were four sub-components: policies; course syllabi and textbooks; technological infrastructure; and professional development, support and incentives. The group of contributory factors were sociocultural and economic ones: the first principally involved Confucian teaching traditions, while the second related to Vietnam's economic situation as a middle-income country. This conceptual framework suggests that the implementation of blended learning is more likely to be successful when all its three components are positive. The findings from this study also suggest that the personal and institutional factors are closely related and can be remedied by effective leadership to meet lecturers'

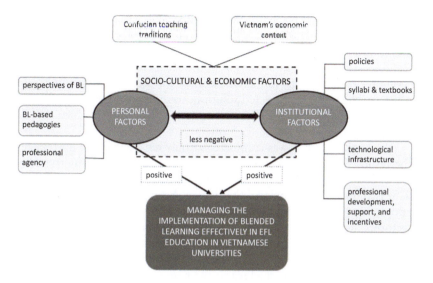

Fig. 11.1 A conceptual framework for the Vietnamese university lecturers to manage their implementation of blended learning in EFL education

needs. When the two main sets of factors are positively aligned, BL is likely to be effective; when the two main factors are negatively aligned, lecturers will likely fail to manage their implementation of BL effectively. Finally, dealing with the vestiges of Confucian teaching practices is also possible. Economic matters may be more difficult to address, but the experience of the more effective lecturers still suggests that prudent management and leadership can manipulate capital resources to the advantage of teaching effectively with BL. Thus, reducing the negative impact of the contributory factors is crucial to make the conceptual framework work well.

Conclusion

The chapter reveals the implementation of BL in Vietnamese EFL higher education was confusing and ineffective. Of the five types of BL stated by the 20 lecturers, the most dominant one was a mix of face-to-face learning as the main component and online learning as a supportive one.

Most of the lecturers admitted that they were not able to manage their implementation of BL successfully in their teaching practice. Their success or failure was closely connected with three underlying sets of factors.

228   T. N. LE

Among those three sets, personal and institutional factors contributed to an effective implementation of BL when both of them were positive. On the contrary, when either of those two sets of factors was negative, the lecturers' success was limited. The third set including sociocultural and economic factors mostly hindered the quality of lecturers' implementation of BL, so the lecturers expected solutions to reduce the negative impact of this contributory set of factors on their teaching practice in BL environments.

Although the study was conducted at only ten Vietnamese universities, the results sketch a general picture of the process of innovating the delivery of English teaching and learning by applying BL at those institutions. This is at least a positive signal that BL has been gradually recognized and adopted in Vietnamese EFL higher education. In reality, Vietnamese EFL lecturers do not easily accept a technology-enhanced delivery mode because they have experienced the strong influence of long-standing traditional methods along with other barriers. Thus, the lecturers' acceptance of BL must come from changes in their mindsets, leading to follow-up changes in their actions. In the present study, there was evidence of this positive change evident in the lecturers' perceptions of benefits of BL as well as motivating and obstructive factors that affected their implementation of BL. These changed perceptions can lead to an increased acceptance and adoption of this technology-enhanced delivery mode in Vietnamese tertiary contexts in the future.

IMPLICATIONS

This study offers some implications to relevant stakeholders including the Vietnam's Ministry of Education and Training, the universities, the faculties/departments of English language, and the EFL lecturers with the aim at increasing the quality of implementing BL in their EFL higher education.

The Vietnam's Ministry of Education and Training is expected to release clear policies for implementing BL in higher education, especially in EFL education. The uniformity across the country is important, but flexibility for different universities to adapt policies to their specific characteristics and conditions is also essential. National government policy makers need to consider the influence of all three groups of factors in the design and introduction of BL-related policies.

The universities need to keep the personal and institutional factors positive to guarantee an effective implementation of BL. There should be explicit policies, detailed syllabi, and clear procedures for implementing BL to support EFL lecturers to apply this delivery mode. More importantly, there should be adequate and appropriate training so that all academic staff feel competent, empowered, and confident to apply BL. Universities and faculties/departments of English language cannot rely on lecturers developing their skills by osmosis; instead, carefully tailored learning opportunities to meet their lecturers' demands is essential.

Economic factors will impact universities' ability to provide high quality technological infrastructure, online resources, textbook-based websites, and computer laboratories. The implementation of BL cannot occur if universities do not provide good Internet connection, technology, and facilities. Also, regular updates and maintenance of equipment and facilities are required to facilitate the use of BL.

The current design of English course syllabi in many Vietnamese universities has been significantly influenced by traditional teaching methods, which have not facilitated and supported the EFL lecturers in implementing BL. The problems also come from the reliance on textbooks, full face-to-face teaching hours, inappropriate assessments, and unrealistic workloads that still overemphasize classroom-based, face-to-face teaching. Thus, there is also a need for a careful review of long-standing syllabus documents, teaching methods, and traditional assessment practices that were conceived in earlier times but are outdated or inappropriate. Accordingly, online elements should be supplemented and attached to those in order to facilitate the successful use of BL.

Necessary changes in payments can motivate EFL lecturers to implement BL in their teaching. Because online teaching is not officially recognized and remunerated in many Vietnamese universities, EFL lecturers often lose interest and motivation. Again, institutional policies need to be reworked to ensure fair wages for both face-to-face and online teaching. Nevertheless, it will put increasing demands on limited financial resources for institutions

The EFL lecturers themselves are required to maintain their personal factors positive. They should continue to improve their understanding of BL, and, especially, to become aware of, and apply effective BL-based pedagogies. To increase personal competence and confidence as well as a sense of personal agency, the lecturers can broaden their understanding through reading professional texts and participating in further training courses. Moreover, to update and improve their pedagogies in BL environments, the EFL lecturers can be guided toward doing research to investigate and improve their teaching practices and students' learning outcomes. Writing journal articles to publish findings or making presentations at international conferences are fruitful ways to enhance the lecturers' experience of using BL. In addition, the lecturers should make the most use of the existing infrastructure and technology to implement BL flexibly.

REFERENCES

Albiladi, W. S., & Alshareef, K. K. (2019). Blended learning in English teaching and learning: A review of the current literature. *Journal of Language Teaching and Research, 10*(2), 232–238. https://doi.org/10.17507/jltr.1002.03

Alebaikan, R. A. (2010). *Perceptions of blended learning in Saudi universities.* [Doctoral dissertation, University of Exeter]. Research Repository. https://ore.exeter.ac.uk/repository/bitstream/handle/10036/117486/AlebaikanR.pdf?sequence=2

Al-Saleh, R. S. S. (2018). EFL teacher's attitudes towards blended learning in Tabuk, Saudi Arabia. *International Journal of Information Research and Review, 5*(1), 5065–5071. https://www.ijirr.com/sites/default/files/issues-pdf/2605.pdf

Alsowayegh, N., Bardesi, H., Garba, I., & Sipra, M. (2019, July 15). Engaging students through blended learning activities to augment listening and speaking. *Arab World. English Journal, 5,* 267–288. https://doi.org/10.24093/awej/call5.18

Bojović, M. D. (2017). Blended learning as a foreign language learning environment. *Teme -Časopis za Društvene Nauke, 41*(4), 1017–1036. https://doi.org/10.22190/TEME1704017B

Bouilheres, F., Le, L. T. V. H., McDonald, S., Nkhoma, C., & Jandug-Montera, L. (2020). Defining student learning experience through blended learning. *Education and Information Technologies, 25*(4), 3049–3069. https://doi.org/10.1007/s10639-020-10100-y

Bowyer, J., & Chambers, L. (2017). Evaluating blended learning: Bringing the elements together. *Research Matters: A Cambridge Assessment Publication, 23,* 17–26. https://www.cambridgeassessment.org.uk/Images/375446-evaluating-blended-learning-bringing-the-elements-together.pdf

Bui, T. H. (2022). *EFL undergraduate students' perspectives and experiences of the flipped classroom at a Vietnamese university.* [Doctoral Dissertation, Edith Cowan University]. Research Online. https://ro.ecu.edu.au/theses/2512

Chen, W. S., & Yao, A. Y. T. (2016). An empirical evaluation of critical factors influencing learner satisfaction in blended learning: A pilot study. *Universal Journal of Educational Research, 4*(7), 1667–1671. https://doi.org/10.13189/ujer.2016.040719

Copriady, J. (2015) Self-motivation as a mediator for teachers' readiness in applying ICT in teaching and learning. *Procedia-Social and Behavioral Sciences, 176*, 699–708. https://doi.org/10.1016/j.sbspro.2015.01.529

Creswell, J. W. (2012). *Educational research: Planning, conducting, and evaluating quantitative and qualitative research* (4th ed.). Pearson Education.

Eshreteh, M. K. M., & Siaj, A. H. (2017). Attitudes of English-major students and teachers towards using blended learning in the English department at Hebron University. *International Journal of Research in English Education, 2*(4), 51–65. http://ijreeonline.com/article-1-66-en.html

Futch, L. S., deNoyelles, A., Thompson, K., & Howard, W. (2016). "Comfort" as a critical success factor in blended learning courses. *Online Learning, 20*(3), 140–158. https://files.eric.ed.gov/fulltext/EJ1113303.pdf

Garner, R., & Rouse, E. (2016). Social presence—connecting pre-service teachers as learners using a blended learning model. *Student Success, 7*(1), 25–36. https://doi.org/10.5204/ssj.v7i1.299

Graham, C. R., Woodfield, W., & Harrison, J. B. (2013). A framework for institutional adoption and implementation of blended learning in higher education. *The Internet and Higher Education, 18*, 4–14. https://doi.org/10.1016/j.iheduc.2012.09.003

Hamzah, F., Phong, S. Y., Sharifudin, M. A. S., Zain, Z. M., & Rahim, M. (2020). Exploring students' readiness on English language blended learning. *Asian Journal of University. Education, 16*(4), 161–170. https://doi.org/10.24191/ajue.v16i4.11948

Hayati, S., Armansah, Y., & Ismail, S. (2021). Teachers experiences on blended learning: a case study of a group of secondary school teachers in Malaysia and Indonesia. *Jurnal Kependidikan: Jurnal Hasil Penelitian dan Kajian Kepustakaan di Bidang Pendidikan, Pengajaran dan Pembelajaran, 7*(4), 767–777. https://doi.org/10.33394/jk.v7i4.4102

Hoang, N. T. (2015). *EFL teachers' perceptions and experiences of blended learning in a Vietnamese university.* [Doctoral Dissertation, Queensland University of Technology] QUT ePrints, https://eprints.qut.edu.au/83945/1/Ngoc%20Tue_Hoang_Thesis.pdf

Horn, M. B., & Staker, H. (2011). *The rise of K-12 blended learning.* Innosight Institute. https://www.christenseninstitute.org/wp content/uploads/2013/01/The-rise-of-K-12-blended-learning.pdf

Hosseinpour, N., Biria, R., & Rezvani, E. (2019). Promoting academic writing proficiency of Iranian EFL learners through blended learning. *Turkish Online Journal of. Distance Education, 20*(4), 99–116. https://doi.org/10.17718/tojde.640525

Ibrahim, M. M., & Nat, M. (2019). Blended learning motivation model for instructors in higher education institutions. *International Journal of Educational Technology in Higher Education, 16*(1), 1–21. https://doi.org/10.1186/s41239-019-0145-2

232   T. N. LE

Ivanova, E., Polyakova, M., & Abakumova, M. (2020). Implementing a blended learning approach to foreign language teaching at SPbPU. In *IOP Conference Series: Materials Science and Engineering* (pp. 1–12). IOP Publishing. https://doi.org/10.1088/1757-899x/940/1/012138

King, A. (2016). *Blended language learning: Part of the Cambridge Papers in ELT series*. Cambridge University Press. https://www.cambridge.org/us/files/2115/7488/8334/CambridgePapersinELT_BlendedLearning_2016_ONLINE.pdf

Koehler, M. J., & Mishra, P. (2009). What is technological pedagogical content knowledge? *Contemporary Issues in Technology and Teacher Education, 9*(1), 60–70. https://citejournal.org/wp-content/uploads/2016/04/v9i1general1.pdf

Koşar, G. (2016). A study of EFL instructors' perceptions of blended learning. *Procedia-Social and Behavioral Sciences, 232*, 736–744. https://doi.org/10.1016/j.sbspro.2016.10.100

Le, Q. A. (2017). The impact of globalisation on the reform of higher education in Vietnam. *International Journal of Business and Economic Affairs, 1*(1), 29–35. https://doi.org/10.24088/ijbea-2016-11005

McGee, P. (2014). Blended course design: where's the pedagogy? *International Journal of Mobile and Blended Learning, 6*(1), 33–55. https://doi.org/10.4018/ijmbl.2014010103

Miles, M. B., Huberman, A. M., & Saldaña, J. (2014). *Qualitative data analysis: A methods sourcebook*. Sage.

Mishra, P., & Koehler, M. J. (2006). Technological pedagogical content knowledge: A framework for teacher knowledge. *Teachers College Record, 108*(6), 1017–1054. http://one2oneheights.pbworks.com/f/MISHRA_PUNYA.pdf

Mozelius, P., & Hettiarachchi, E. (2017). Critical factors for implementing blended learning in higher education. *International Journal of Information and Communication Technologies in Education, 6*(2), 37–51. https://doi.org/10.1515/ijicte-2017-0001

Mulyono, H., Ismayama, D., Liestyana, A. R., & Komara, C. (2021). EFL teachers' perceptions of Indonesian blended learning course across gender and teaching levels. *Teaching English with Technology, 21*(1), 60–74. https://files.eric.ed.gov/fulltext/EJ1283385.pdf

Musdalifah, I., Agusriandi, S., & Elihami. (2021, February). *Blended learning method to optimize English language learning in non-English language education departments at Muhammadiyah University of Enrekang* [Paper Presentation]. International Virtual Conference on Science, Technology and Educational Practices, Gorontalo, Indonesia. https://papers.euroasiaconference.com/index.php/eac/article/view/209/226

Ngo, V. G. (2016). *Towards an effective integration of ICT in an EFL setting in a Vietnamese higher education context.* [Doctoral Dissertation, University of

Adelaide]. DSpace. https://digital.library.adelaide.edu.au/dspace/handle/2440/103499

Nguyen, G. H. (2017). *Teachers' roles in EFL blended language learning at tertiary level in Vietnam: Their views, their practice* [Doctoral Dissertation, University of Canberra]. Research System. https://researchsystem.canberra.edu.au/ws/portalfiles/portal/33682307/file

Nguyen, T. H. (2019). *Oral corrective feedback in a blended learning environment: Challenges and contradictions faced by teachers in a Vietnamese university* [Doctoral Dissertation, The University of Waikato]. Research Commons. https://hdl.handle.net/10289/13110

Norberg, A., Dziuban, C. D., & Moskal, P. D. (2011). A time-based blended learning model. *On the Horizon, 19*(3), 207–216. https://doi.org/10.1108/10748121111163913

Nuri, H. S. M., & Bostanci, H. B. (2021). Blended learning to improve university students' language skills in the Iraqi context. *Turkish Journal of Computer and Mathematics Education, 12*(2), 246–255. https://turcomat.org/index.php/turkbilmat/article/view/708/506

O'Donoghue, T. (2007). *Planning your qualitative research project: An introduction to interpretivist research in education.* Routledge.

O'Donoghue, T. (2018). *Planning your qualitative research thesis and project: An introduction to interpretivist research in education and the social sciences* (2nd ed.). Routledge.

Okaz, A. A. (2015). Integrating blended learning in higher education. *Procedia-Social and Behavioral Sciences, 186,* 600–603. https://doi.org/10.1016/j.sbspro.2015.04.086

Partridge, H., Ponting, D., & McCay, M. (2011). *Good practice report: Blended learning.* Australian Learning and Teaching Council. https://eprints.qut.edu.au/216216/1/47566.pdf

Pillay, S., & James, R. (2014). The pains and gains of blended learning—social constructivist perspectives. *Education + Training, 56*(4), 254–270. https://doi.org/10.1108/ET-11-2012-0118

Radia, B. (2019). Approaching a reading course via Moodle-based blended learning: EFL learners' insights. *Modern Journal of Language Teaching Methods, 9*(11), 1–12. https://doi.org/10.26655/mjltm.2019.11.1

Rahim, M. N. (2019). The use of blended learning approach in EFL education. *International Journal of Engineering and Advanced Technology, 8*(5), 1165–1168. https://doi.org/10.35940/ijeat.E1163.0585C19

Riel, J., Lawless, K. A., & Brown, S. W. (2016). Listening to the teachers: Using weekly online teacher logs for ROPD to identify teachers' persistent challenges when implementing a blended learning curriculum. *Journal of Online Learning Research, 2*(2), 169–200. https://ssrn.com/abstract=2820338

Sheerah, H. A. H. (2020). Using blended learning to support the teaching of English as a Foreign Language. *Arab World. English Journal Special Issue on CALL, 6*, 191–211. https://doi.org/10.24093/awej/call6.13

Sulaiman, N. A. (2018). Implementing blended learning and flipped learning models in the university classroom: A case study. *Teaching English with Technology, 18*(4), 34–47. https://files.eric.ed.gov/fulltext/EJ1195820.pdf

Tawil, H. (2018). The blended learning approach and its application in language teaching. *International Journal of Language and Linguistics, 5*(4), 47–58. https://doi.org/10.30845/ijll.v5n4p6

Taylor, S. J., Bogdan, R., & DeVault, M. (2016). *Introduction to qualitative research methods: A guidebook and resource* (4th ed.). John Wiley & Sons.

Tran, L. T. H. (2020). *Factors affecting the teaching and learning of English in a blended learning environment in a Vietnamese university* [Doctoral Dissertation, The University of Waikato]. Research Commons. https://hdl.handle.net/10289/14050

Vymetalkova, D., & Milkova, E. (2019). Experimental verification of effectiveness of English language teaching using MyEnglishLab. *Sustainability, 11*(5), 1–15. https://doi.org/10.3390/su11051357

Wang, N., Chen, J., Tai, M., & Zhang, J. (2019). Blended learning for Chinese university EFL learners: learning environment and learner perceptions. *Computer Assisted Language Learning, 34*(3), 297–323. https://doi.org/10.1080/09588221.2019.1607881

Wright, B. M. (2017). Blended learning: Student perception of face-to-face and online EFL lessons. *Indonesian Journal of. Applied Linguistics, 7*(1), 64–71. https://doi.org/10.17509/ijal.v7i1.6859

Wu, J., & Liu, W. (2013). An empirical investigation of the critical factors affecting students' satisfaction in EFL blended learning. *Journal of Language Teaching & Research, 4*(1), 176–185. https://doi.org/10.4304/jltr.4.1.176-185

Zaim, M., & Mudra, H. (2019). Blended English language learning as a course in an Indonesian context: An exploration toward EFL learners' perceptions. In *Proceedings of the 2019 8th International Conference on Educational and Information Technology* (pp. 209–216). ICEIT. https://doi.org/10.1145/3318396.3318435

Zhang, D., & Zou, Y. (2020). Fostering multiliteracies through blended EFL learning. *International Journal of Linguistics, Literature and Translation, 3*(2), 40–48. https://doi.org/10.32996/ijllt.2020.3.2.5

CHAPTER 12

Innovation in Language Teaching in Vietnam and Cambodia: Key Themes

Linh Phung, Hayo Reinders, and Vu Phi Ho Pham

Innovation in the field of language teaching (Reinders, Coombe, et al., 2019a; Reinders, Ryan, & Nakamura, 2019b) is a response to the ever-changing dynamics and demands of our globalized world. This book has showcased some innovative projects that institutions and educators in Vietnam and Cambodia have implemented in their language teaching contexts. These innovations have been guided by evolving teaching methodologies in the field and influenced by disruptive events and technological advancements. This concluding chapter synthesizes the key themes that have emerged throughout this book and emphasizes the crucial role of teacher empowerment and support in ensuring the success of these innovations.

L. Phung (✉)
Eduling International, Pittsburgh, PA, USA

H. Reinders
Faculty of Liberal Arts, King Mongkut's University of Technology Thonburi, Bangkok, Thailand

V. P. H. Pham
Faculty of Foreign Languages, Van Lang University, Ho Chi Minh City, Vietnam

© The Author(s), under exclusive license to Springer Nature Switzerland AG 2024
L. Phung et al. (eds.), *Innovation in Language Learning and Teaching*, New Language Learning and Teaching Environments,
https://doi.org/10.1007/978-3-031-46080-7_12

235

Implementing Contemporary Teaching Methodologies

Innovation in language teaching is generally driven by a quest for effective methodologies to bring about better learning outcomes and meet changing needs (Carless, 2012). This quest is clearly demonstrated by the chapters in this book in response to the evolution of pedagogical methodologies and concepts discussed in the field. There is a general trend to move away from traditional, teacher-centered approaches to embrace learner-centric ones under the umbrella of communicative language teaching (CLT). CLT prioritizes communication over knowledge of the target language as a structure, emphasizing the practical use of language in authentic contexts (Nunan, 1989; Savignon, 1997; Wilkins, 1976). T. L. Nguyen's chapter on Communicative Pronunciation Teaching (CPT) illustrates this very attempt to develop and implement communicative activities in the classroom, which was found to heighten student awareness of pronunciation issues and increase their engagement. Students' positive feedback and requests for more similar activities underscore the necessity of fulfilling the principles of CLT in the classroom through a systematic application of CLT materials, tasks, and teaching techniques, signaling a departure from traditional teaching methods that rely on rule presentations and mechanical exercises devoid of authentic communication.

Moreover, English Medium Instruction (EMI) (e.g. Macaro et al., 2018) was a reason for an innovation reported by T. N. Nguyen and Dinh, where the entire English curriculum was revamped to better prepare students for their business Bachelor programs. Through systematic and thorough environment and needs analyses, the authors highlight the demand for more robust English courses that better prepare students for the EMI courses in the later phase of their study. Similarly, in the K-12 setting, Content and Language Integrated Learning (CLIL) was cited as a guiding pedagogy for Louw and Reaksmey's innovation in establishing a K-12 school in Siem Reap, Cambodia. The integration of language and content engages students in meaning-focused activities where they treat language as a tool, which is an important distinction between CLT and traditional approaches. In addition, students are able to apply their language skills in real-world contexts, ensuring a more holistic and authentic learning experience.

Multilingualism and inclusive pedagogies have also emerged as powerful frameworks for language teaching innovation. Embracing linguistic diversity and fostering multilingual education acknowledges the rich tapestry of languages spoken in Vietnam and Cambodia and reflects the "multilingual turn" in language education worldwide (Meier, 2016). By acknowledging and leveraging students' mother tongues, educators can create a linguistically and culturally responsive pedagogy that respects the diverse backgrounds of their learners (Gay, 2010; Hollie, 2018). Specifically, Louw and Reaksmey's innovation involves the establishment of a trilingual K-12 program in Cambodia in Khmer, English, and Chinese. In a different vein, Do et al.'s chapter reports on a materials development innovation that explicitly adopted a culturally and linguistically responsive approach. The materials developed in the project include texts and illustrations that represent the students' cultural values and practices to facilitate their development of Vietnamese as a second language. Overall, these innovations align with contemporary demands for practical language skills and acknowledgment of the cultural and linguistic assets that multilingual students bring to the classroom. They aim to prepare students for integration into the wider society as well as communication and employment across borders in an interconnected world.

The Effects of Disruptive Events

Innovation rarely occurs in a vacuum; it often springs from disruptive events and changing geopolitical landscapes. The Covid-19 pandemic served as an unprecedented catalyst for innovation in education worldwide, including in Vietnam and Cambodia (Reimers & Opertti, 2021). The sudden shift to remote and online learning compelled educators to explore innovative digital tools and adapt their teaching methods. As reported in Vu's study, amid the Covid-19 outbreak, English language teachers in Vietnam were "forced" by the circumstances to conduct online classes. Embracing various online technologies, Vu's innovation focused on promoting group work and student engagement in a graduate-level course by following a thoughtful design framework for online group collaboration. Students expressed positive attitudes toward online group collaboration and embraced its benefits to promote communication, collaboration, critical thinking, and academic content comprehension.

Similarly, seizing the increased acceptance of online learning and rising opportunities to collaborate with virtual educators and English Language Fellows from the U.S. Department of State due to the pandemic, Ng and Mannion reported on a successful creation of a new MA in English program in Sihanoukville, Cambodia. The chapter illustrates how innovation can arise through the fortuitous confluence of planned and unplanned factors as a result of globally disruptive events like the Covid-19 pandemic.

Also in the context of the pandemic, Le reports increased openness to a new way of organizing instruction and offering blended learning at Vietnamese universities. However, her chapter clearly demonstrates that lasting change is only possible if other critical factors affecting the implementation of an innovation are aligned. These factors include personal factors (e.g. teachers' awareness and willingness to implement BL), institutional factors (e.g. support given to teachers to adopt a new instructional approach), and sociocultural factors (e.g. the influence of Confucianism on how teachers and students position themselves in the classroom). In other words, successful innovation depends not only on capitalizing on enabling factors, but also on overcoming barriers that are teacher related, system-related, and school related.

Other geopolitical developments, such as the rise of China's influence in Cambodia has had a profound impact on language teaching in the country. As reported by Louw and Reaksmey, the demand for Chinese language proficiency has surged, prompting the development of a trilingual school that offers Chinese alongside English and Khmer, the students' native language. This expansion demonstrates how geopolitical shifts can shape language education priorities and stimulate innovative approaches to meet evolving demands. Moreover, owing to the economic relations between Japan and Vietnam, Japanese has emerged as the second most widely studied foreign language in Vietnam after English (Statistica, 2023), which underscores the significance of the establishment of a Bachelor of Japanese Language program at RMIT University in Vietnam as reported in Yamato's chapter.

In addition, emerging and disruptive technologies, such as mobile learning, artificial intelligence, and virtual reality, have begun to permeate language teaching (Pikhart, 2020; Parmaxi, 2020; Zou et al., 2023). These technologies hold the promise of creating engaging learning experiences and promoting language acquisition. With the undeniable prominence of such learning apps as Duolingo and Memrise, teachers and students in Vietnam report frequent use of these apps and acknowledge their potential impact on student engagement and language learning outcomes, as reported by Tran et al.

Overall, the chapters affirm that innovation in language teaching is not only a response to disruptive events and geopolitical changes but also an embracement of cutting-edge technologies to advance education in Vietnam, Cambodia, and beyond.

Assessing the Impact and Involving Stakeholders

Innovation is a multifaceted and dynamic process, one that requires ongoing assessment and continuous improvement (Fullan, 2001). A fundamental aspect of this process is the collection of feedback from key stakeholders representing a range of perspectives, including students, educators, and school administrators. It is encouraging to note that, throughout the chapters in this book, a data-driven approach to evaluating innovation is consistently employed. Various instruments, including course assessments, questionnaires, and in-depth interviews, have been used to evaluate the impact and effectiveness of the innovation detailed in each chapter.

Of particular significance is the prominence given to student feedback across the chapters, highlighting a commitment to improving student learning outcomes and placing students at the center of educational innovations. Encouragingly, many chapters, such as those authored by Yamato, T. L. Nguyen, N. Nguyen, Vu, and Tran et al., prioritize students' invaluable feedback and incorporate insights gained from this feedback in future innovations. In tandem with the data gathered from students is feedback from educators who are at the forefront of implementing these innovations. Their perspectives, experiences, and feedback are essential components in the evaluation process. Chapters authored by Le, Tran et al., T. L. Nguyen, Do et al., and T. N. Nguyen and Dinh collect and analyze the input of these educators, generating lessons that can sustain and improve these innovative practices as well as insights that are helpful for other contexts.

Also important are school administrators, who serve as the custodians of essential resources, coordinators of efforts, and providers of professional training opportunities necessary for the success of educational innovations. Louw and Reaksmey's chapter, for instance, analyzes rich data drawn from interviews with department heads in English, Khmer, and Chinese, illuminating their perspectives, successes, and challenges in the execution of the school vision and goals. Furthermore, it is noteworthy that other stakeholders, such as industry partners, have been engaged and consulted. The collaborative efforts with these external stakeholders are exemplified in the curriculum project detailed by Yamato, signifying the multifaceted nature of innovation that extends beyond the immediate environment of the classroom and into the broader socioeconomic context where graduates will be working.

In sum, the chapters collectively demonstrate the pivotal role of stakeholder engagement, feedback, and collaboration in the innovation process. This multifaceted approach not only ensures that innovations align with the diverse needs and perspectives of those who have a stake in the innovation but also facilitates continuous improvement and adaptation.

EMPOWERING AND SUPPORTING TEACHERS

At the heart of successful innovation in language teaching are empowered and supported teachers (Wedell & Grassick, 2020). No matter how advanced the methodologies or technologies, it is teachers who bridge the gap between the innovation as a mandate from the ministry of education, school leaders, department chairs in a top-down approach and innovation as a process happening in the classroom. More often than not, educational reforms starting from the top fail to lead to actual changes in teacher attitudes and practices as well as student outcomes because there is insufficient training and support for teachers.

This case is illustrated clearly in Le's chapter regarding blended learning, which concludes that its implementation in Vietnamese EFL higher education was confusing and ineffective as most lecturers in her study admitted that they were not able to manage its use successfully in their teaching practice. This was due to the lack of clarity in what the approach meant in their context, the heavier workload involved, and the comfort of continuing traditional teaching arrangements. Although there was evidence of increased recognition of the benefits of blended learning in providing more language learning opportunities to students beyond the classroom, the lack of clarity and support affected its implementation.

Similarly, Do et al.'s chapter acknowledges the need to train teachers in teaching Vietnamese as a second language to effect changes in their teaching practices. In addition, materials development is only the starting point in implementing linguistically and culturally inclusive pedagogical practices. T. L. Nguyen's chapter illustrates the effectiveness of offering intensive training to teachers to implement Communicative Pronunciation Teaching in the classroom. Adequate training seems to be the key to empowerment and effective implementation because only then do teachers feel they have the knowledge and the tools to innovate and bring about change.

CONCLUSION

In conclusion, this exploration of innovative language teaching practices in Vietnam and Cambodia underscores a dynamic response to global shifts. The chapters reveal a commitment to contemporary teaching methodologies, notably a move toward learner-centric approaches under Communicative Language Teaching (CLT). This departure from traditional methods emphasizes the systematic application of CLT principles, materials, and teaching techniques, signaling a transformative shift in language education. Disruptive events, particularly the Covid-19 pandemic, acted as catalysts, compelling educators to embrace digital tools and new approaches to learning. Geopolitical and economic changes, such as China's growing influence and the Japanese labor market, have also shaped language education priorities.

The assessment of innovation impact by stakeholders emerges as significant. Incorporating student feedback, teacher perspectives, and external stakeholder input ensures a comprehensive evaluation process, fostering continuous improvement and alignment with diverse needs. At the core of successful innovation is the empowerment and support of teachers. The chapters emphasize that effective implementation relies on adequately trained and supported educators, highlighting the key role teachers play in bridging the gap between top-down mandates and transformative processes in the classroom. These insights extend beyond regional borders, offering valuable lessons for educators globally in navigating and leading innovation in language education.

REFERENCES

Carless, D. (2012). Innovation in language teaching and learning. In *The encyclopedia of applied linguistics.* https://doi.org/10.1002/9781405198431.wbeal0540

Fullan, M. (2001). *The new meaning of educational change.* Teachers College Press.

Gay, G. (2010). *Culturally responsive teaching: Theory, research, and practice.* Teachers College Press.

Hollie, S. (2018). *Culturally and linguistically responsive teaching and learning: Classroom practices for student success* (2nd ed.). Shell Education.

Macaro, E., Curle, S., Pun, J., An, J., & Dearden, J. (2018). A systematic review of English medium instruction in higher education. *Language Teaching, 51*(1), 36–76.

Meier, G. S. (2016). The multilingual turn as a critical movement in education: Assumptions, challenges and a need for reflection. *Applied Linguistics Review, 8*(1), 131–161. https://doi.org/10.1515/applirev-2016-2010

Nunan, D. (1989). *Designing tasks for the communicative classroom.* Cambridge University Press.

Parmaxi, A. (2020). Virtual reality in language learning: A systematic review and implications for research and practice. *Interactive Learning Environments, 31*(1), 172–184. https://doi.org/10.1080/10494820.2020.1765392

Pikhart, M. (2020). Intelligent information processing for language education: The use of artificial intelligence in language learning apps. *Procedia Computer Science, 176,* 1412–1419.

Reimers, F., & Opertti, R. (Eds.). (2021). *Learning to build back better futures for education: Lessons from educational innovation during the Covid-19 pandemic.* UNESCO: International Bureau of Education.

Reinders, H., Coombe, C., Littlejohn, A., & Tafazoli, D. (Eds.). (2019a). *Innovation in language learning and teaching: The case of Middle East and North Africa.* Palgrave Macmillan.

Reinders, H., Ryan, S., & Nakamura, S. (Eds.). (2019b). *Innovation in language teaching and learning: The case of Japan.* Palgrave Macmillan.

Savignon, S. J. (1997). *Communicative competence: Theory and classroom practice.* Addison-Wesley Publishing Company.

Statistica Research Department. (2023, November 8). Leading second languages to learn among people in Vietnam as of June 2021. *Statistica.* https://www.statista.com/statistics/1248183/vietnam-popular-foreign-languageto-learn-among-people/

Wedell, M., & Grassick, L. (2020). Innovation in language teaching and learning. *The encyclopedia of applied linguistics.* https://doi.org/10.1002/9781405198431.wbeal0540.pub2

Wilkins, D. A. (1976). *Notional syllabuses.* Oxford University Press.

Zou, B., Reinders, H., Thomas, M., & Barr, D. (2023). Editorial: Using artificial intelligence technology for language learning. *Frontiers in Psychology, 14.* https://doi.org/10.3389/fpsyg.2023.1287667

INDEX

A

Active learning, 157, 160
Adaptive algorithms, 185
Additional type, 17
Adult learner, 37, 48
AI/ML-based language learning apps, 186
Artificial intelligence, 238
Assessment, 137, 138, 140–143, 148–150
Authentic assessment, 33–36, 38, 41–44, 47, 48
Autonomous learning, 184

B

Backward design, 18
Belt and Road Initiative (BRI), 75, 78, 83
Bilingual education, 56
Bilingualism, 94
Blended learning, 238, 240
Bottom-up innovation, 2, 6, 10

C

Cambodia, 51, 52, 55, 56
Collaborative learning, 157–179
Collaborative tools, 176
Common European Framework of Reference (CEFR), 5
Communication tasks, 126, 129
Communication tools, 161, 163, 168
Communicative framework, 120, 121, 124, 125
Communicative pronunciation teaching (CPT), 116, 119–121, 124–129
Constructivism, 159
Content and Language Integrated Learning (CLIL), 236
Cooperative learning, 158
COVID-19 pandemic, 74, 75, 70, 01
Culturally and linguistically responsive pedagogy, 96, 97
Cumulative programs, 17
Curriculum design, 95
Curriculum development, 18, 19, 22–23

© The Author(s), under exclusive license to Springer Nature Switzerland AG 2024
L. Phung et al. (eds.), *Innovation in Language Learning and Teaching*, New Language Learning and Teaching Environments, https://doi.org/10.1007/978-3-031-46080-7

243

244 INDEX

D
Doi Moi (Renovation), 4

E
Educational policies, 34, 44, 48
Emerging technologies, 188, 191, 193, 195, 202–204
English as a Medium of Instruction (EMI), 3, 5, 6, 10, 15–17, 22–27, 29, 30
English intensive course, 16
English Language Fellow (ELF) (USA), 74, 81
English Medium Instruction (EMI), 236
Environment analysis, 19, 23
Ethnic minority primary students, 99, 100, 107, 109, 110
Evaluation, 239, 241

F
Face-to-face learning, 211, 212, 215, 219, 225, 227
Feedback, 38, 39, 43, 44, 46, 48
Flipped classroom, 35, 38–41, 44, 47

G
Gamification features, 185, 193
Global integration, 3

H
Hybrid, 83, 84, 86–88
Hybrid-mode, 35, 38

I
Immersion, 51, 54–57, 59, 69
Inclusive pedagogies, 236
Industry partners, 239

Infrastructure, 73, 84, 88
Innovation in language teaching, 235–241
Institutional factors, 214, 216, 218, 221, 223, 225, 226, 228
Intended learning outcomes (ILOs), 18, 26, 29, 30
Intercultural communicative ability, 2
International collaboration, 15
Internationalization, 15, 30
Internship, 135–151

K
K-12 program, 51–70

L
Language policy, 94
Learner autonomy, 3
Learner-centered approaches, 4, 5, 9
Learner-centeredness, 3
Learner-focused techniques, 184
Learner engagement, 2
Learner motivation, 2
Learning Management System (LMS), 36, 38, 39, 43
Learning outcomes, 236, 238, 239
Learning styles, 2
Linguistically and culturally responsive pedagogy, 237
Linguistic diversity, 236

M
Materials development, 237, 240
Meaning-focused activities, 236
Minority languages, 93, 94, 99, 109
Mobile language learning applications, 184
Mobile learning, 238

Mock conference (MC), 135–151
Motivation, 160, 171, 175,
176, 178
Multilingualism, 236
Multilingual turn, 237
Multimodal learning, 2

N
National Foreign Language Project
(NFLP) 2020, 5
Needs analysis, 19–24, 26

O
Online, 75, 76, 78–80, 82–84,
86–88
Online collaborative
learning, 157–179
Online group work, 158, 160–163,
166, 176–177
Online learning, 209, 210, 212,
214–216, 219, 223, 225, 227
Oral communication, 115, 116, 118,
119, 126
Outcome-based learning (OBL),
16–19, 26, 30

P
Performance, 137–139, 141–150
Personal factors, 218, 221,
223, 229
Personalized Interaction, 101
Phenomenology, 58
Phonetic instruction, 122, 125, 130
Project 2020, 5, 9

R
Reflection, 40, 43, 47
Reflective interviews, 58, 59, 66
Replacement programming, 17

S
Second language acquisition (SLA),
95, 98, 99, 108
Siem Reap, 51–70
Sihanoukville (Cambodia), 73–88
Situated learning, 136–140, 143,
147, 150
Situation analysis, 19
Sociocultural and economic factors,
224–226, 228
Social interdependence, 159
Soft skills, 35, 36, 42
Stakeholders, 35, 45–48, 239–241
Strategic partnerships, 74, 80
Student-centered education, 185
Student-centered learning, 160

T
Teacher-centered approaches, 236
Teacher professional learning (TPL),
117, 119, 120, 129
Top-down innovation, 2, 4–6, 9
Traditional teaching methods, 236
Training, 116, 117, 130
Translanguaging, 98
Translation, 135–151
Transnational program, 16, 30
Trilingual education, 69
Trilingual K-12 program, 237

V
Vietnamese as a second
language, 93–110
Virtual and augmented realities (VR/
AR), 186
Virtual reality, 238

W
Web-based technologies, 214,
215, 220

Printed by Libri Plureos GmbH
in Hamburg, Germany